IMAGES
*of America*

# SHELBY TOWNSHIP

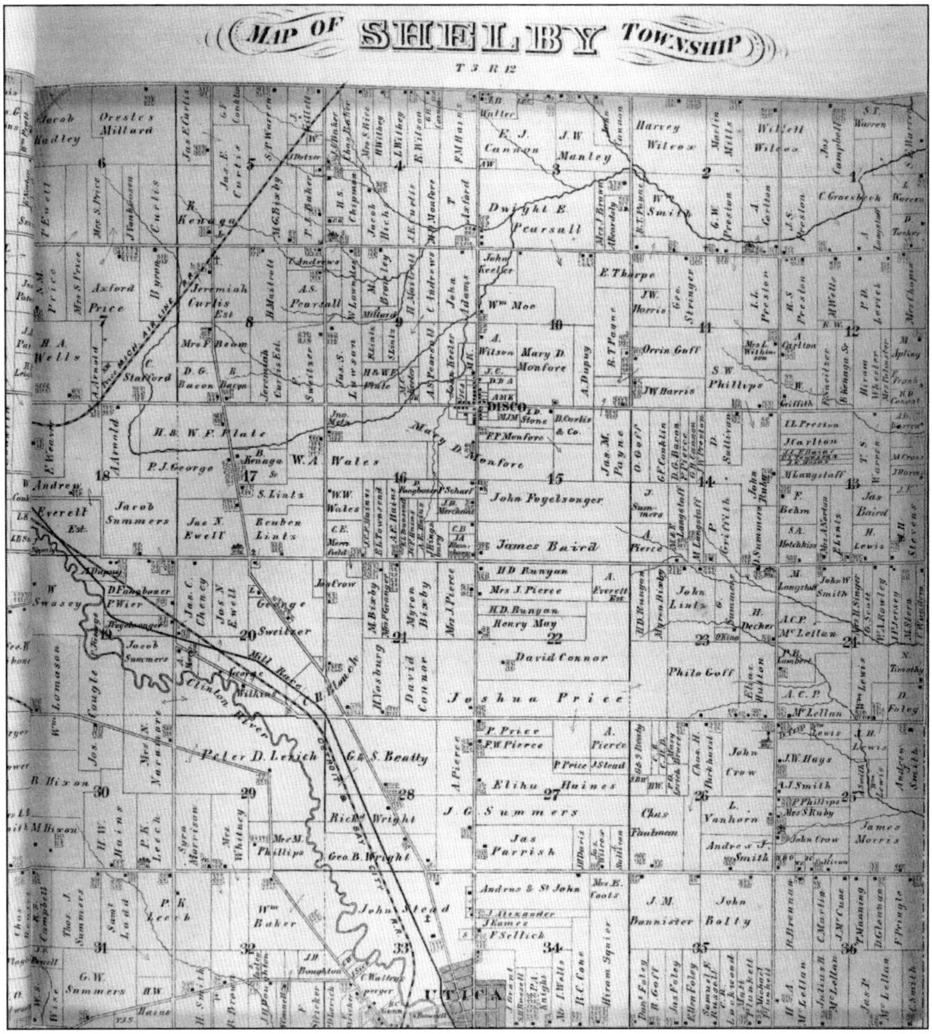


This map of Shelby Township is from *The Historical Atlas of Macomb County, Michigan* compiled by D. J. Stewart of Philadelphia, Pennsylvania, in 1875. The township is made up of 36 square-mile sections that are numbered beginning with Section 1 in the northeast corner. The east-west section roads begin at the southern boundary with Hall Road (mile road no. 20) and count up to 26 Mile Road marking the northern boundary. The roads that generally follow the north-south section lines are, beginning on the western boundary of the township, Dequindre Road, Ryan Road, Mound Road, Van Dyke Avenue (center), Jewell Road, Schoenherr Road, and Hayes Road, which marks the eastern boundary. Shelby Road runs diagonally through the western part of the township from Section 5 to Utica. Ryan Road only runs south of 23 Mile Road. Mound Road runs between Shelby and 26 Mile Roads. Jewell Road only runs north of 24 Mile Road.

**ON THE COVER:** Three unidentified young men enjoy lunch alongside the old canal around 1907. The Clinton and Kalamazoo Canal was initially built to connect Lake Michigan to the eastern waterways through Lower Michigan. The project was a failure and never completed. The section of canal that ran through Shelby Township was used as a millrace. (Douglas Harvey; photograph by Burt Harvey.)

IMAGES
*of America*

# Shelby Township

Hilary Davis for the
Shelby Township Historical Committee

ARCADIA
PUBLISHING

ISBN 978-0-7385-8428-7

Published by Arcadia Publishing
Charleston, South Carolina

Printed in the United States of America

Library of Congress Control Number: 2009943884

For all general information, please contact Arcadia Publishing:
Telephone 843-853-2070
Fax 843-853-0044
E-mail sales@arcadiapublishing.com
For customer service and orders:
Toll-Free 1-888-313-2665

Visit us on the Internet at www.arcadiapublishing.com

*This book is dedicated to the residents of Shelby Township, past, present, and future.*

# Contents

# ACKNOWLEDGMENTS

First and foremost, I thank the members and volunteers of the Shelby Township Historical Committee for their help with images and information. Their huge collection of historical books, maps, papers, and photographs is now housed at the one-room Andrews Schoolhouse on the Shelby Township municipal grounds.

I am grateful for the time, patience, and generosity of the many township residents, former and present, who shared their family photographs and histories, including Patricia Sabol of the George Roberts and Hugh Switzer family; Marie, Debbie, and Bill Remer; Lynn and Grace Drake of the Lagodna family; Lillian Powerski; George Wellhausen Jr.; Lynn Warren; Craig Nickel; David and Roberta Mocabee; Delores Strouse Metro; Michael and Christy Meyer; Douglas Falls; Dolores Schmidt; members and friends of the Carleton Fuhrman family; and members of the Smith family, who are Gary and Mary Bradt, Gayle Jocks, and Joyce Clark.

Many hours were spent working with the fine folks at the Detroit Public Library, the Mount Clemens Public Library, the Walter P. Reuther Library, the Sterling Heights Public Library, the Utica Public Library, and the Utica Heritage Association. I appreciate their help and patience.

I also thank Louis Resner, Richard Meitz, Frank Shepherd of the defunct *Utica Sentinel* and *Daily Sentinel* newspapers, and Richard Kelley of the *Macomb Daily* for access and permission to use images from their collections.

I am especially grateful to Douglas Harvey for sharing his marvelous collection of photographs taken by his uncle Burt Harvey and for helping me with the cover image.

Thanks go to my editor, Anna Wilson, for answering my questions and putting my mind at ease and to my family for accepting my long absences while I worked on this book.

The majority of the images in this book are individually credited and to all those people I did not mention above, I give heartfelt thanks for your permission to use them. Other image credits are abbreviated as follows: Shelby Township Historical Committee (STHC), the National Automotive History Collection at the Detroit Public Library (NAHC), the Walter P. Reuther Library at Wayne State University (WPRL), and the *Macomb Daily* (MD).

# INTRODUCTION

The Shelby Township Historical Committee is pleased to introduce this photographic collection of persons, places, and things of Shelby Township from the mid-1800s to the 1970s. We are grateful to the persons who have donated and loaned these images, provided the information concerning them, and given permission for their use.

In 1796, the United States acquired areas of the Midwest from the British. In 1805, the boundaries of the territory of Michigan were defined. Several tribes of Native Americans were living in the area as they had done for thousands of years. The federal government made treaties with the various tribes for ownership of the land, thus paving the way for exploration, survey, and settlement.

Settlers, mostly from New England and New York, began arriving in the territory before government surveyors officially surveyed the area. In the winter of 1816 and 1817, Nathaniel Burgess became the first person to build a house in what was to become Section 34 of Shelby Township. Nathaniel Squires, while traveling along the Clinton River in 1817, came upon a high point of ground where two Native American trails crossed near the banks of the river. There he built a cabin for his family, and they became the first to settle in what would become the village of Utica.

It was during the winter of 1817 and 1818 that Shelby Township was surveyed into sections and quarter sections. Known first by its public land survey system designation as Town 3 North, Range 12 East, land in the township became available for sale from the United States General Land Office in Detroit in 1818. The cost per acre was $2 at first, then after 1820 it was $1.25 cash per acre with an 80-acre minimum purchase. Blake Curtis was the first property buyer in the township purchasing the southwest quarter of Section 7 on May 24, 1819.

When the Erie Canal opened in 1825, travel from the East became easier and more settlers began to arrive in the township. More acreage was purchased, land was cleared for farms, and houses and barns were built. Saw mills and gristmills were built along the Clinton River and the smaller streams that cut through the township. Roads were improved, the first railroad tracks were laid, and a canal for boat transportation was dug through the township.

The first schools were started in log cabins around the township as early as 1818, and the continuing importance of education for township children is evident in the development of the many schools and school districts over the years. An academy for higher learning was built in the village of Disco in 1850. Ten years later, a union school for schooling beyond the primary grades was established in Utica.

Shelby Township was formally organized in April 1827. It was one of the first five townships into which Macomb County was originally divided. Like many who came to the township in the first half of the 19th century, the first settlers saw opportunity and a chance for a new start. While early survey reports stated that the area was comprised of nothing but barren soil and malarial swamps, the settlers saw instead the land's true potential as good farmland with abundant water resources that could power mills. What none of them could visualize were nearly 200 years of hardship, endurance, and innovation that would become the Shelby Township known today. The timber frame home Ezra Burgess built on Dequindre Road bares witness to all this history and still stands as a monument to those early pioneers.

Shelby Township has been recognized by the State of Michigan through its Historical Marker Program with three markers. One located within our River Bends Park marks the location of Spring Hill Farm and tells of its owners, the Lerich family, who made the farm a stop on the Underground Railroad prior to and during the Civil War. In later years, Joe Louis, the world-famous boxing champion, owned the farm. When the property was purchased by the State of Michigan and added to the state park system, portions were used for a Nike missile base during the Cold War period, as the marker notes.

Another state historic marker is located at the Packard Proving Grounds. While the test track is gone, the buildings, many of which were designed by the famous architect Albert Kahn, remain. A restoration process continues and the buildings and grounds are open to the public on many occasions throughout the year. The Packard Proving Grounds historic site is also listed on the National Register of Historic Places.

A Michigan State Historical Marker is also located at the Utica Cemetery. A walk through this cemetery and through the other cemeteries within the township is in itself a lesson in history, for they are the final resting places of many of our early settlers.

The 1940s and 1950s were the beginning of a change for Shelby Township. The former village of Utica had become a separate municipality in 1937. Farms were being replaced with subdivisions and businesses needed for the increasing number of residents. Police and fire departments were organized and placed in operation. A township hall was built in 1948 to house those departments and the municipal offices. As the departments and need for township services expanded, the township offices and police department moved into a new municipal building in 1972. On November 7, 1978, the township status was changed to that of a charter township, giving it more control over its destiny.

Readers are encouraged to think of the generations who settled here, cleared the land, produced the crops, operated the businesses, and lived in an environment that we today would find most difficult. Shelby Township's history is nothing more than typical and nothing less than unique. They are the people to whom this book is dedicated.

It is our story.

—Clendon Mason and Daniel Lehman
Chairman and Vice Chairman
Shelby Township Historical Committee

# *One*

# Tracing the Pioneers

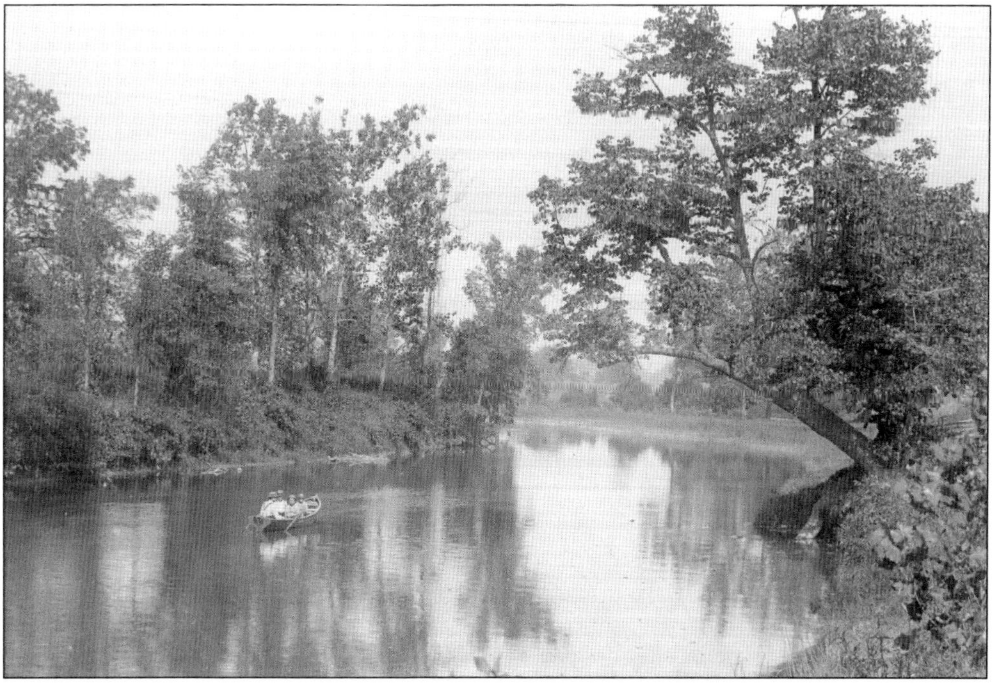

Boaters around 1890 enjoy a leisurely cruise on the Clinton River, which winds diagonally through the southwest corner of Shelby Township. The river and its feeders provided the first settlers access to the township's interior and power for their saw and gristmills. The river continued to power mills into the 20th century and has provided a source of recreation to this day. (Mount Clemens Public Library.)

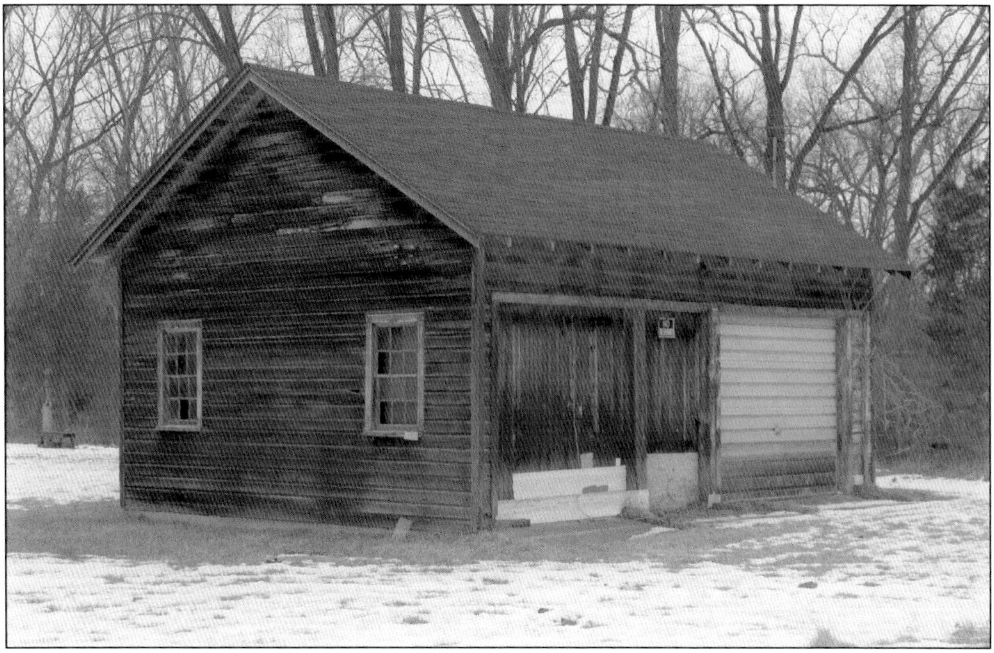

The settlers usually built log cabins for their first dwellings while they cleared the land and raised crops. Once the farm was established, the log cabin would be replaced by a timber frame house such as this one, which was built by Ira Preston around 1830. Preston built a larger house in 1843 and converted this cabin to a barn. (Jamie Fuhrman; photograph by Richard Mayer.)

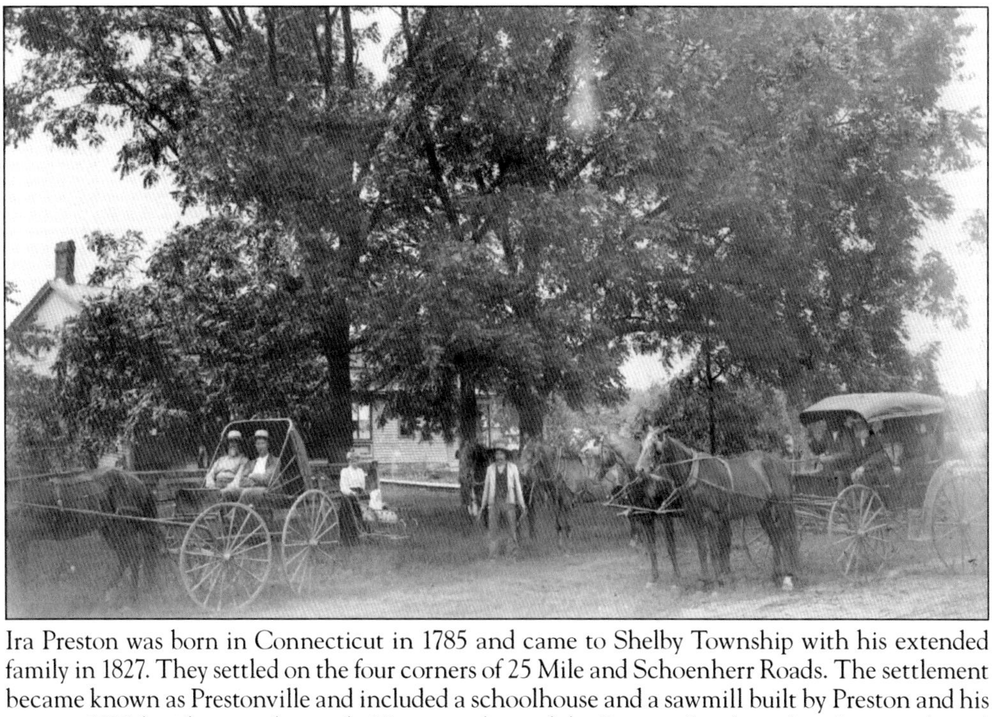

Ira Preston was born in Connecticut in 1785 and came to Shelby Township with his extended family in 1827. They settled on the four corners of 25 Mile and Schoenherr Roads. The settlement became known as Prestonville and included a schoolhouse and a sawmill built by Preston and his sons in 1828 beside a nearby creek. Here members of the Preston family gather for an informal portrait around 1894. (STHC.)

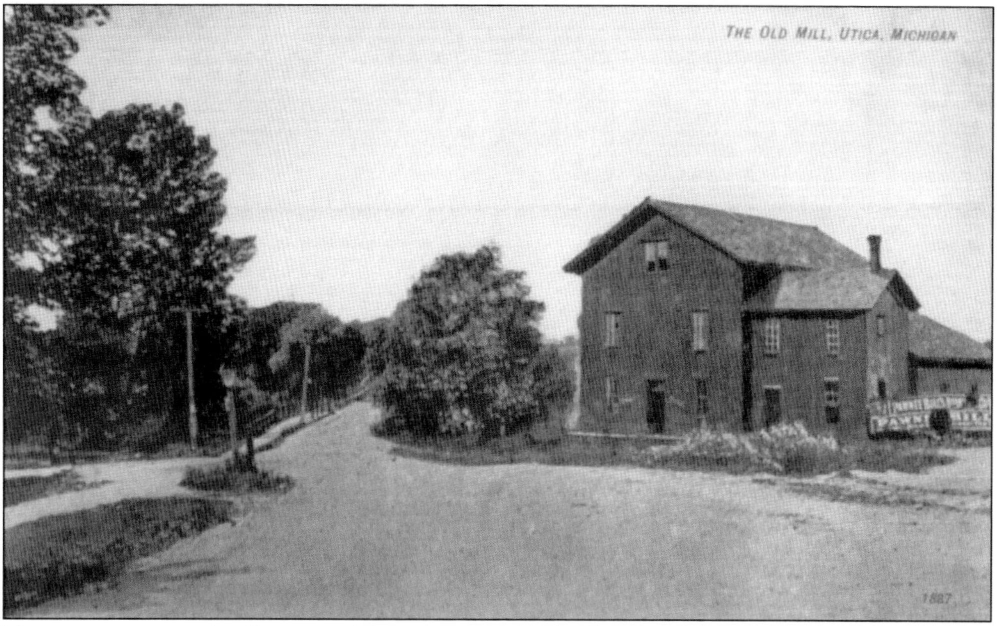


The construction of mills to grind grain was one of the first priorities of the early settlers. This postcard from the late 1800s shows one of the earliest gristmills built on the banks of the Clinton River by brothers Adam and Jacob Price around 1828. It was located on Main Street in the village of Utica beside the bridge that crossed the river. (Louis Resner.)

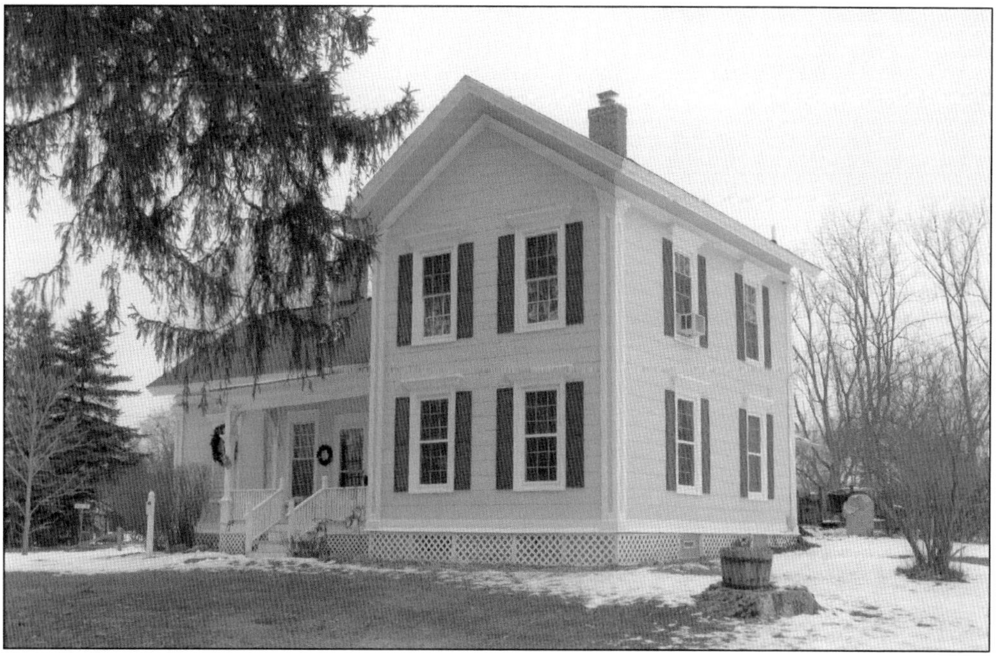

Section 7 was considered to have the best farmland in Shelby Township. The 160 acres that Blake Curtis purchased in this section were sold to Samuel and Lydia Wells, who moved from New York around 1824 with their 14 children and established a prosperous wheat farm. Son Harmon Wells took over the farm and built this house on 24 Mile Road around 1860. (Richard Milks; photograph by Richard Mayer.)

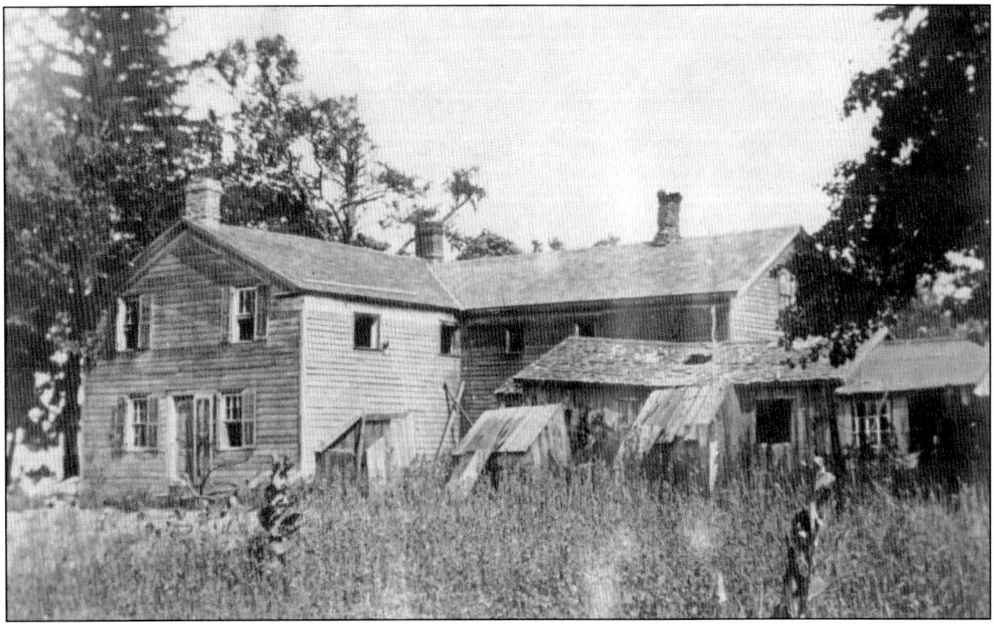

Section 7, with its gently rolling terrain and well-drained soils, also appealed to Ezra Burgess, a settler from New York, who purchased an 80-acre piece of it in 1823. Here he settled his family, built this house, and established a farm. Pictured here around 1900 and apparently abandoned, the Burgess house, thought to be the oldest house in the township, now stands restored on Dequindre Road. (Vikki Papesh.)

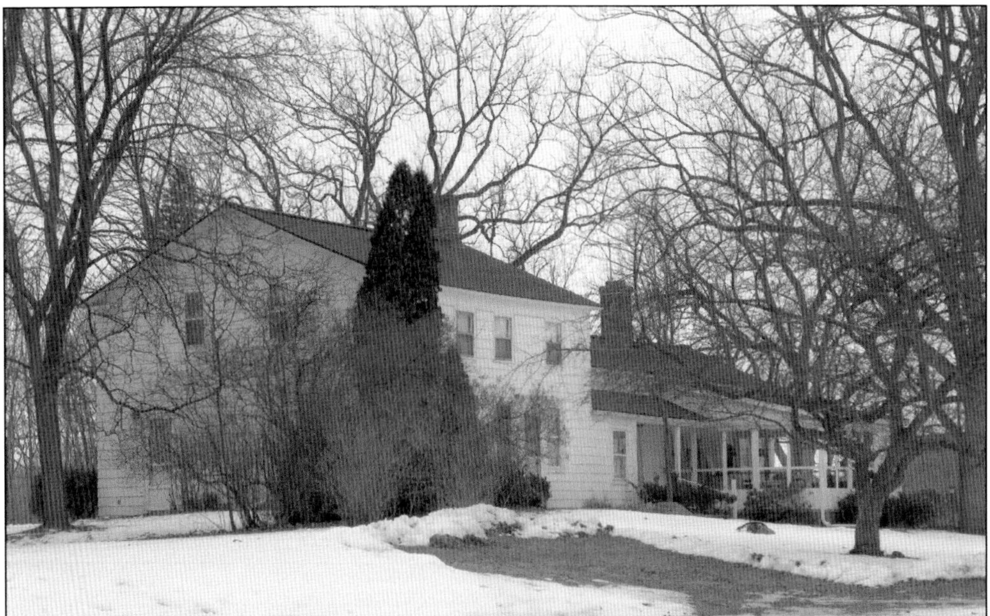

Samuel Axford bought the remaining pieces of Section 7 beginning in 1823. Axford was an attorney and gentleman farmer from New Jersey who came to Shelby Township with his wife, Rachel, and their nine children. He served as township supervisor from 1828 to 1835 and as a state representative from 1839 to 1843. He built this house on 25 Mile Road around 1833. (STHC.)

Abel Warren is pictured at right with his wife, Sarah, shortly before his death in 1862. Warren was one of the earliest settlers in Shelby Township, arriving from New York in 1824 with his wife and children. In that same year, he purchased 80 acres of land in Section 4. He was a Methodist Episcopal minister as well as a farmer and was the first man licensed to preach in the territory of Michigan. In their later years, the Warrens lived with their youngest son, Samuel Warren, on a farm in Section 4. Samuel Warren is pictured below with his wife, Mary Jane, around 1900. Other children of Abel Warren, along with his brother Asa Warren and several of his cousins, also settled in the northern part of the township. (Both, Lynn J. Warren.)

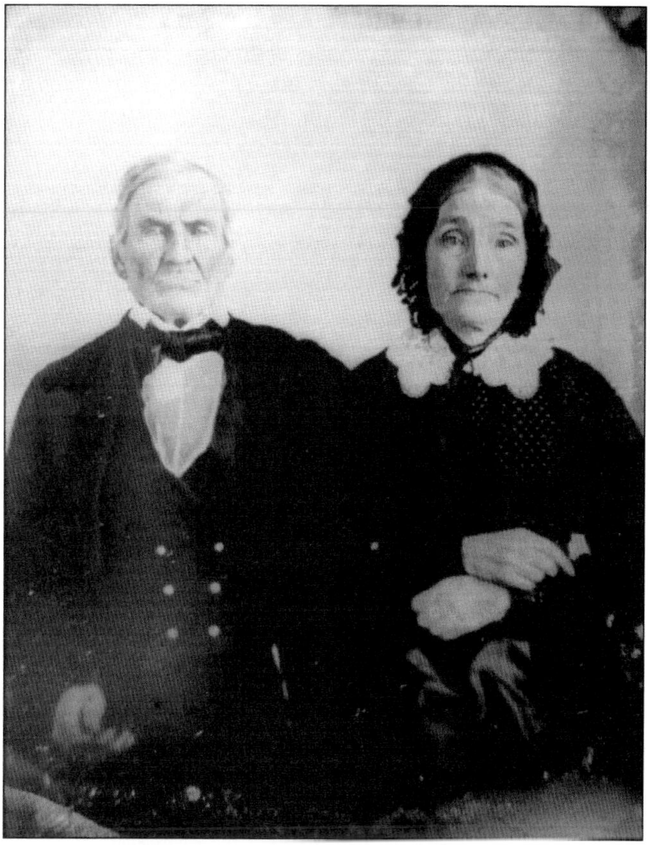

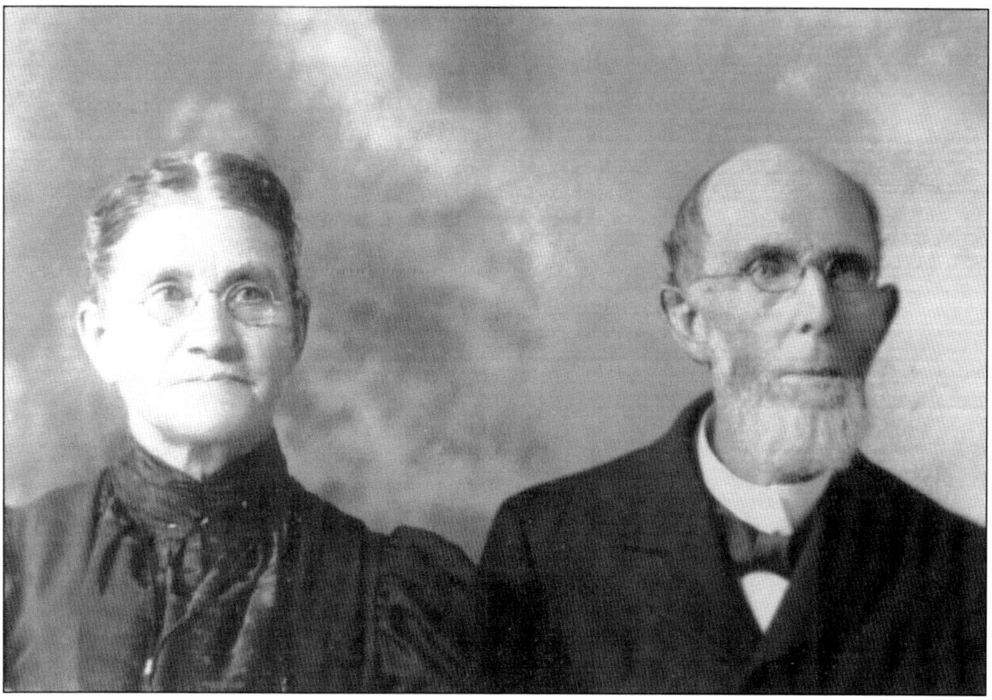

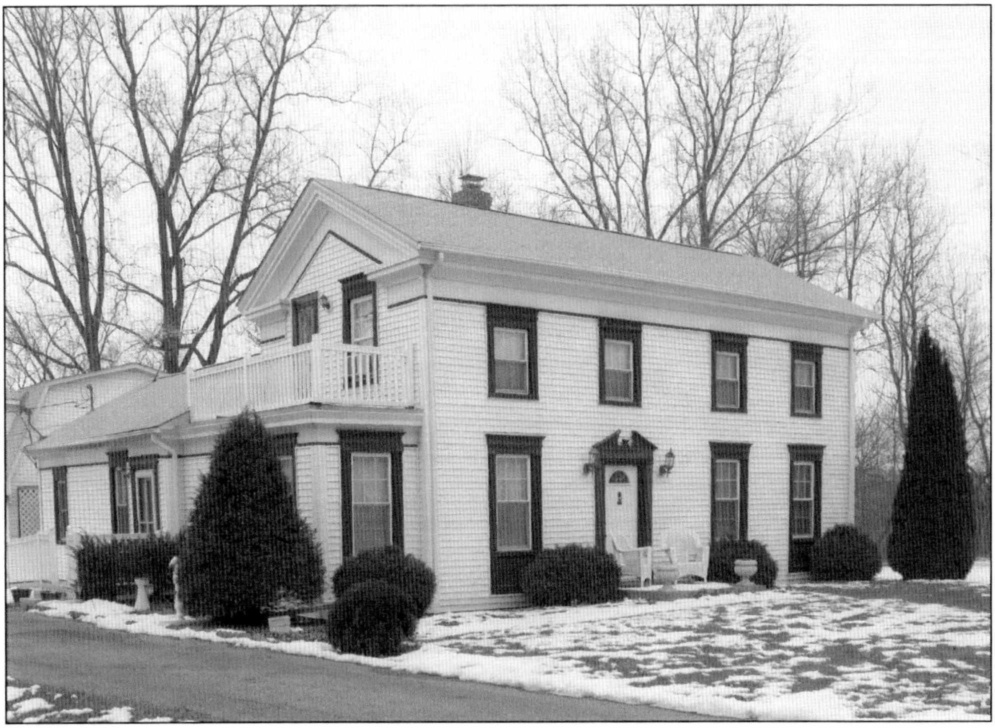

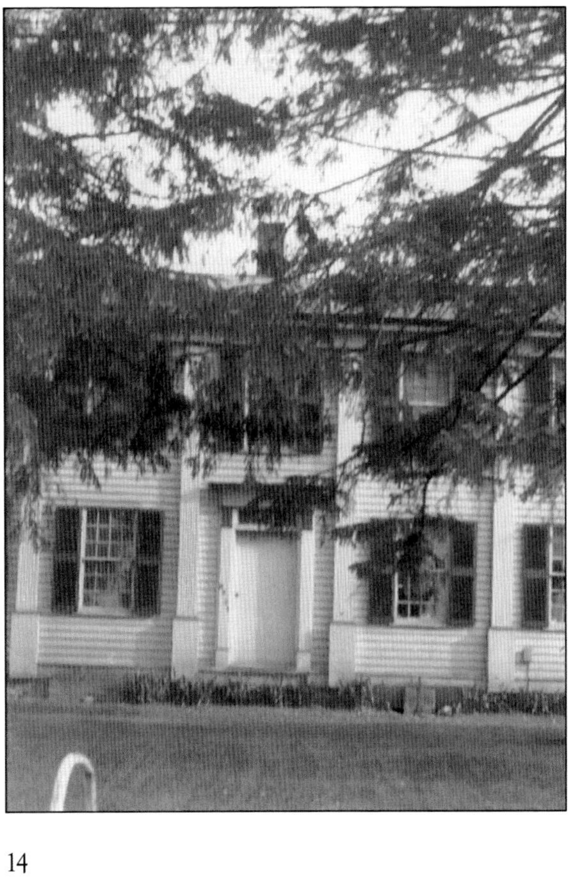

Sometime between 1860 and 1875, Samuel Warren purchased a farm on 26 Mile Road in Section 5 and built this farmhouse where he lived until his death in 1908. His descendants lived here into the mid-20th century. The house, which had fallen into disrepair, was moved to its present location on Jewell Road in 1985 and restored by a group of Shelby Township firefighters. (John Millichamp; photograph by Richard Mayer.)

The Wilcox brothers from New York, Elias and David, also settled in the northern part of Shelby Township, purchasing 80-acre parcels of land in Section 2 in the early 1830s. David Wilcox built this house on 26 Mile Road and established a farm. The house, shown here in the early 1940s, was moved to California in 2004 to save it from demolition. (Delores Strouse Metro.)

Andrew Jackson Smith came to Shelby Township from New York with his wife, Aurilla, shortly after 1850 and settled on a 40-acre farm on Schoenherr Road in Section 25. Aurilla died in 1854, one year after son Orville was born. Andrew Smith, shown here around 1890, was a successful farmer and a member of the Methodist congregation in the village of Disco. (Barbara Gaskill Presti.)

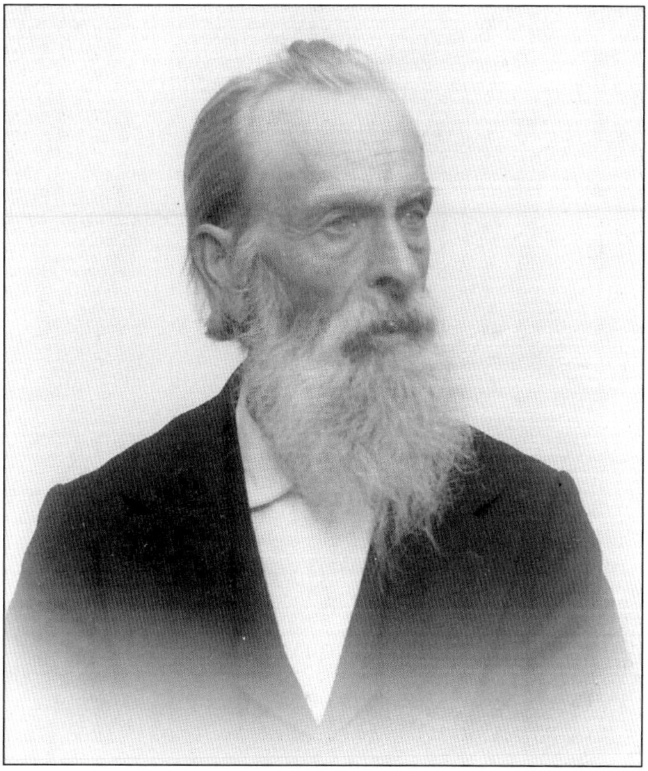

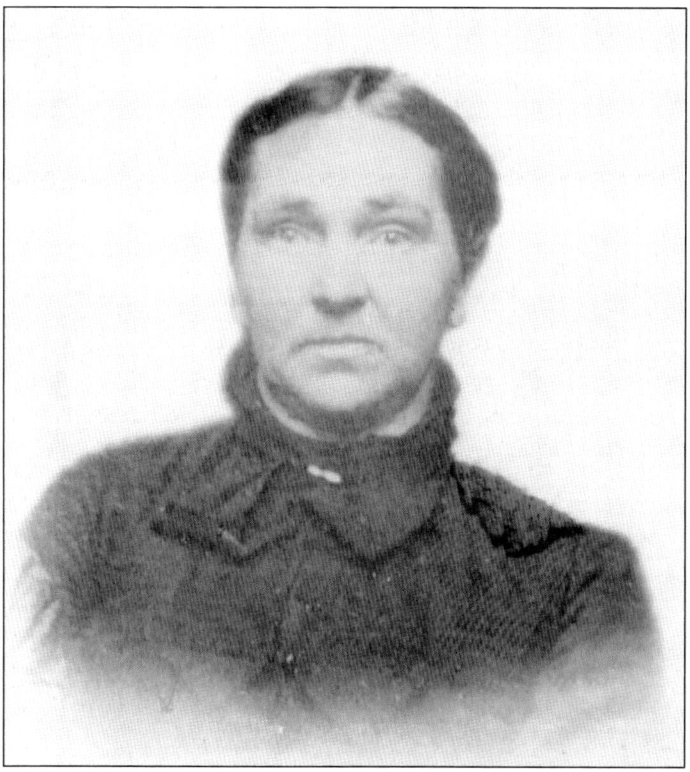

Esther Ann Arnold Smith, pictured here around 1890, was the daughter of Alvah Arnold, one of the early settlers of Shelby Township. She was born in the township in 1834. Around 1856, she became the second wife of Andrew Jackson Smith and bore him eight children. A year after Esther Ann died in 1895, her widowed sister Ellen Lewis became Smith's third wife. (Barbara Gaskill Presti.)

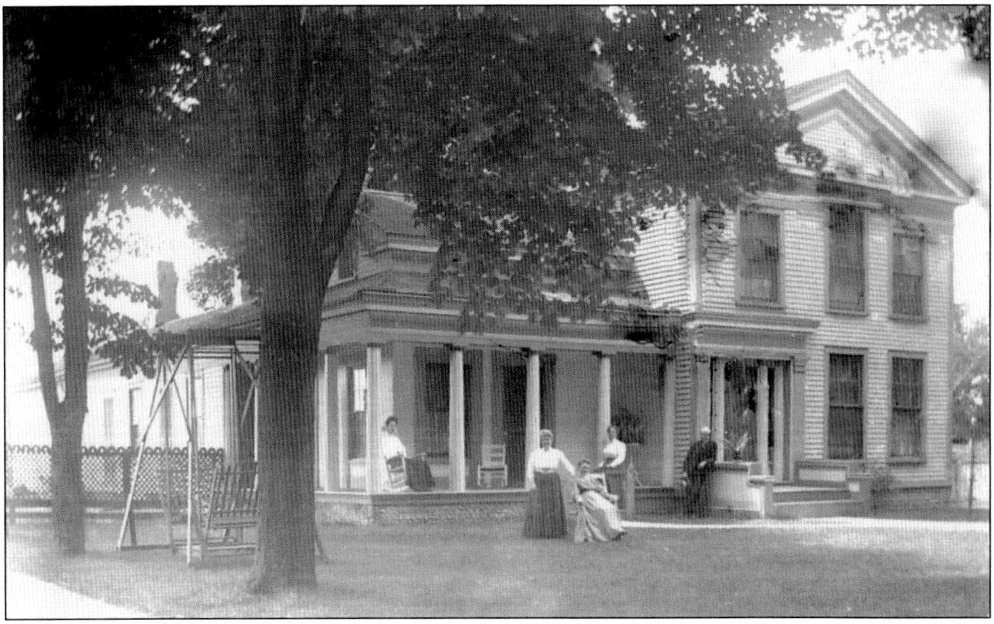

John Young came to Shelby Township around 1844, established a general store in Utica, and built this house on Cass Avenue around 1852. He was elected the first village president in 1877. In the early 1900s, when this photograph was taken, Young's brother-in-law and business partner, Ralph Wilcox, occupied the house. Wilcox stands to the right of four unidentified women. (Douglas Harvey; photograph by Burt Harvey.)

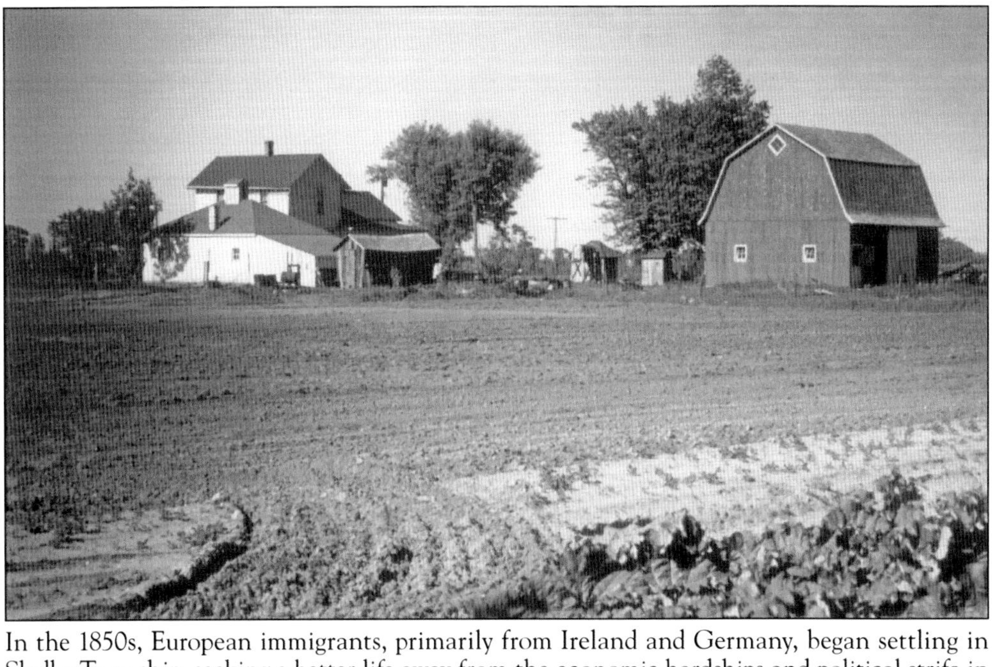

In the 1850s, European immigrants, primarily from Ireland and Germany, began settling in Shelby Township, seeking a better life away from the economic hardships and political strife in their birth countries. Richard and Judith Brennan came from Ireland, bought 80 acres of land in Section 36, and built this house on 21 Mile Road around 1851. The farmstead is pictured here in the 1940s. (STHC.)

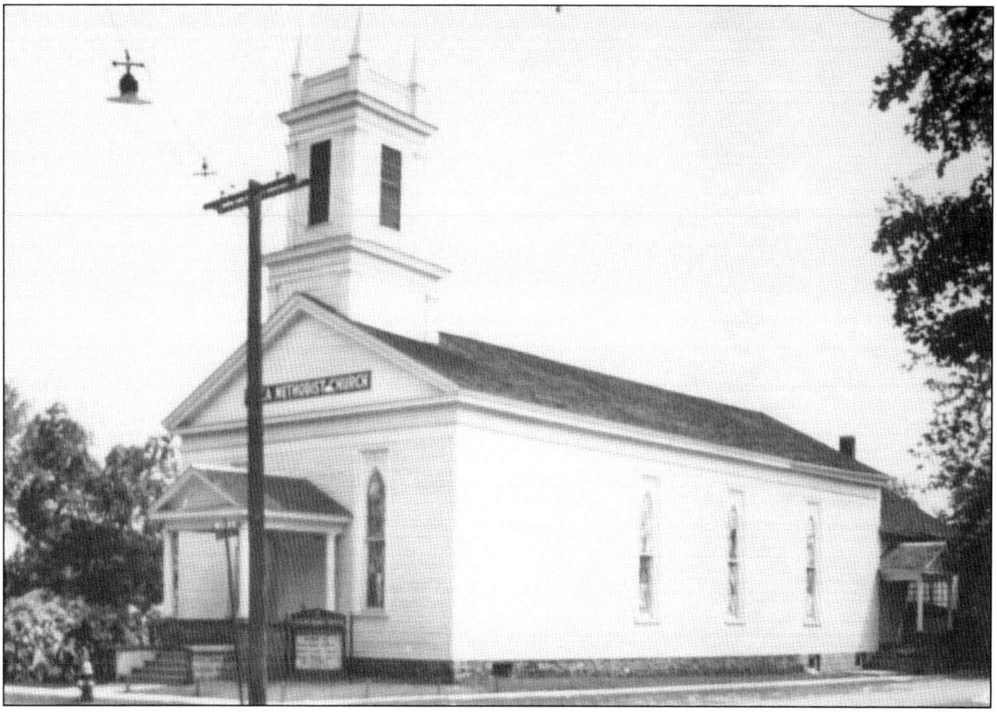

Homes and schoolhouses served as places of worship in the earliest days of settlement. A few churches were built in the mid-19th century around Shelby Township, including this one for the Methodists. Built in Utica in 1839, this building was moved to its present location on Cass Avenue in 1855. Many township residents attended this church, which continues to hold religious services. (Utica Public Library.)

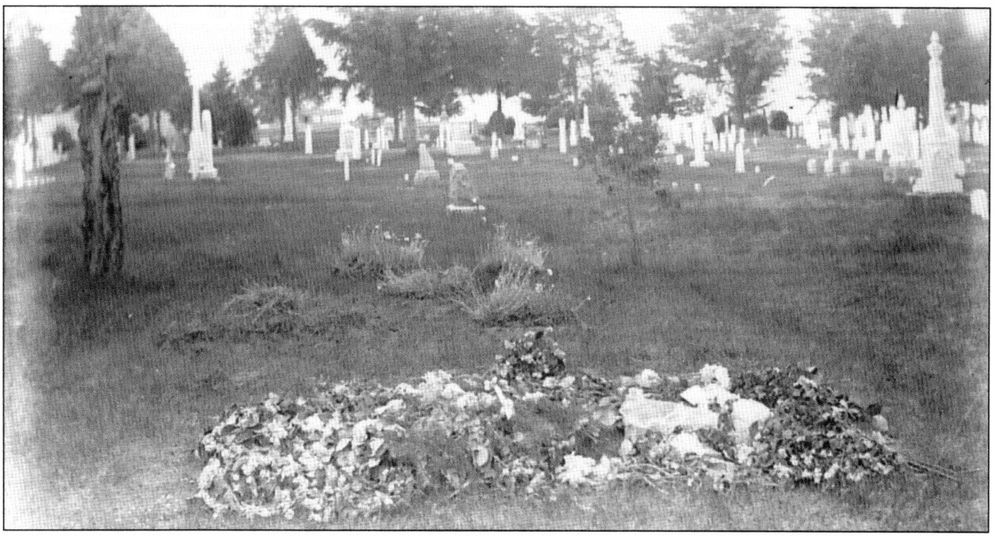

By 1859, there were five cemeteries in Shelby Township, including the Utica Cemetery shown in this photograph of an unknown burial from 1908. The Utica Cemetery was established in the 1820s on Shelby Road and is one of the oldest cemeteries in Michigan. Many of the township's first settlers are buried here, their headstones telling tales of hardship and endurance. (Douglas Harvey; photograph by Burt Harvey.)

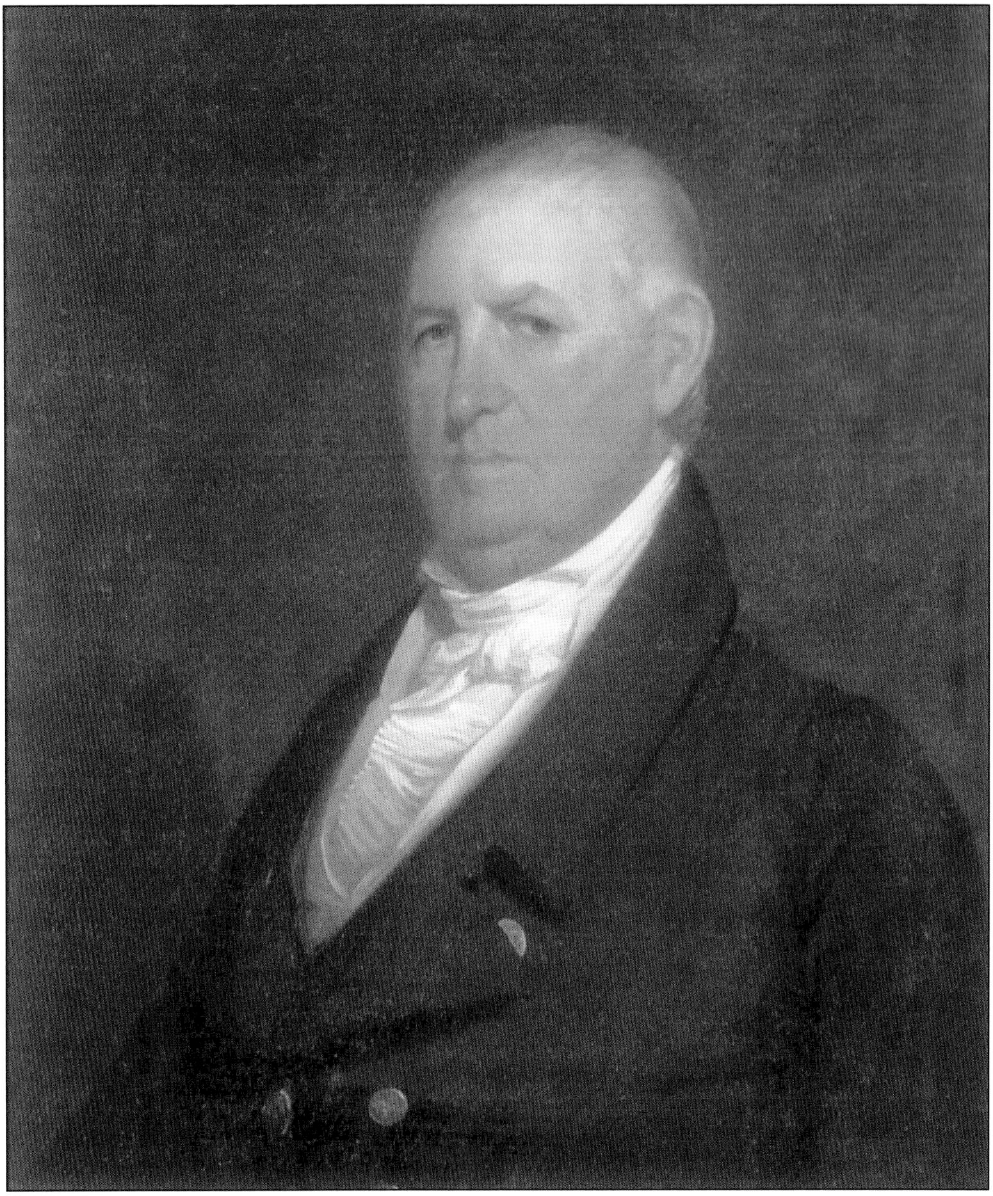

Legend has it that Shelby Township was named for Isaac Shelby, the famous Revolutionary War officer and the first and fifth governor of Kentucky. A hero to early Michigan residents, Governor Shelby contributed a large number of troops from Kentucky to fight a significant battle in the War of 1812, and their victory secured the territory of Michigan from British occupation. After Shelby Township was organized in 1827, the first meeting to elect a government was held at the log house of Perez Swift in Section 21. Joseph Lester became the first township supervisor. Other residents were elected to various posts, including Abel Warren, who became township clerk, and Elias Wilcox, who became an overseer of highways. According to the U.S. census records, 55 families were living in Shelby Township in 1830. Many more would arrive over the next decades, lured by tales of productive farmland, thriving businesses, and schooling for children. By 1850, the number of residents in Shelby Township had more than tripled. (Kentucky Historical Society.)

# *Two*

# The Villages of Disco and Utica

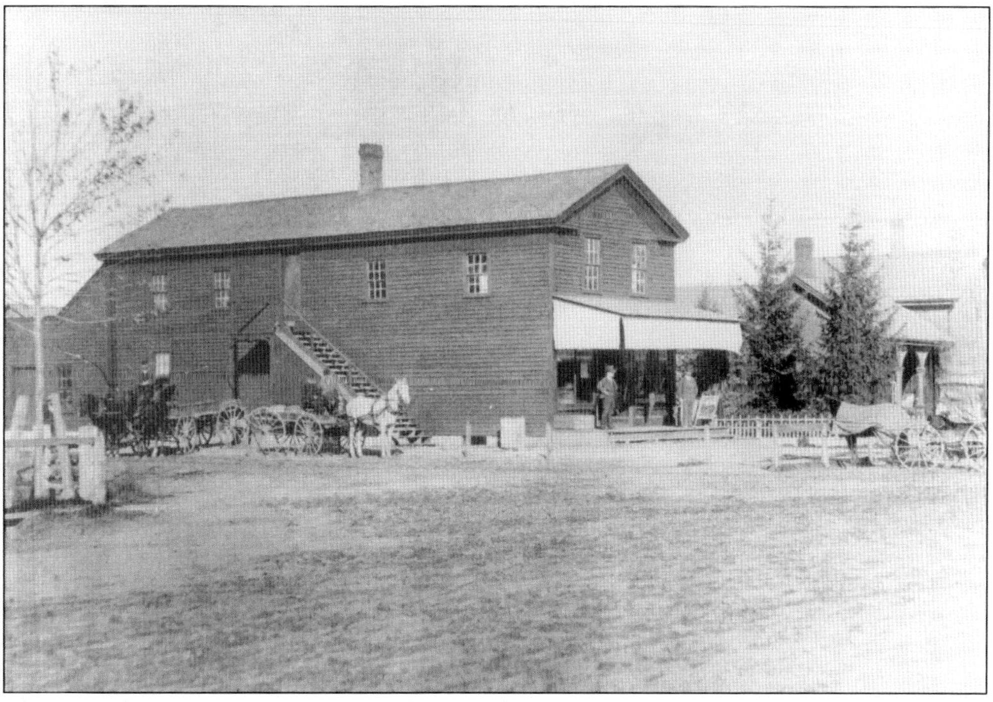

The general store in Disco is pictured here in the late 1800s. The villages of Disco and Utica offered Shelby Township residents central locations for services such as markets, mills, hotels, transportation facilities, doctors, post offices, and churches as well as employment opportunities and social activities. (Hugh Switzer and George Roberts family.)

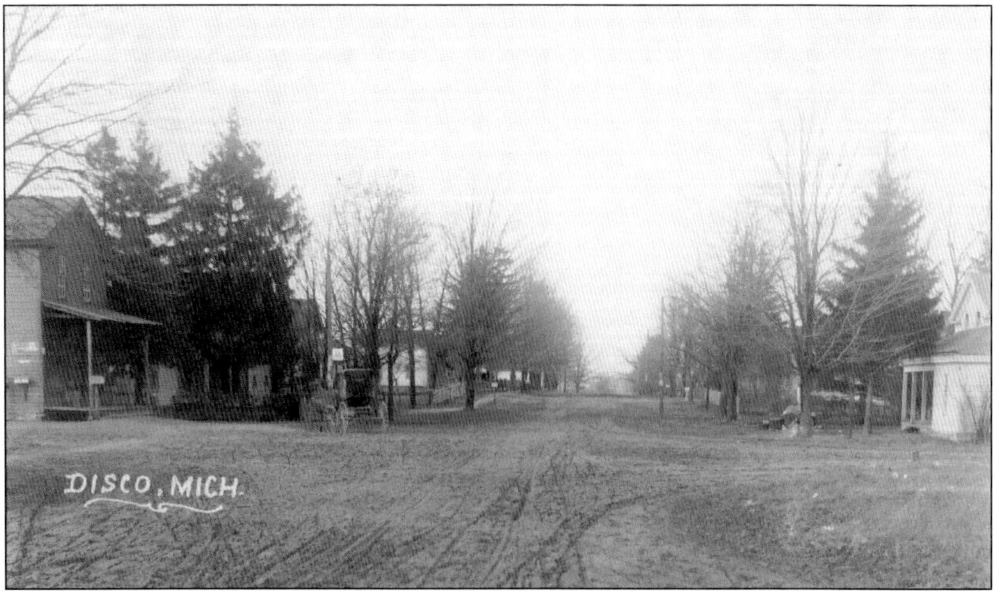


This is Disco looking north on Van Dyke Avenue at 24 Mile Road in the early 1900s. The general store is on the left. Isaac Monfort, Chauncy Church, John Keeler, and others settled the village in the early 1830s. First called "English Town" but later named Disco, possibly from the Latin word *discere,* ("to learn"), it was platted in 1849 as an academy town. (Louis Resner.)

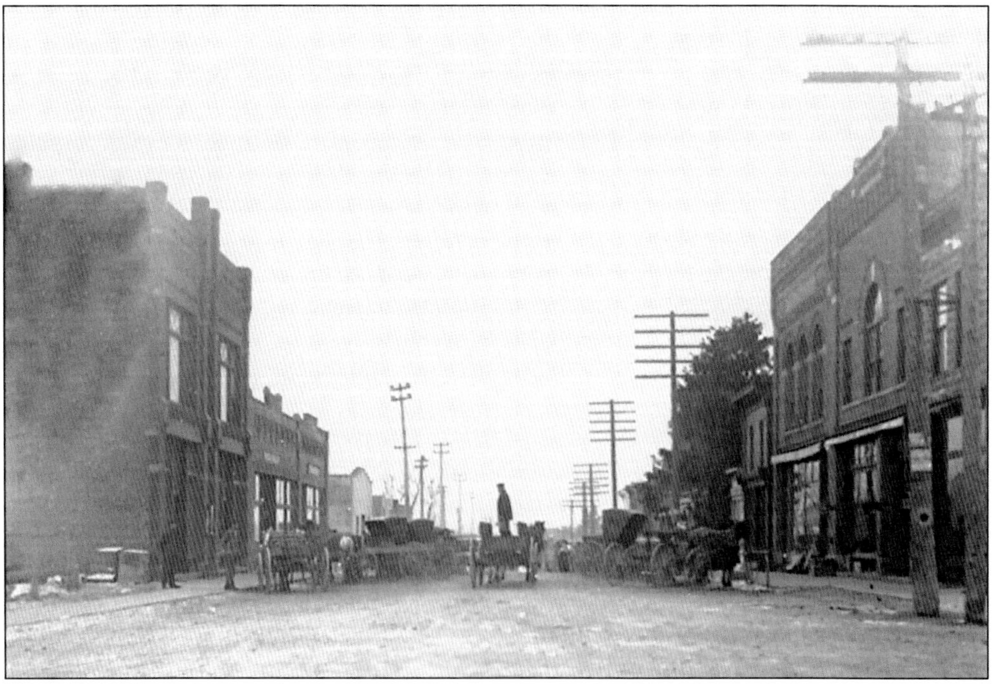

In 1817, Nathaniel Squire brought his family to the southern border of Shelby Township near the Clinton River. The village, which soon sprang up here, was platted and named Harlow by another early settler, Joseph Stead, in 1829. Its name was changed to Utica in 1833. This c. 1907 photograph shows Main Street at Cass Avenue looking west. (Douglas Harvey; photograph by Burt Harvey.)

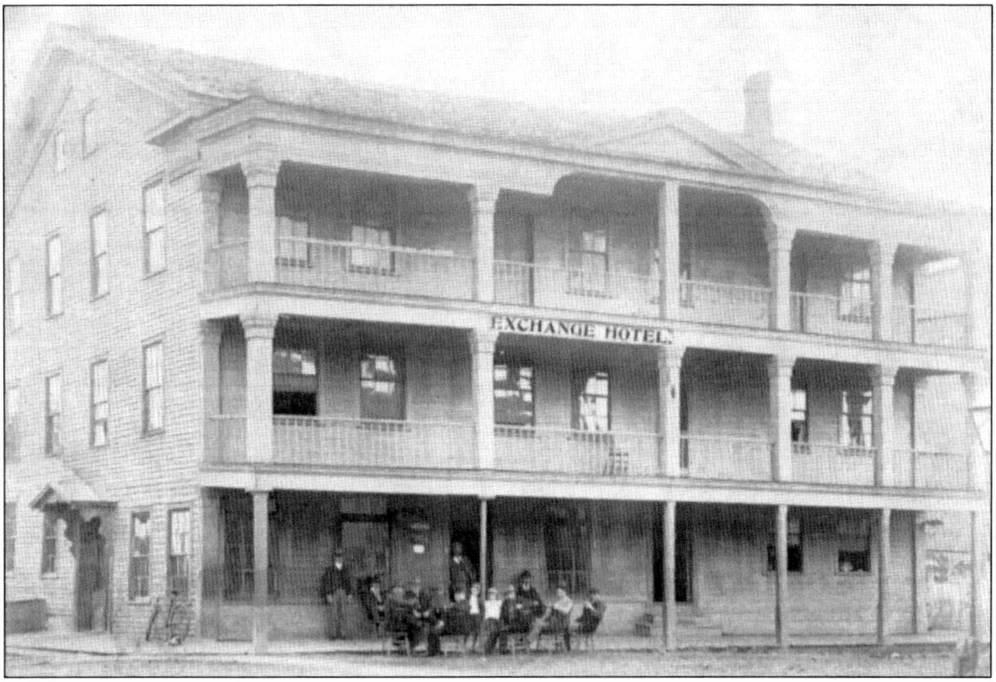


The Exchange Hotel was built in 1831 at the southwest corner of Cass Avenue and Main Street in Utica. Payne K. Leech built the first two stories with the top two stories added later. In this photograph from the 1800s, a large group has gathered out front. The hotel was a center of village activity as well as a stop for travelers. (MD.)

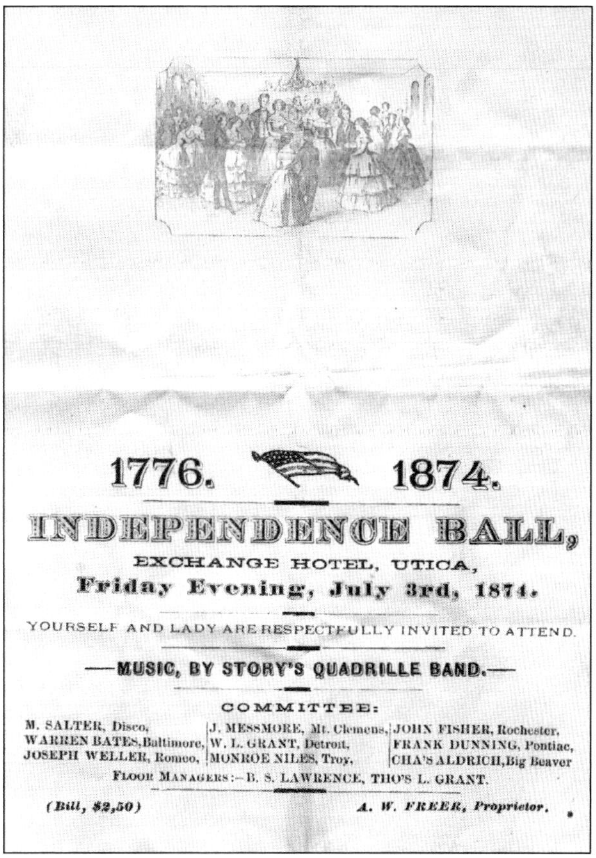

1776. 1874.

INDEPENDENCE BALL,

EXCHANGE HOTEL, UTICA,

Friday Evening, July 3rd, 1874.

YOURSELF AND LADY ARE RESPECTFULLY INVITED TO ATTEND.

—MUSIC, BY STORY'S QUADRILLE BAND.—

COMMITTEE:

| | | |
|---|---|---|
| M. SALTER, Disco, | J. MESSMORE, Mt. Clemens, | JOHN FISHER, Rochester, |
| WARREN BATES, Baltimore, | W. L. GRANT, Detroit, | FRANK DUNNING, Pontiac, |
| JOSEPH WELLER, Romeo, | MONROE NILES, Troy, | CHA'S ALDRICH, Big Beaver |

FLOOR MANAGERS:—B. S. LAWRENCE, THO'S L. GRANT.

*(Bill, $2,50)* *A. W. FREER, Proprietor.*

The third floor of the Exchange Hotel contained a ballroom. The hotel, along with many other buildings in Utica, burned in the spring of 1904 in the worst fire in village history. A new brick hotel was built on the site in 1915, and the building still stands today. (STHC.)

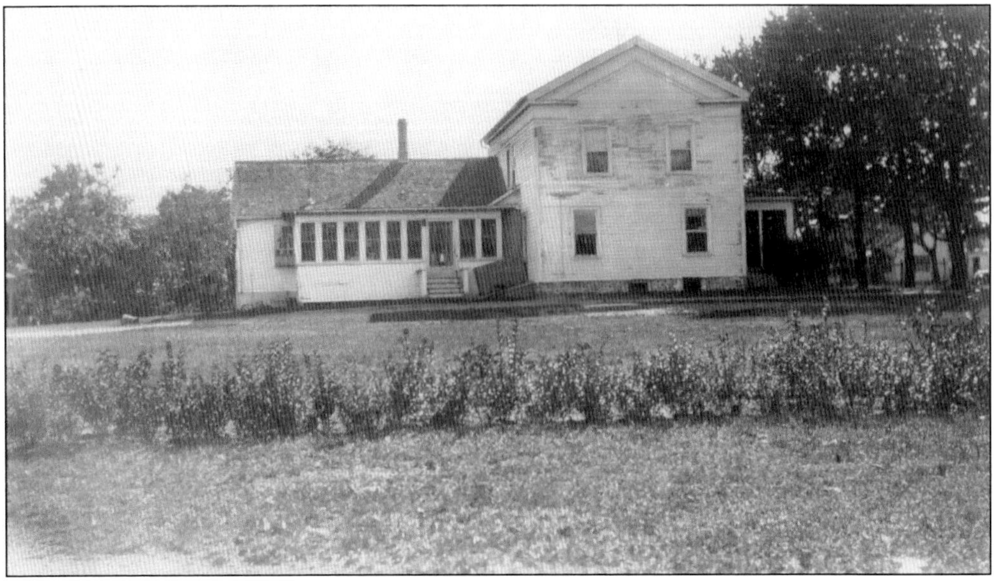

The Disco Hotel was located near the southeast corner of 24 Mile Road and Van Dyke Avenue and accommodated travelers on the stagecoach run from Almont to Royal Oak in the mid- to late 1800s. Concord coaches hauled by four-horse teams could shuttle travelers from Almont to parts south and back in a day. (Hugh Switzer and George Roberts family.)

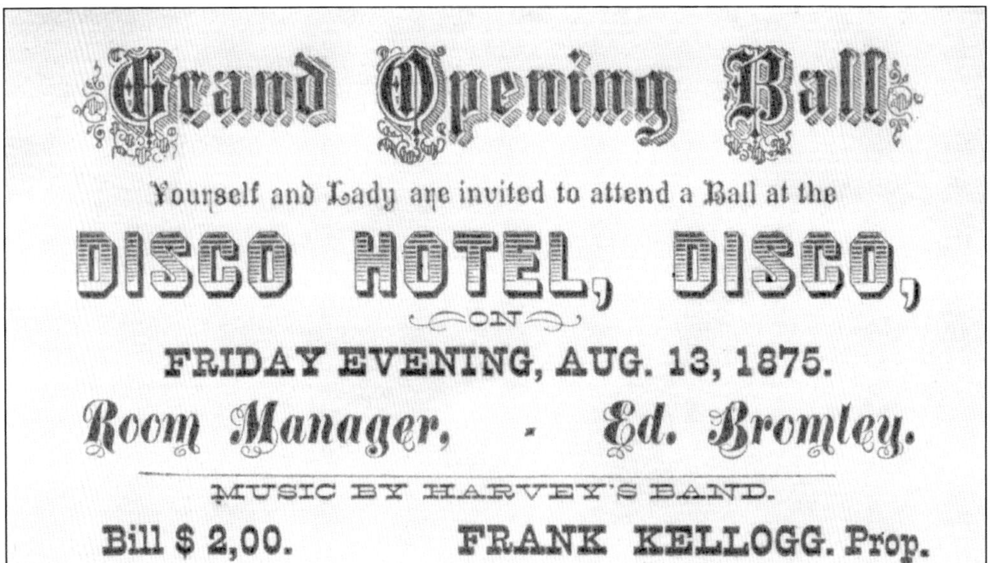


Like the Exchange Hotel in Utica, the Disco Hotel also hosted parties and dances as indicated by this ticket from 1875. After the stagecoach line ceased operations, the hotel became a private residence. The building was torn down around the middle of the 20th century to make way for a shopping center. (Louis Resner.)

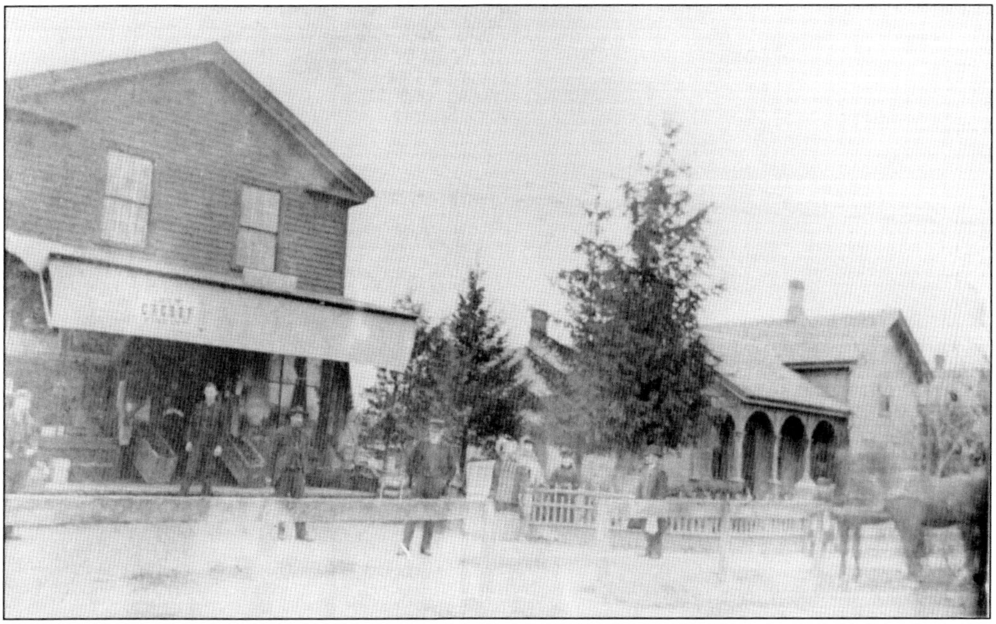

From the time it was established by the Pearsall family around the 1840s, the Disco General Store was a gathering place for villagers as evident in this photograph from the late 1800s. The business was purchased by John Switzer in 1880 and became known as the Switzer Store. The building was continuously used as a store until the 1990s. (Hugh Switzer and George Roberts family.)

## TIME MARCHES ON!

The reproduced letter which follows was sent out by my father on the occasion of the opening of his store.

*Disco, Mich., July 1st, 1880.*

*Dear Sir: I would respectfully inform you that I have opened a General Store at this place, where can be found an entirely new and fresh stock of goods, which I will sell at the lowest price, and when convenient I should be pleased to have you call and look through the store, whether you wish to purchase or not.*

*I have a fair assortment of Dress Goods, Hosiery, Cloths, Cassimeres, Hats and Caps, Boots and Shoes, a full line of Domestic Goods, Wall Paper, Yankee Notions, and all the latest Novelties.*

*I also keep a good stock of Shelf Hardware, Tinware, Machine, Plow and Carriage Bolts, Nails, Putty, Glass, Varnishes, Oils, and all shades and colors of Paints and Driers.*

*I also have a good line of Groceries, Crockery, Glassware, Patent Medicines, &c.*

*The highest market price paid for Butter and Eggs.*

*Soliciting a fair share of your patronge, I remain yours very truly*

*JOHN W. SWITZER.*

56 years have elapsed. A tribute to the founder and the ideals which have been carefully fulfilled. I now invite you to inspect my new store. I have set aside Thursday, December 17, 1936, between six and nine P.M., as open house at

Hugh G Switzer's

DISCO, MICH.

The 19th-century Switzer Store featured a variety of goods, including hardware, clothing, groceries, and patent medicine. This pamphlet, which was issued by John Switzer at the opening of his store, was reissued by his son Hugh Switzer in 1936 for the grand opening of his general store. Hugh modernized the store with new display cases and the latest items. (Hugh Switzer and George Roberts family.)

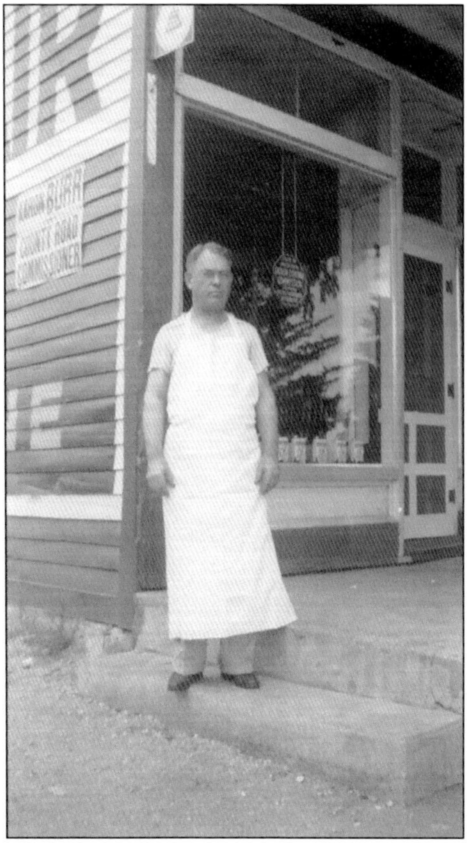


Hugh Switzer stands in front of his general store in Disco around 1936. Hugh owned and operated the store, which continued to offer a wide variety of goods and services to local farmers and families until around 1953, when the business was sold to George Wellhausen. (Hugh Switzer and George Roberts family.)

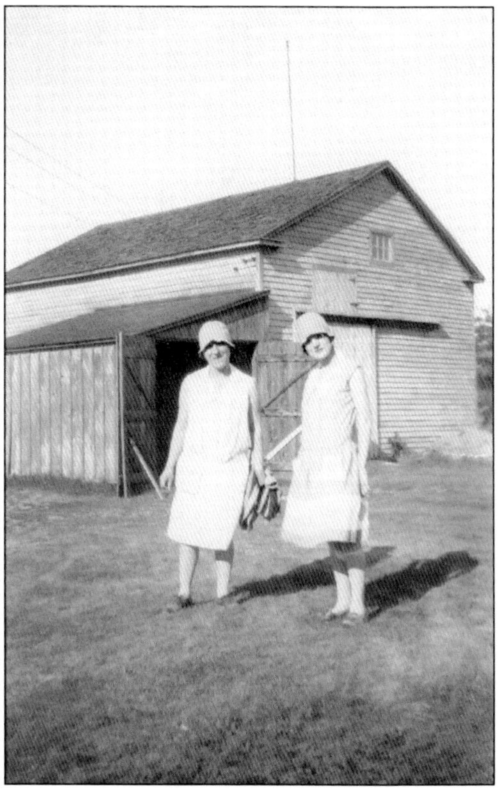

Josephine Roberts Switzer (left), wife of Hugh Switzer, and her friend Ethel Messmore, wife of James Victor Messmore, who ran an auto dealership in Utica, stand in front of the Switzer's barn in Disco around 1925. Hugh Switzer used the barn to store fertilizer that he sold to local farmers. (Hugh Switzer and George Roberts family.)

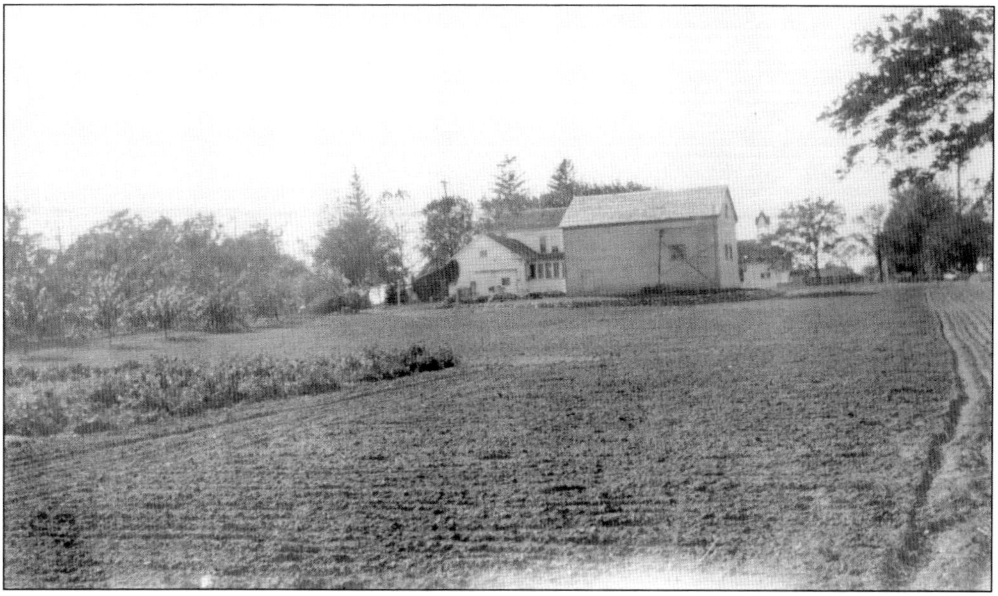

Hugh and Josephine Switzer bought the former Disco Hotel and raised crops on the acreage behind the house and barn. Visible in the background of this 1930s photograph is the Disco schoolhouse across Van Dyke Avenue, where Josephine taught school before she married Hugh. (Hugh Switzer and George Roberts family.)

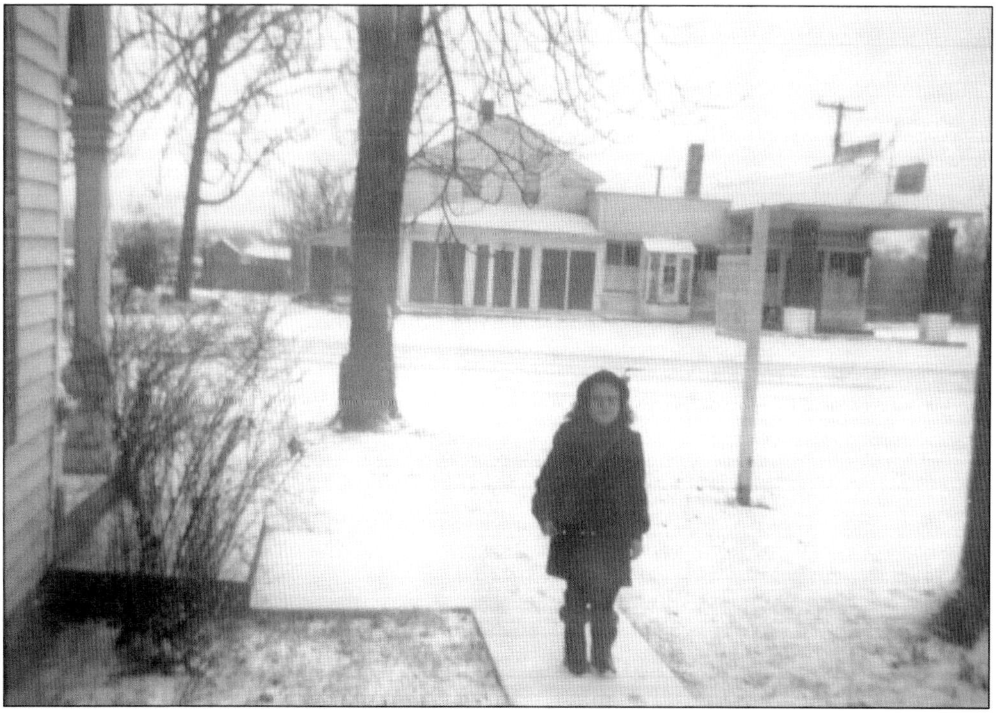

Patricia Roberts, grandniece of Hugh and Josephine Switzer, stands next to her family's house located just north of the Switzer Store. In the background of this 1948 photograph is one of Disco's old homes on Van Dyke Avenue that had been converted into a bar. Hugh Switzer's filling station was located behind the bar on 24 Mile Road. (Hugh Switzer and George Roberts family.)

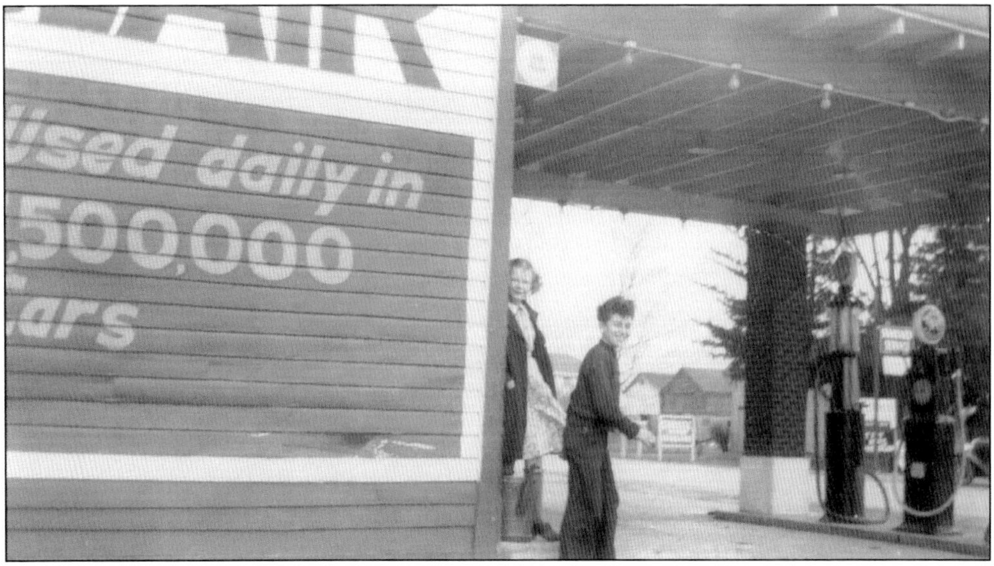

Harriet Brown (left) and ? Millard stand in front of the Switzer Store in Disco around 1936. Note the gasoline pumps and canopy that the Switzers added to the front of the store. These two children were from longtime Disco families. Many generations of families called Disco home, enjoying the neighborliness and business opportunities that come with small-town living. (Hugh Switzer and George Roberts family.)

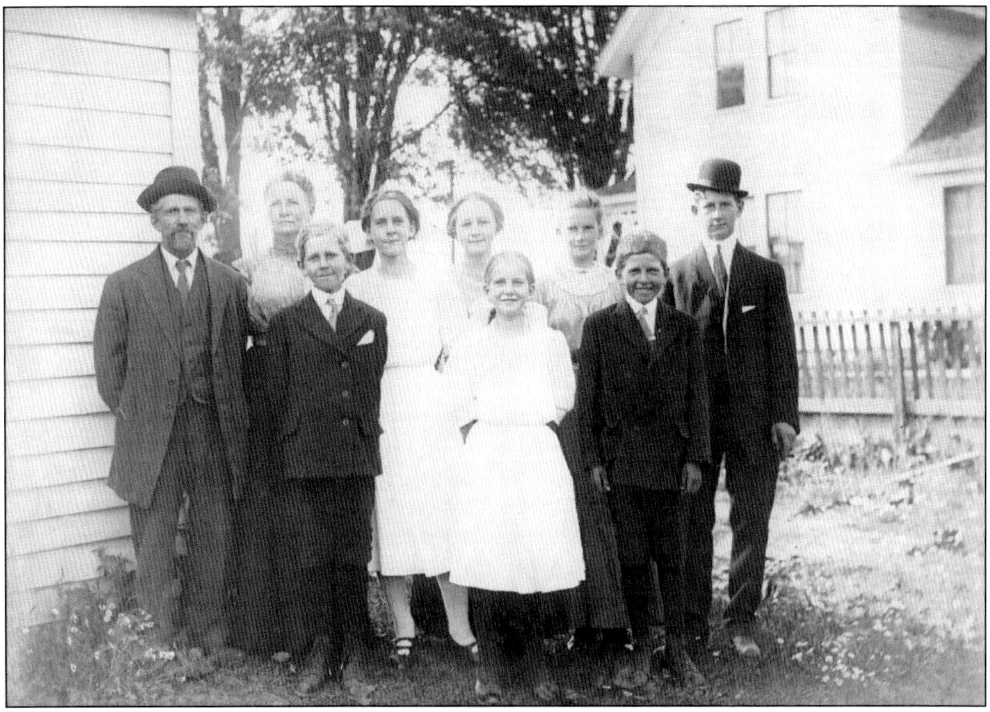

Julius Kirschbaum came to Disco from Prussia in the late 1800s, settling on a small farm east of the village. The family members in this 1910 photograph are, from left to right, (first row) Louis, Emma, and Bill; (second row) Julius, Anna (Julius's wife), Augusta, Flora, Bertha, and Julius Jr. Julius Kirschbaum Jr. became a justice of the peace for Shelby Township. (Lynn and Grace Drake.)

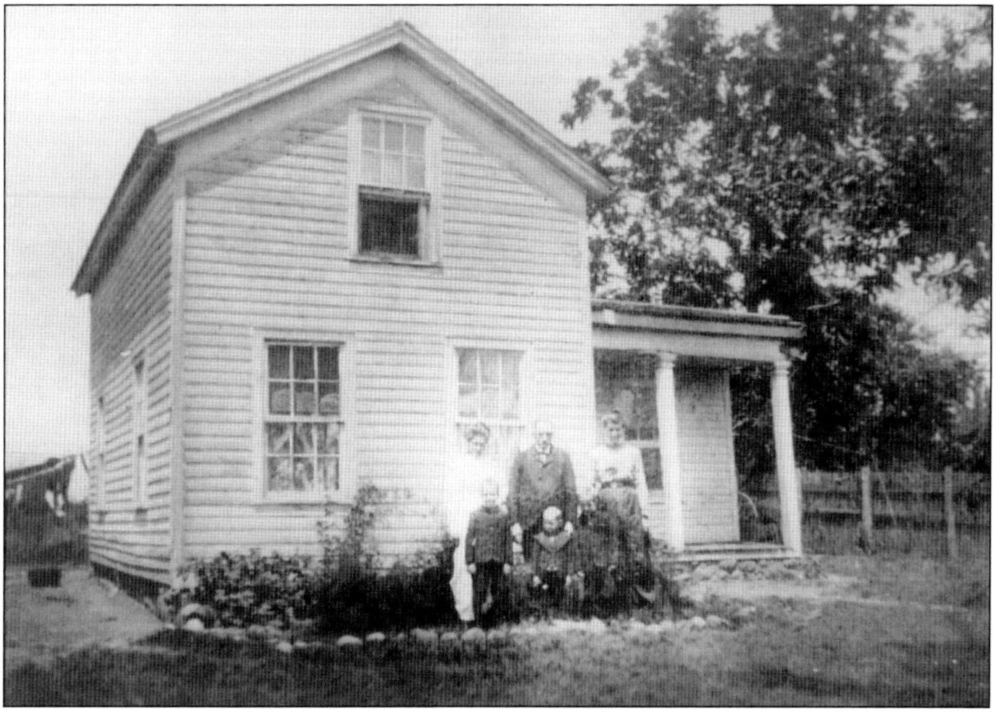

Egbert Herrington came to Disco from New York in the late 1800s and built this house on 24 Mile Road just west of the Switzer store. Egbert supported his family by peddling furs, butchered beef, and fruit. The family members in this 1901 photograph are, from left to right, (first row) Vernon, Edward, and Bernell; (second row) Delilah (Egbert's mother), Egbert, and his wife Harriett. (STHC.)

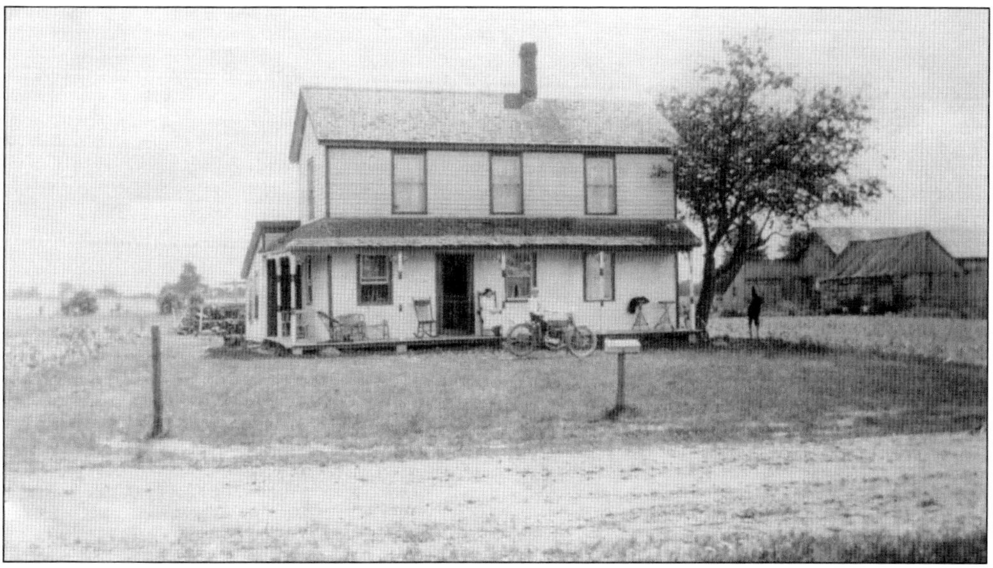

After Egbert Herrington died from an infected spider bite in 1910, young Edward Herrington quit school and went to work at the Switzer Store. His mother, Harriett, later married George Blumberg of Disco and the family moved to this house near the southwest corner of the village. Many members of the Herrington family spent their entire lives in Disco. (STHC.)

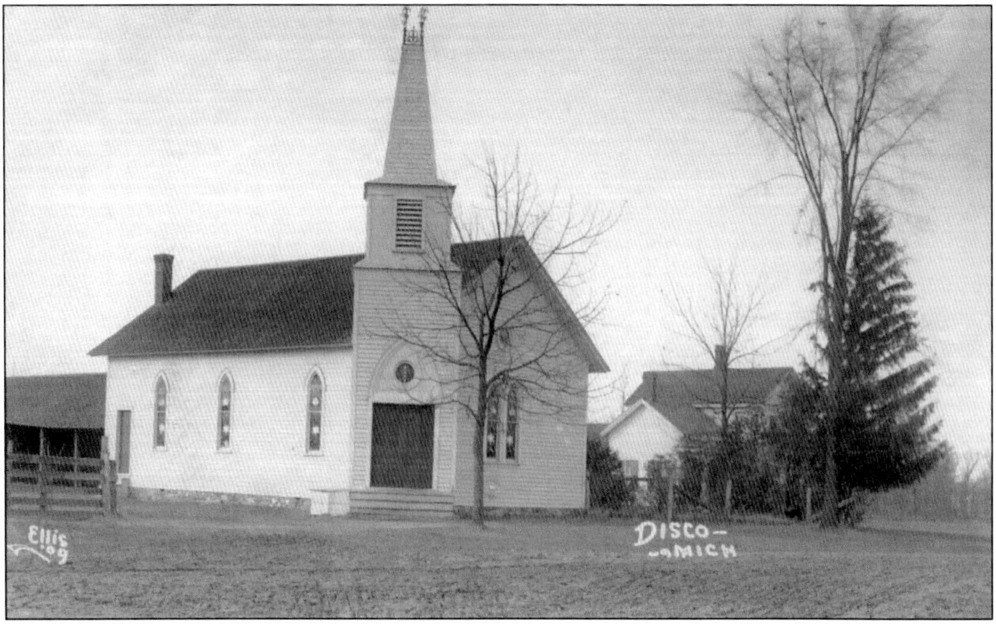

Shown here in a photograph produced by the Ellis Studio in 1909 is the Methodist Protestant Church in Disco. It was built on Van Dyke Avenue north of 24 Mile Road in 1890. Before this, the congregation met in a schoolhouse. When the Methodist congregation decided to build a new church in 1999, the church building was moved onto the Shelby Township municipal grounds. (Louis Resner.)

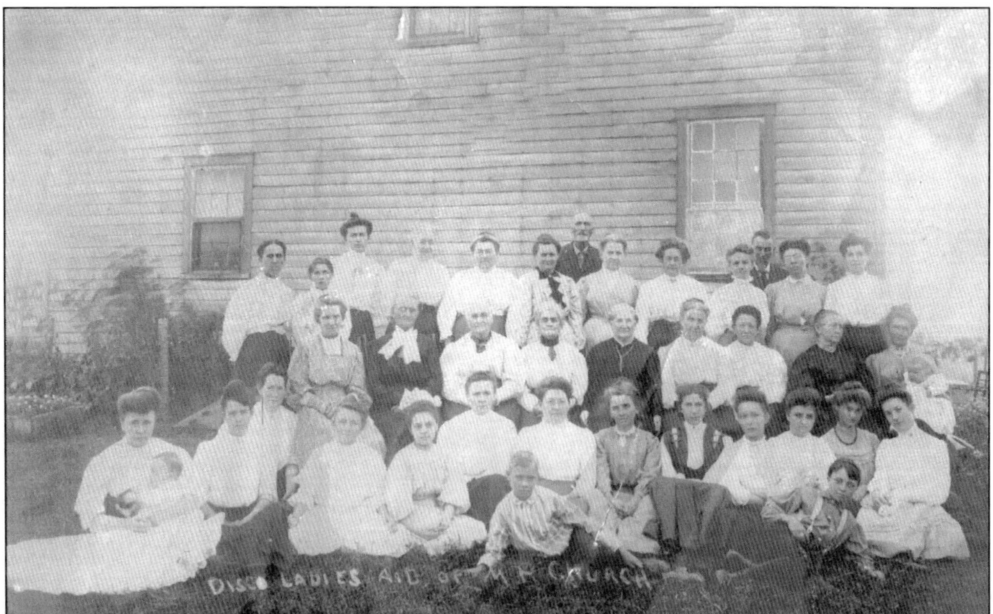

Here in 1907, the members of the Disco Ladies Aid of the Methodist Protestant Church gather for a photograph outside of the school where they held their meetings. Women's organizations like the Ladies Aid Society provided opportunities for local woman to gather for social activities and to engage in fund-raising and charitable works for the church and community. (STHC.)

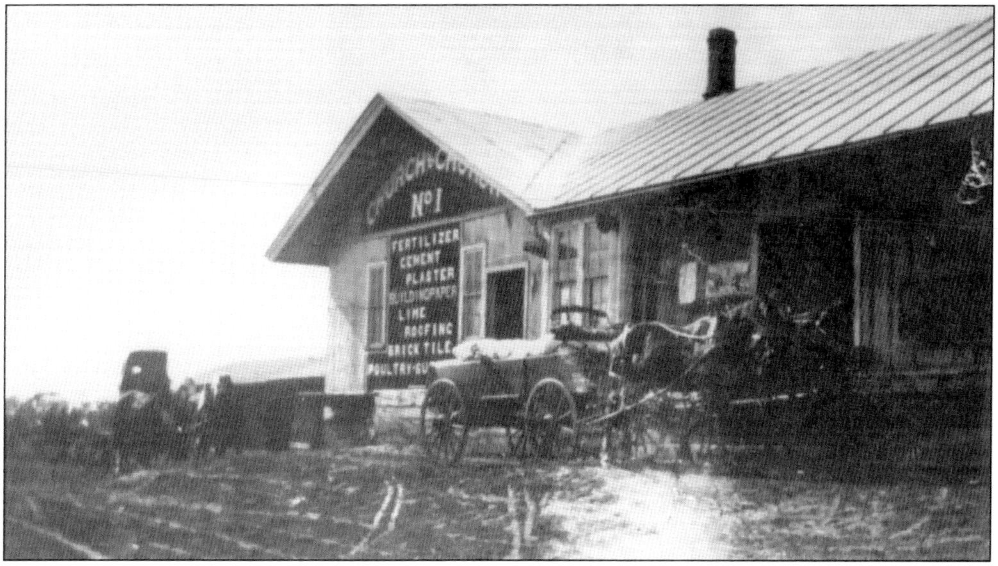


The Church and Church Company was located on West Utica Road near Main Street in Utica. It opened in the late 1890s, catering to the needs of local farmers and tradesmen with items that could not be obtained at the general store. For example, a sewer pipe for the Disco schoolhouse was purchased from this store according to school records from 1919. (Utica Public Library.)

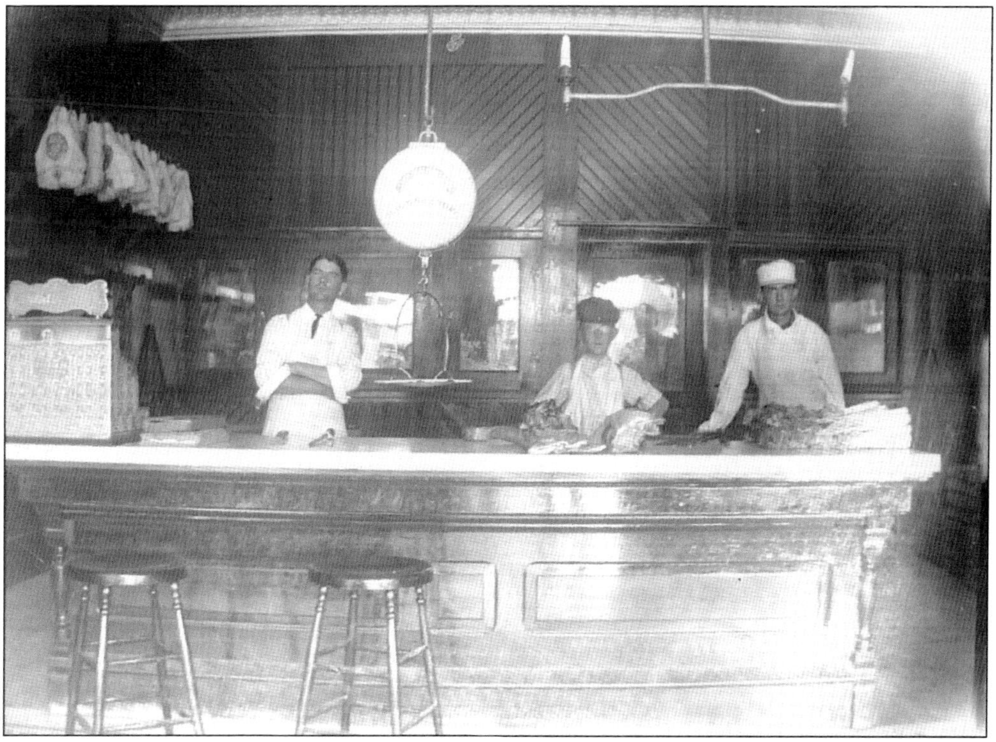

James Messmore bought a meat market in Utica in 1872 and moved the business to a building on the east side of Cass Avenue just south of Main Street in 1897. His son Howard Messmore took over the business in 1902, which stayed in the family until 1931. Three unidentified shopkeepers pose inside the market around 1907. (Douglas Harvey; photograph by Burt Harvey.)

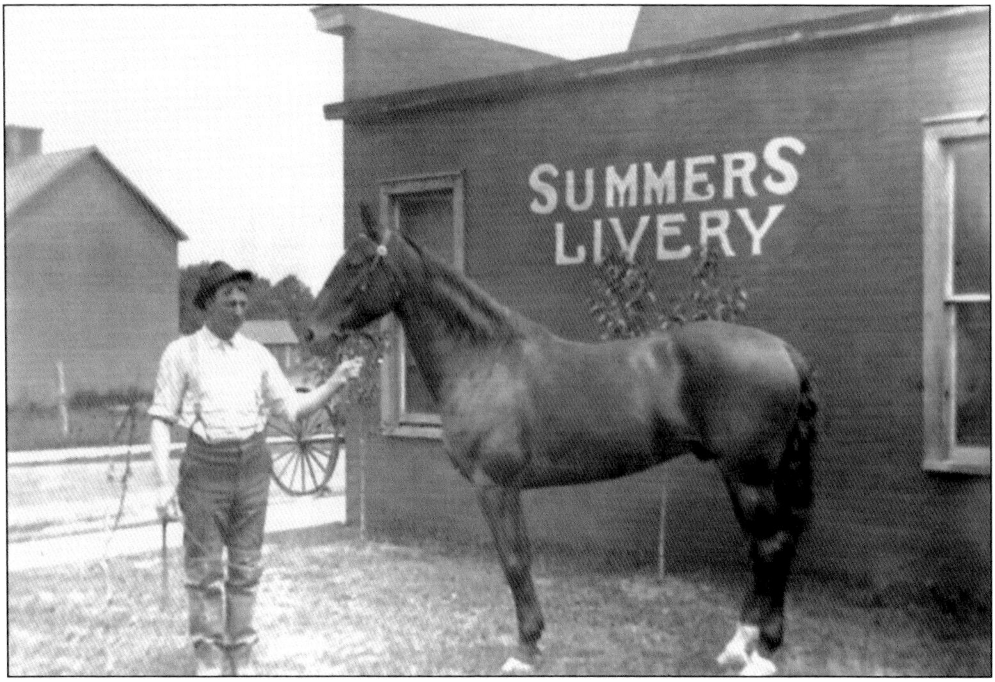


Addison Summers's livery was located on Summers Street between Cass Avenue and Van Dyke Avenue in Utica. Summers was born in 1857 on his father's 160-acre farm on 23 Mile Road in Shelby Township. His grandfather Jacob Summers was one of the township's first settlers. Employee William Simms is shown here with one of the livery horses around 1907. (Douglas Harvey; photograph by Burt Harvey.)

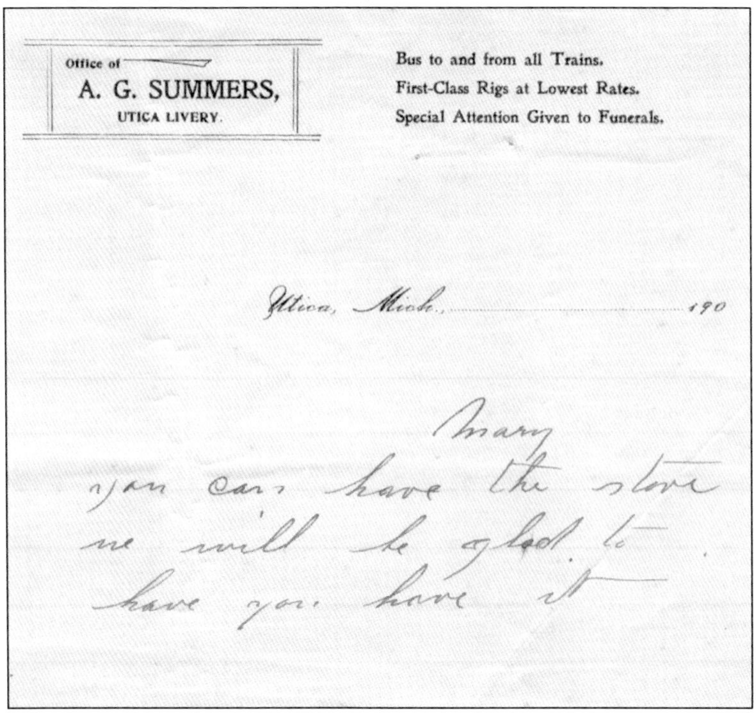

Office of
A. G. SUMMERS,
UTICA LIVERY.

Bus to and from all Trains.
First-Class Rigs at Lowest Rates.
Special Attention Given to Funerals.

Utica, Mich., 190

Mary
you can have the stove
we will be glad to
have you have it

Addison Summers purchased the livery business from Henry Harris in 1891. A horse-drawn bus line operating to and from the Utica train depot with stops at the Exchange Hotel was his primary business. The Summers Livery also provided other sorts of transportation services, according to the business letterhead on this note, and continued to do so until 1911. (STHC.)

The Central Drug and Grocery store is pictured here on Main Street in Utica around 1907. A local physician, Dr. George Roberson, opened a store on this spot in 1898. The original building was moved and Roberson built this new one in 1901. It continued as a drug and grocery store until the end of World War II. (Douglas Harvey; photograph by Burt Harvey.)

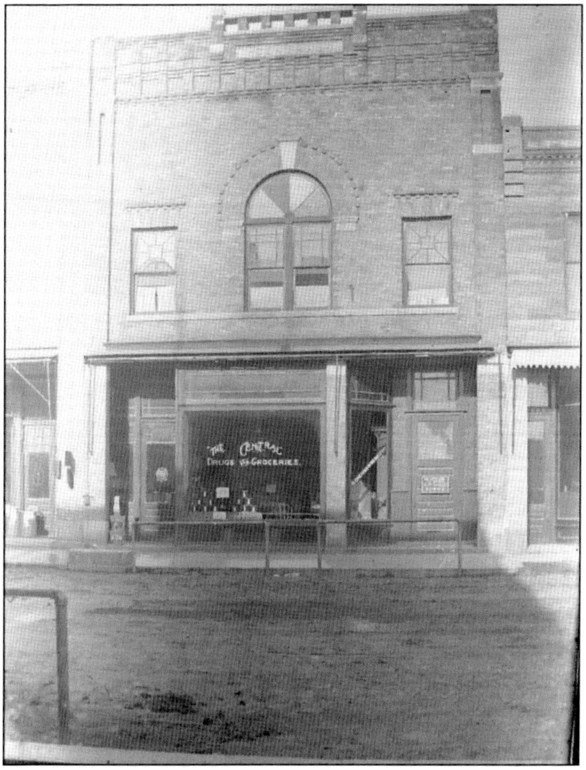

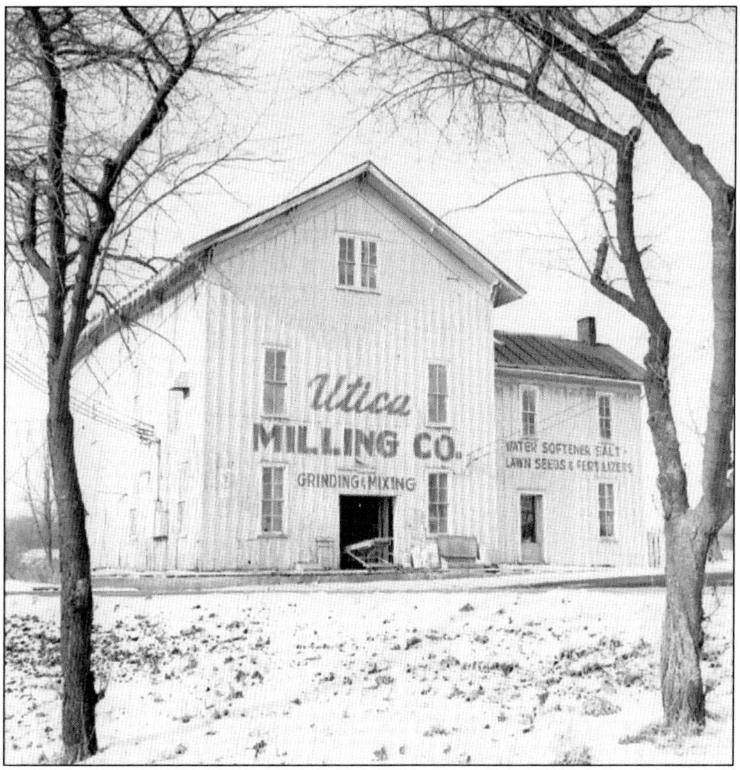


The mill alongside the Clinton River on Main Street in Utica was taken over by the Criesman family in the 1880s and continued to grind grains for farmers throughout Shelby Township. The business also offered other goods and services that met the changing needs of local farmers, which helped it to survive into the latter half of the 20th century. (MD.)

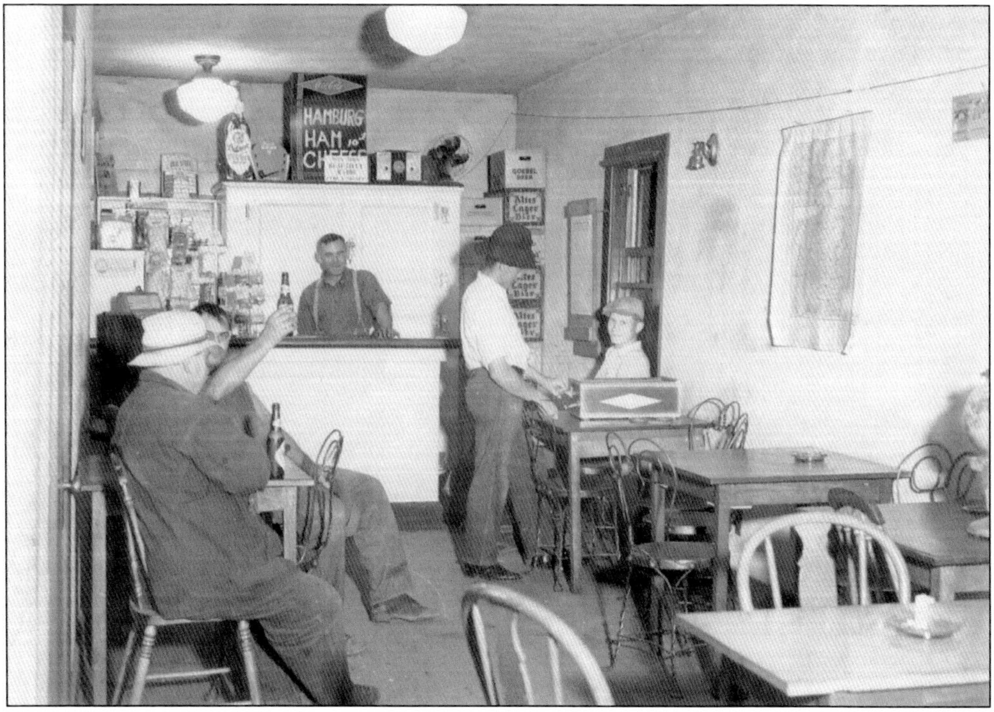


Several businesses popped up between the two villages of Disco and Utica during the 20th century. The Midway Café, located midway between Disco and Utica, opened at 22 Mile Road and Van Dyke Avenue in the early 1900s. Standing behind the counter, proprietor William Frase chats with customers at the café in the late 1930s. (Howard Frase family.)

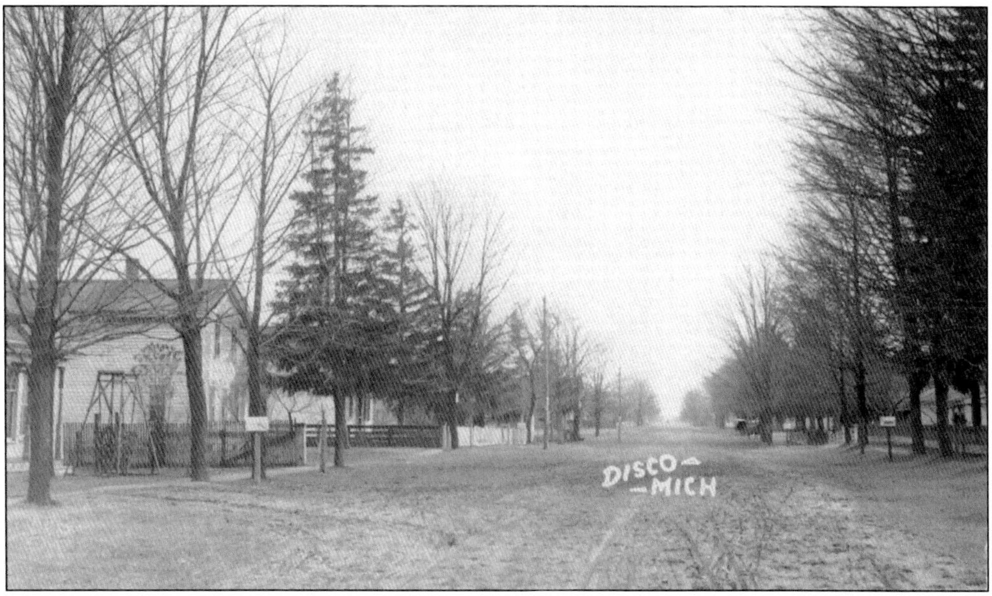


Utica became a city in 1937 and continues to thrive to this day. Disco remained a quiet country crossroads village, as pictured here in this postcard from the early 1900s (looking south on Van Dyke Avenue), well into the 20th century. After World War II, it began a slow decline due, in part, to changes wrought by the advent of the automobile. (STHC.)

# *Three*

# Farms and Families

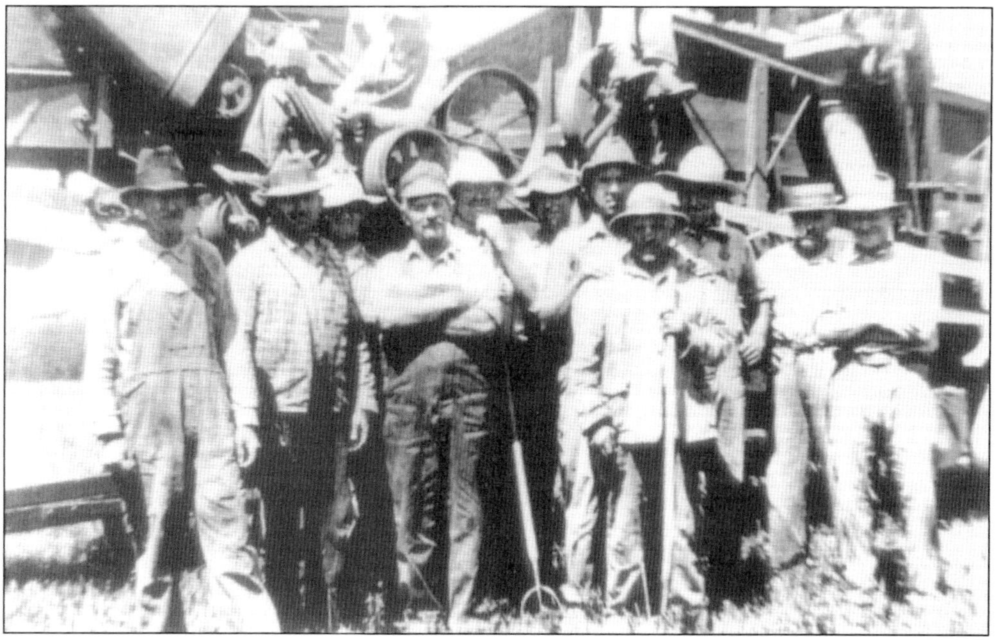

A group of local farmers takes a break in front of an early model threshing machine in this undated photograph. Farming was often a solitary, dawn-to-dusk occupation. But when a community effort was needed to get the crop harvested in time for market day or before winter set in, neighbors pulled together to get it done. (STHC.)

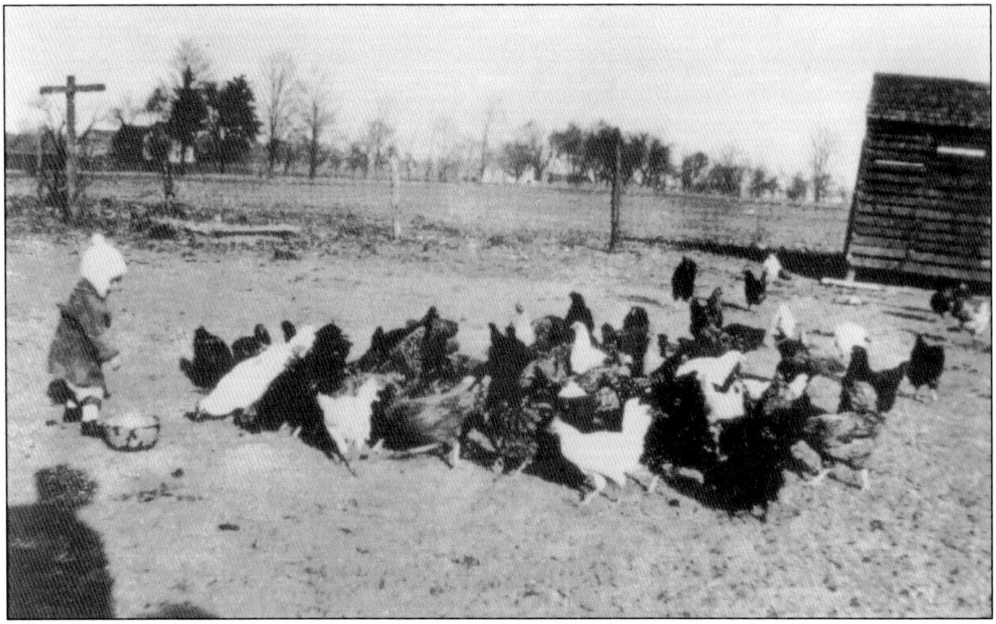

All family members on a farm helped with chores, even the youngest, like this toddler feeding chickens in 1930s Shelby Township. Well into the 1950s, most people in the township made a living farming, raising chickens for eggs, cattle for meat and dairy, and sheep for wool. They grew a variety of crops such as wheat, corn, and potatoes, plus specialty items to meet changing market demands. Farms often stayed in families for generations. The farm below was on 23 Mile Road west of Ryan Road and had been in early settler Jacob Summer's family for three generations before the Foster family acquired it around 1900. Pictured by the farmhouse are, from left to right, unidentified, Jane Foster, unidentified, and John Foster. (Both, STHC.)

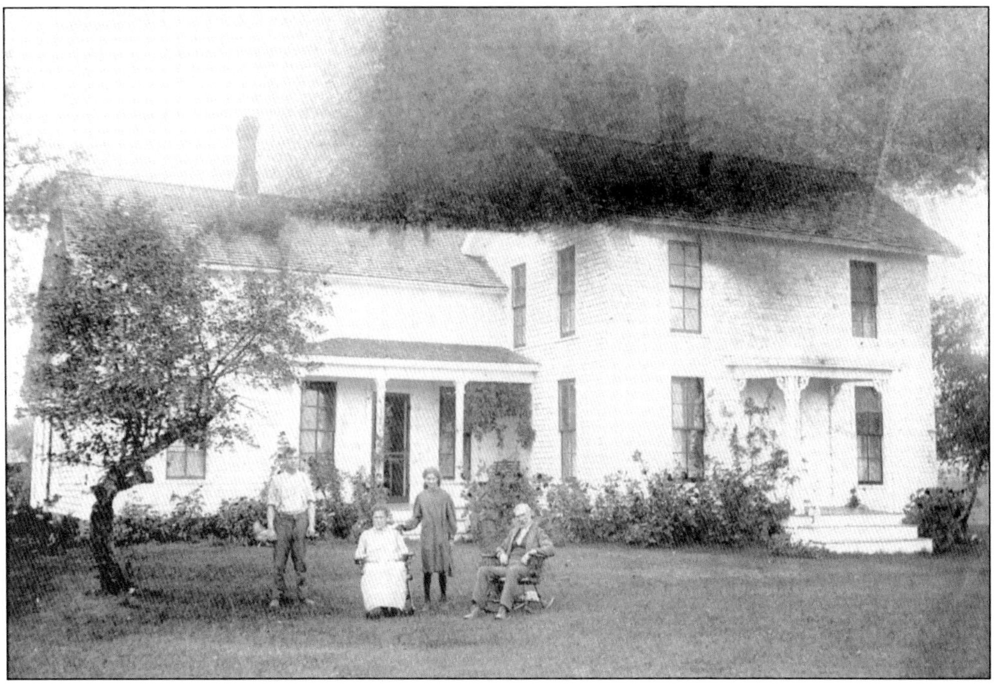

Mary Lagodna, in her late 70s, sits in her farmhouse around 1924. Charles and Mary Lagodna came to Michigan from eastern Prussia in 1881 and settled on a 40-acre farm at the northwest corner of Jewell and 25 Mile Roads. They farmed the land and raised several children who settled on farms of their own in Shelby Township. (Lynn and Grace Drake.)

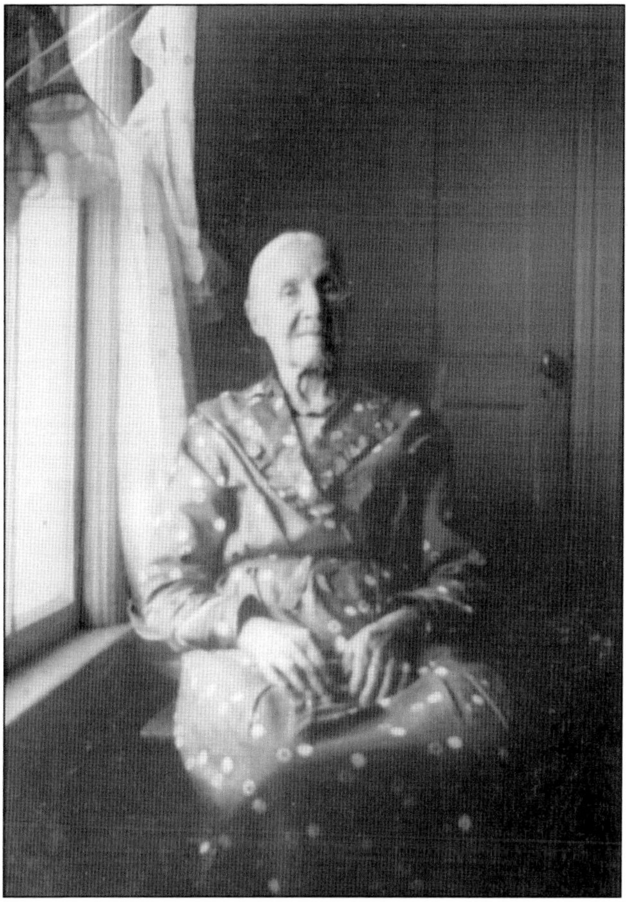

Charles Lagodna Jr. took over the Lagodna farm on Jewell Road. Pictured here on the farm are his five daughters with their cousins around 1925. The oldest daughter, Florence, holds the pump handle. The others are, from left to right, (first row) Shirley, Carl Lagodna, and Ralph Lagodna; (second row) Ruth, Johanna, and Marion. (Lynn and Grace Drake.)

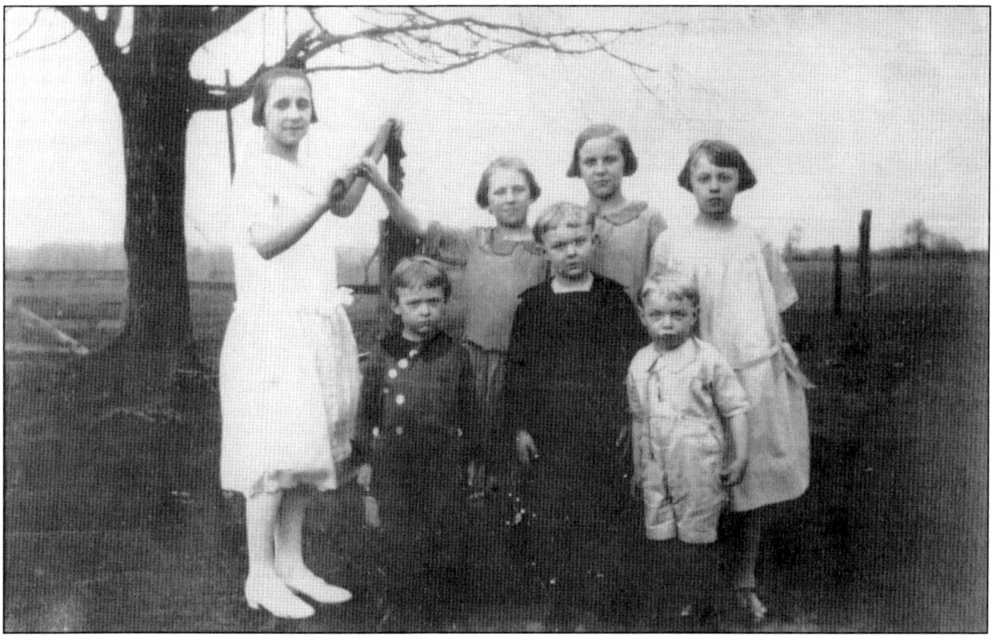

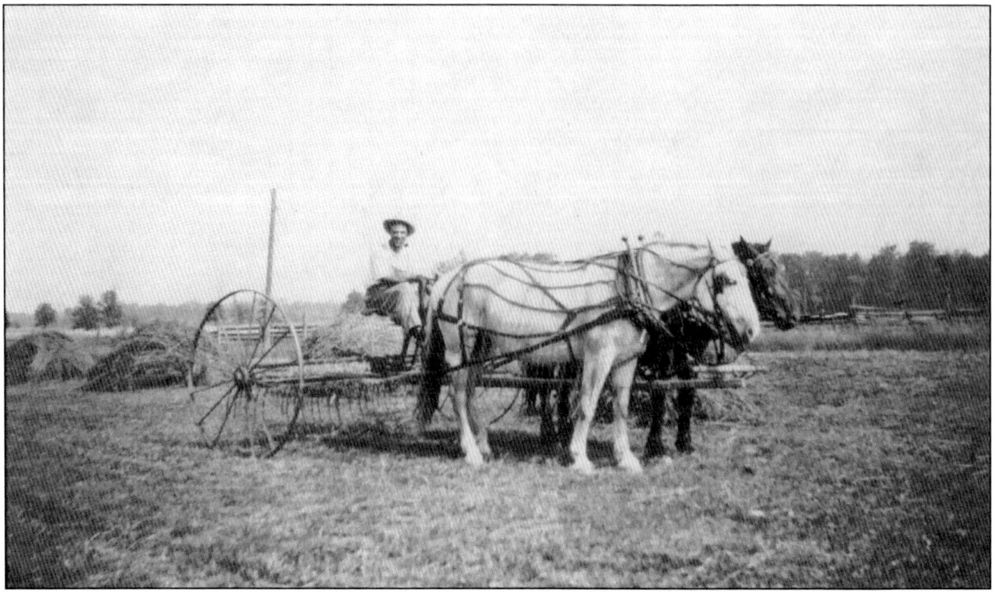

Fred Lagodna, another son of Charles and Mary Lagodna, bought a farm on 22 Mile Road east of Schoenherr Road around 1916. The farm once belonged to early Shelby Township settler Harvey Lewis. Like his mother and father, Fred and his wife, Martha, farmed the land and raised children. The children attended Crowe School, a nearby one-room schoolhouse, and helped out on the farm. In the c. 1925 photograph above, Fred drives a team of horses pulling a hay rake. Below, Martha bundles cornstalks into sheaves. The Lagodnas also grew wheat, vegetables, and other cash crops. (Both, Lynn and Grace Drake.)

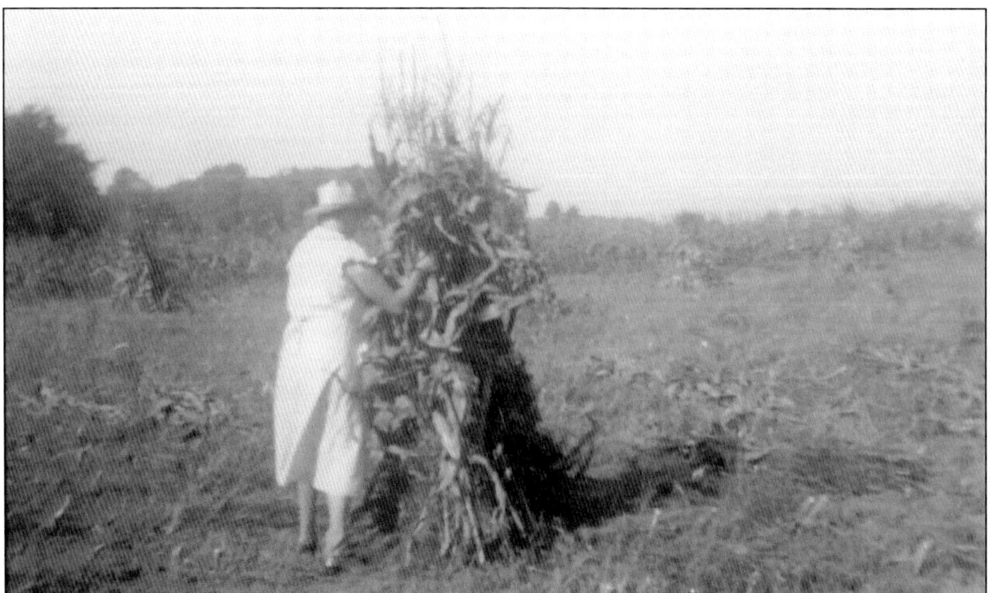

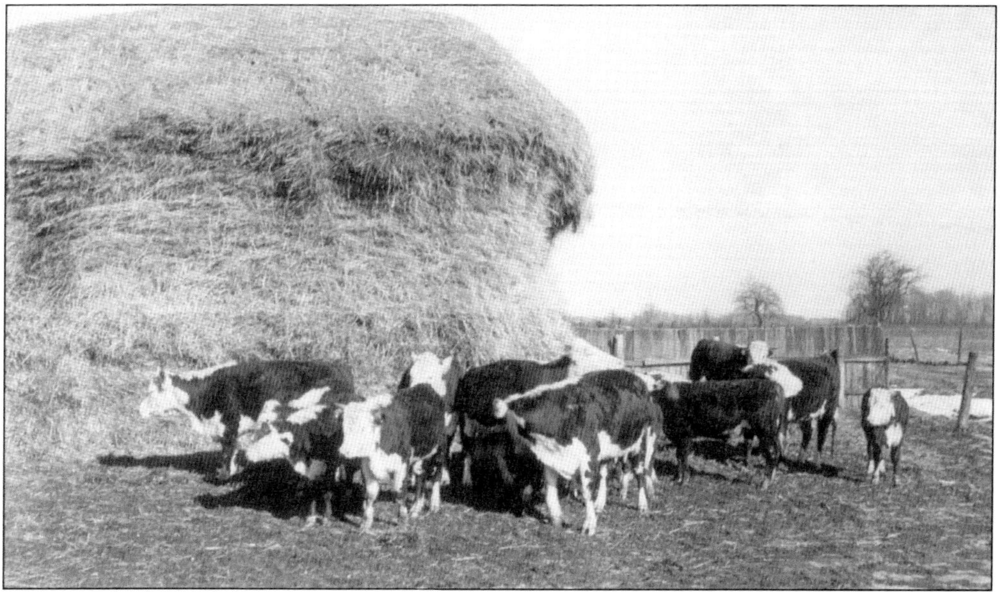

Fred Lagodna raised farm animals like ducks and chickens for meat and eggs. He also had a herd of dairy cattle and grew the hay that fed them. There were many dairy farms in Shelby Township in the early 1900s. But during the Great Depression, the federal government set strict standards on sanitation, milk pricing, and fat content in milk for the nation's dairy industry. Fred and Martha Lagodna found the regulations onerous and switched to raising beef cattle. Above, some of their herd strolls past a large mound of hay on the way to the barn. Below, a formidable-looking bull stares down the photographer. (Both, Lynn and Grace Drake.)

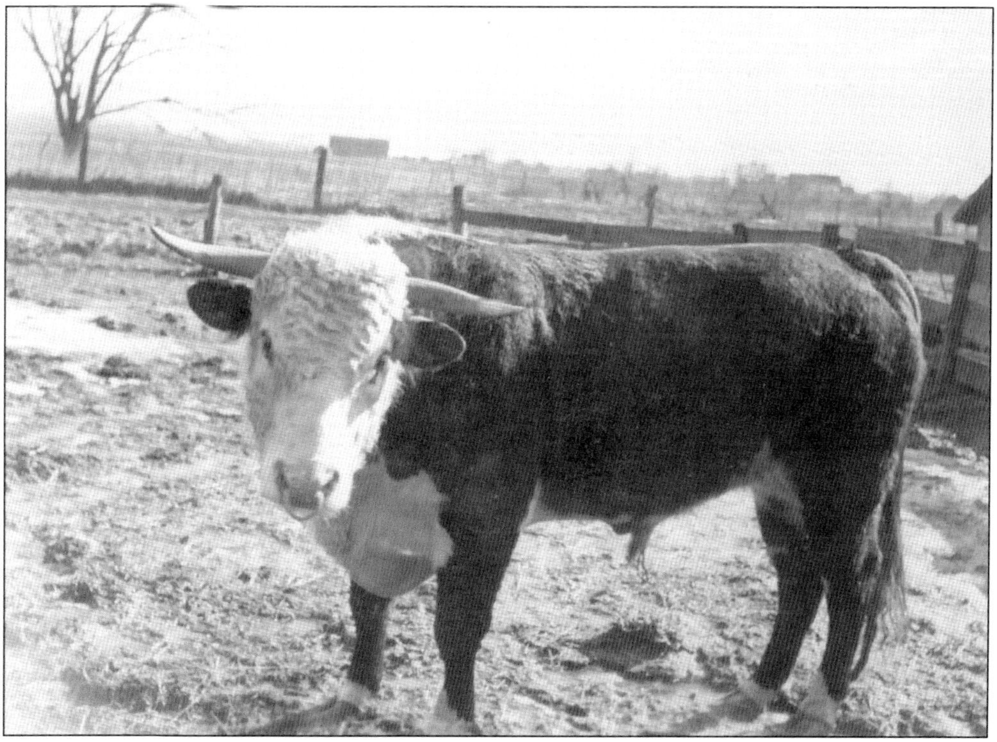

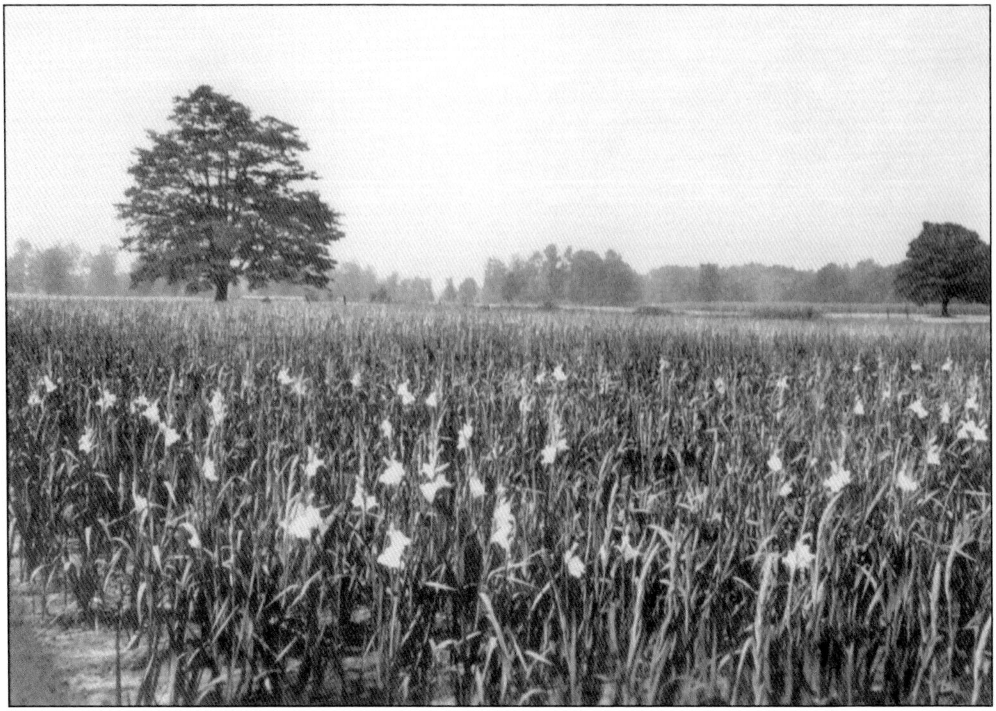

Several acres of the farm were devoted to growing gladiolas, which Martha Lagodna raised with the help of her children. Not only was growing flowers a hobby of Martha's, it was also another source of income for the family. The hand-cut flowers were sorted into containers and transported by flatbed truck to nearby florists and to the farmer's markets in Royal Oak and Detroit. Gladiolas need open fields and bright sunlight for the best blooms, and they thrive in well-drained soil that has been fertilized with manure. All were in abundance on the Lagodna farm. (Both, Lynn and Grace Drake.)

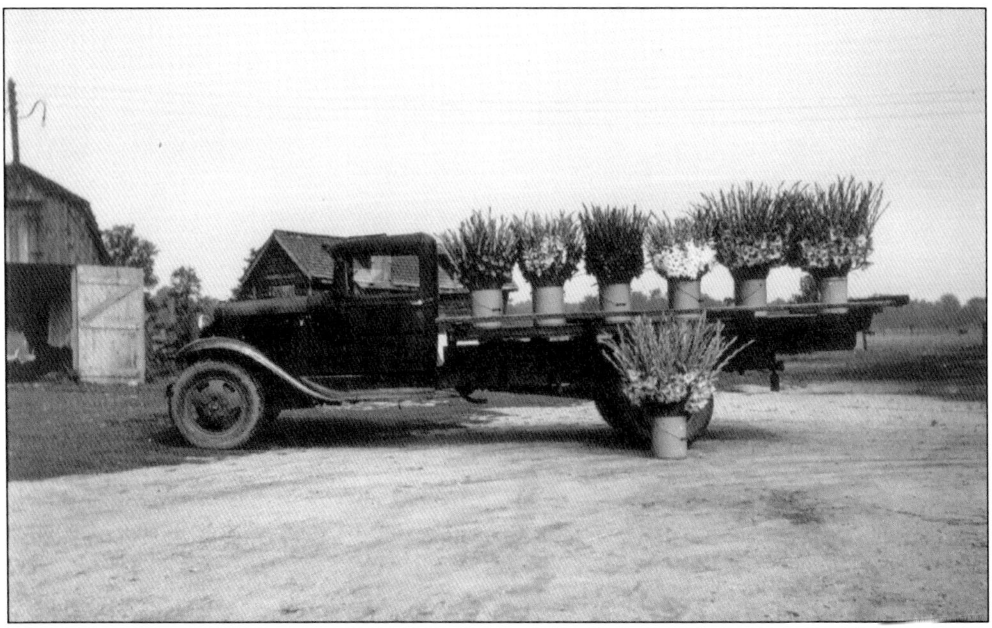

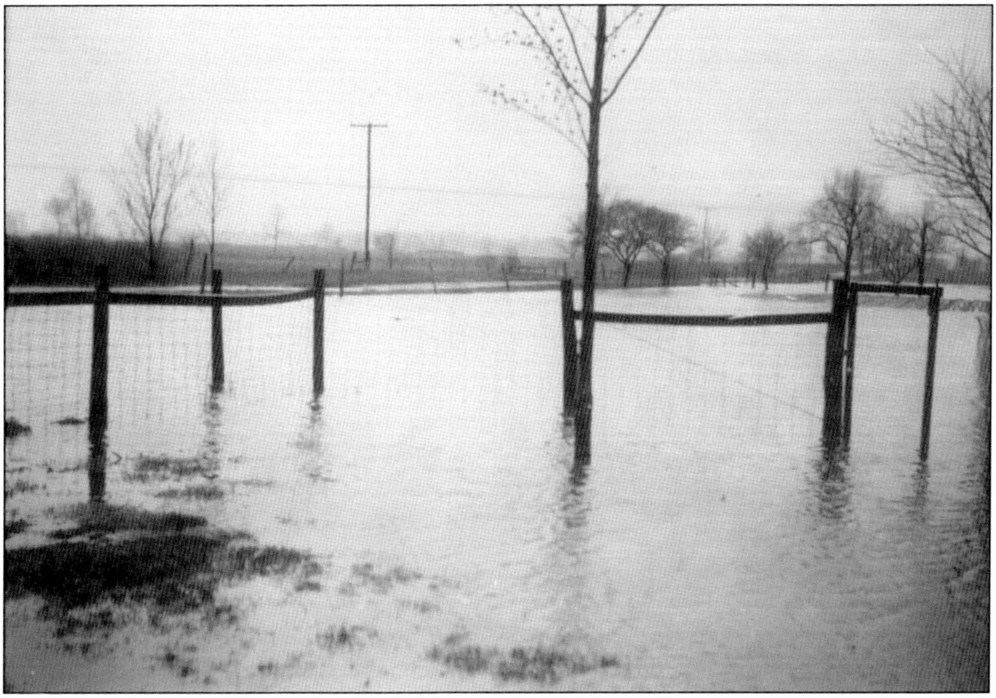

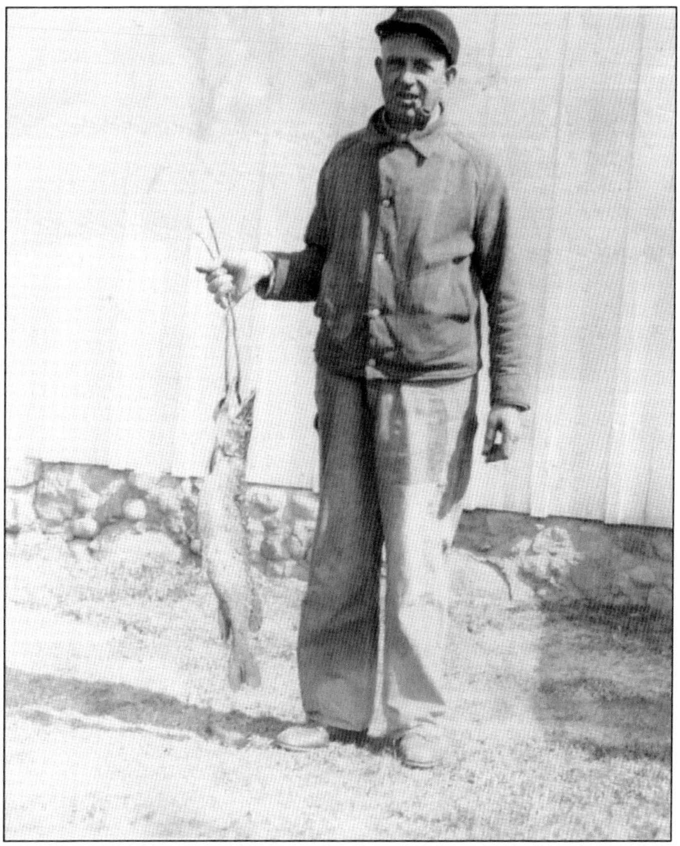

A creek that is part of the Clinton River watershed ran through the Lagodna farm. Like many of the creeks that cut through the farms of Shelby Township, they were used for irrigation, watering livestock, and were often dammed to make ponds for ice. A creek could also be a source of trouble as seen above in this photograph from the late 1930s when the Lagodnas' fields and 22 Mile Road were flooded after very heavy rains. Before the introduction of modern-day pollutants, these creeks were much cleaner, and the abundant fish in them provided sport and food. At right, Fred Lagodna holds a pike that he took out of his creek in the late 1940s, which is known today as the Decker Drain. (Both, Lynn and Grace Drake.)

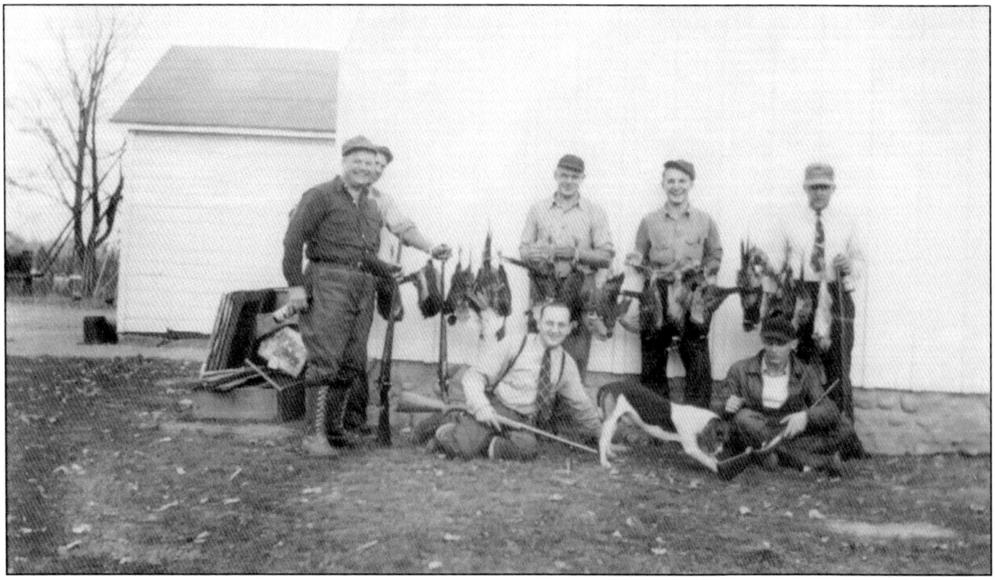

The many acres of open country crisscrossed by fresh creeks, which characterized Shelby Township through the first half of the 20th century, attracted a variety of fowl for farmers to hunt for food and sport. Here a group of unidentified friends, neighbors, and family members gathers at the Fred Lagodna farm after a hunt to have a beer and show off their game. (Lynn and Grace Drake.)

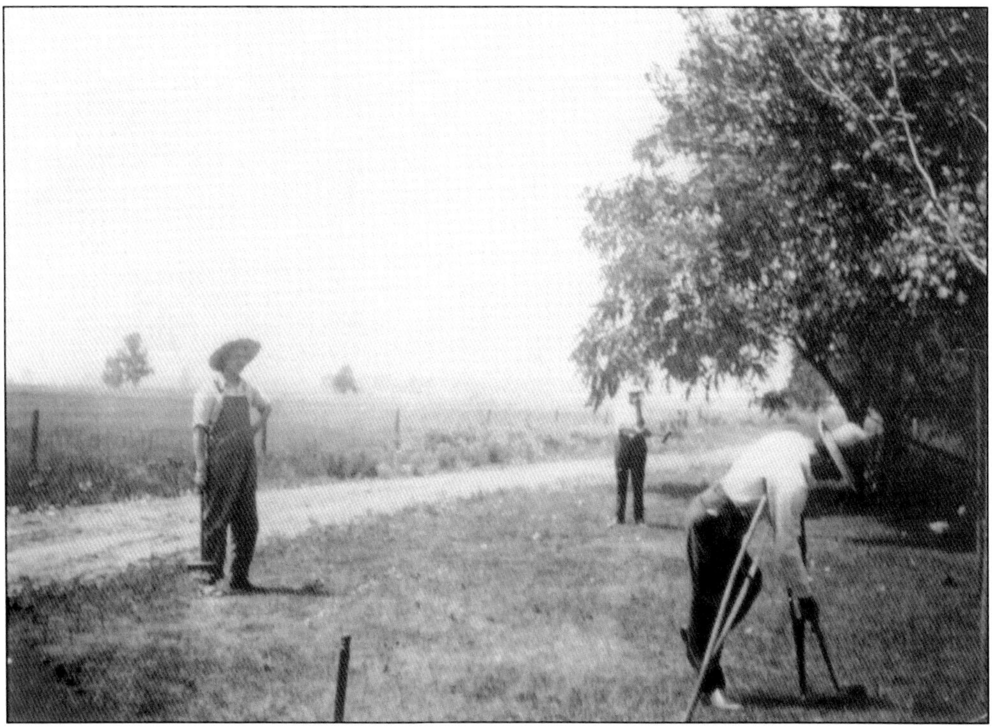

On a sunny day, a farmer could always take time out from working for a game of croquet. Here, around 1918, three men enjoy a game in the front yard at Fred Lagodna's place. Note 22 Mile Road behind them, which at this time was a narrow dirt track. The players are, from left to right, Fred Lagodna, family friend Herman Stuehmer, and neighbor John Lewis. (STHC.)

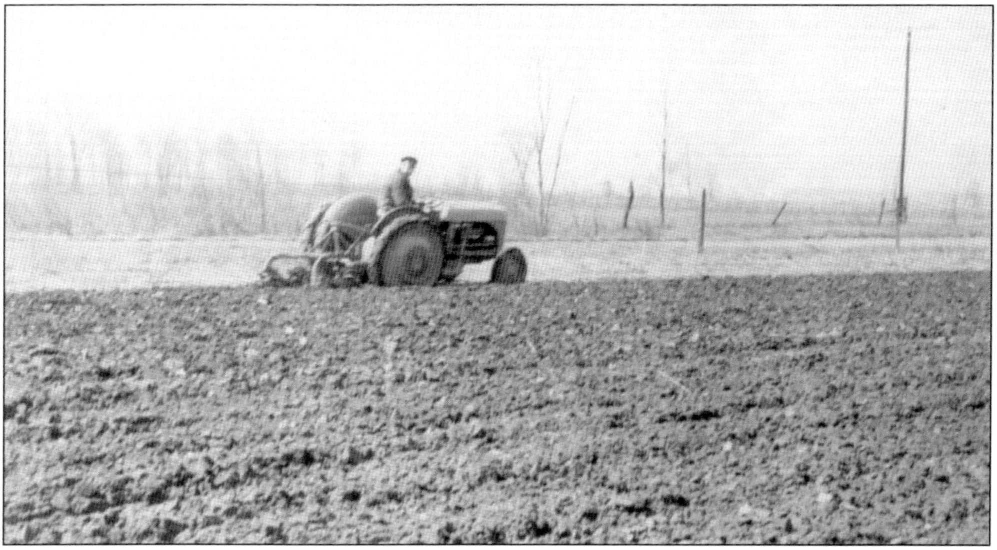

By 1940, Fred Lagodna had traded in his horses and harnesses for the latest gasoline-powered tractor to pull the hay rake, soil tiller, and other farm equipment. Here he is turning over one of his fields for a new planting. He also found time to be active in the community and served as Shelby Township supervisor in the 1940s and 1950s. (Lynn and Grace Drake.)

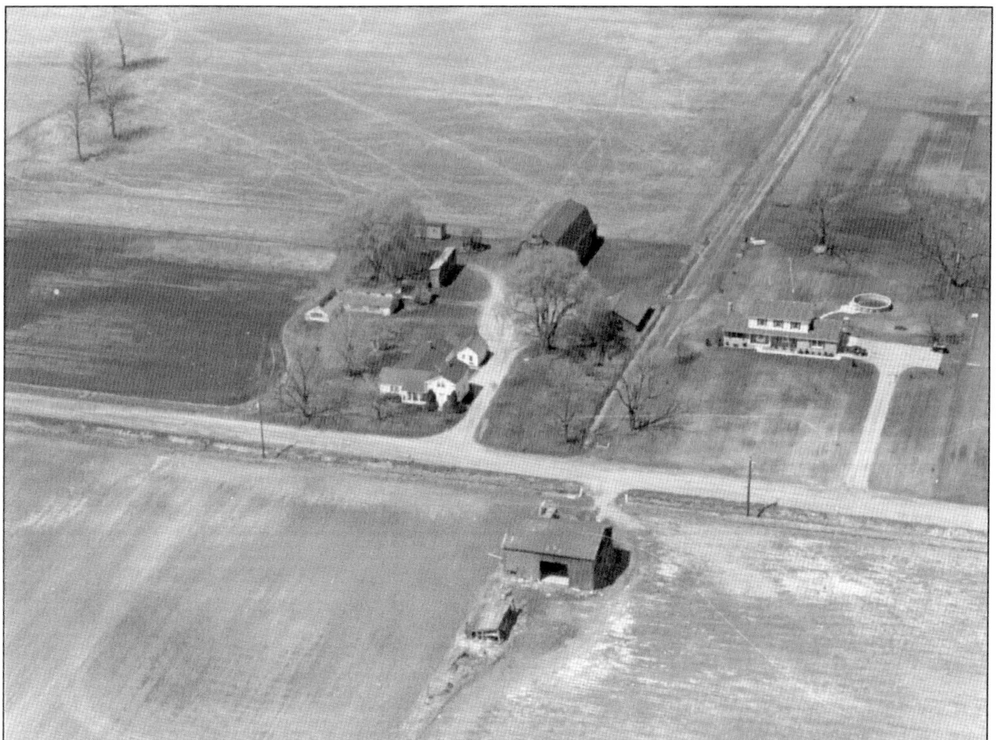

The Lagodna farm, on the north side of 22 Mile Road, is in the center of this photograph taken around 1965 shortly before the buildings were demolished. The Lewis family farmhouse that sat to the east for nearly 120 years had already been demolished and replaced with a modern split-level home. The barn across the street belonged to the Lewis family. (Lynn and Grace Drake.)

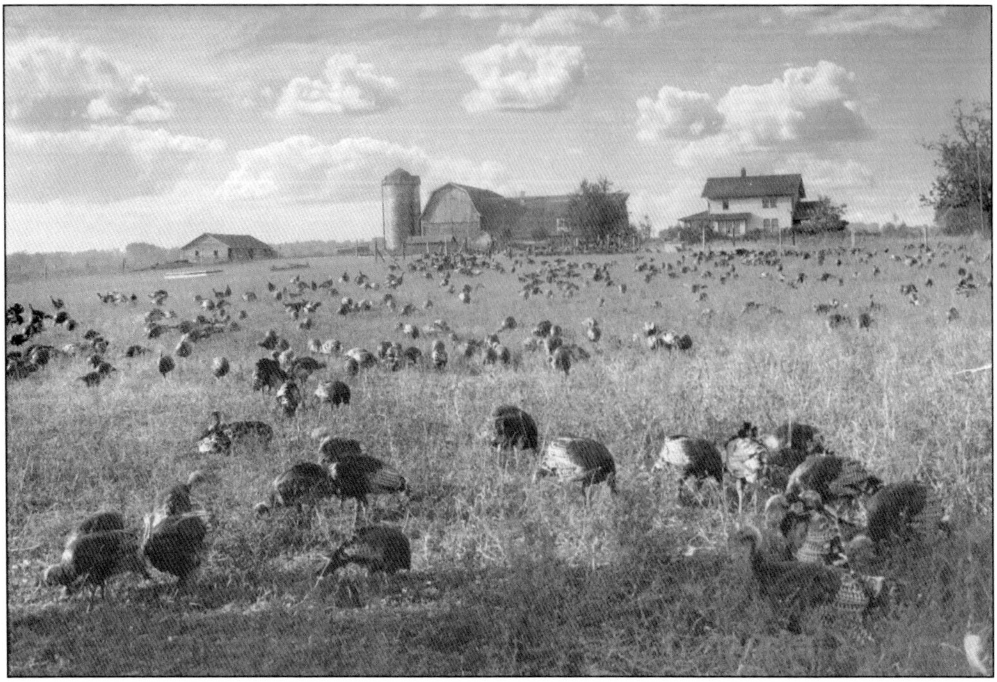

In 1911, Ernest Hardy bought a 120-acre farm at 25 Mile and Shelby Roads and moved his family from Allegan County, Michigan. He joined the growing number of dairy farmers in Shelby Township. The Hardy dairy farm was prosperous until the Great Depression when the Hardy children had to leave school to help raise the turkeys shown here in this photograph of the farm in the 1930s. (Jean Robertson.)

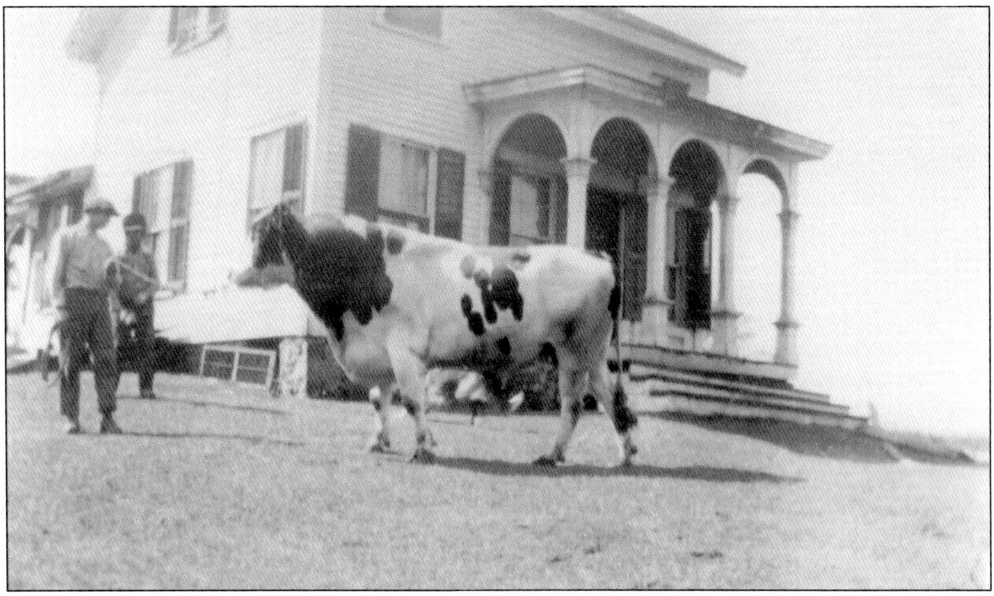

Ernest Hardy owned a premier herd of registered Holsteins, considered to be the best dairy cattle. He and his son James Hardy bought a half interest in a grand champion Holstein bull for $20,000 in the late 1940s. Here two unidentified farm hands display the animal in front of one of the Hardy family farmhouses on 25 Mile Road. (Michael and Christy Meyer.)

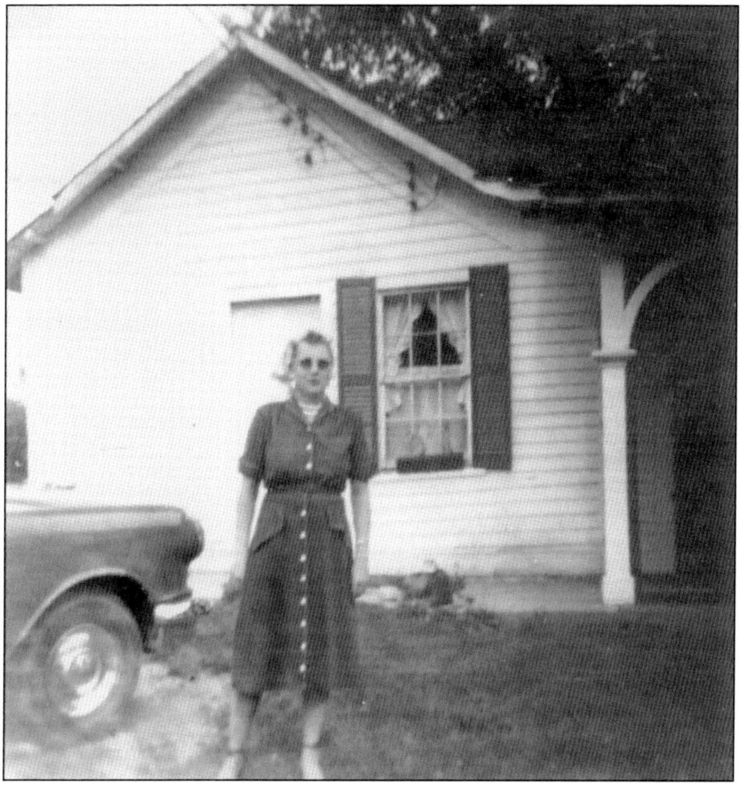

Two of Ernest Hardy's daughters bought farms of their own nearby. Jean Hardy bought the former Samuel Axford farm around 1951. Her sister Jane Pauline (shown here in 1955) bought an adjoining farm with her husband, Gerald Falls, in 1943. Together they raised livestock and grew hay, wheat, and corn. (Michael and Christy Meyer.)

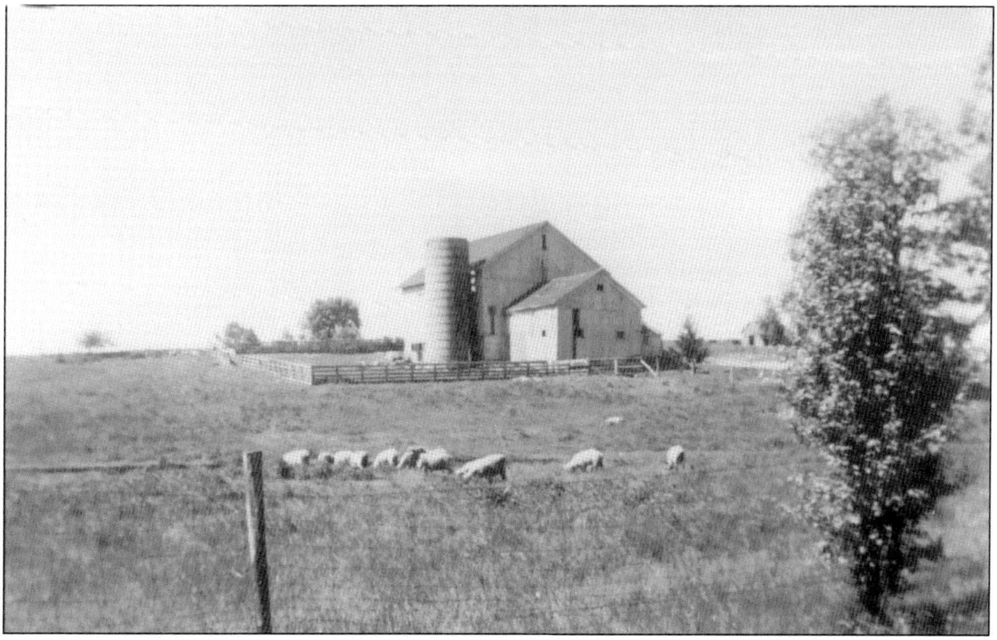

Here is the Falls and Hardy sheep farm around 1950. The sale of sheared wool was an important part of the family income. Today the barns and fences are gone and have been replaced by a modern housing development. Two of the old Hardy family farmhouses still stand on the south side of 25 Mile Road. (Michael and Christy Meyer.)

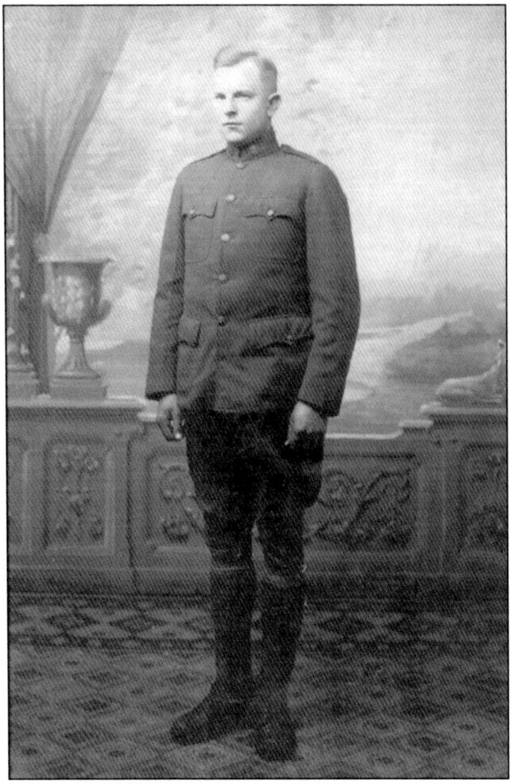

Gustav Streowska poses in his World War I uniform for his portrait in 1918. Gustav was born in Detroit to German and Polish parents in 1893. Drafted in 1917, he served as a cook for the U.S. Army. After his service, Gustav married Laura Klann, bought the former David Wilcox farm in Shelby Township in 1926, and changed his name to Gust Strouse. (Delores Strouse Metro.)

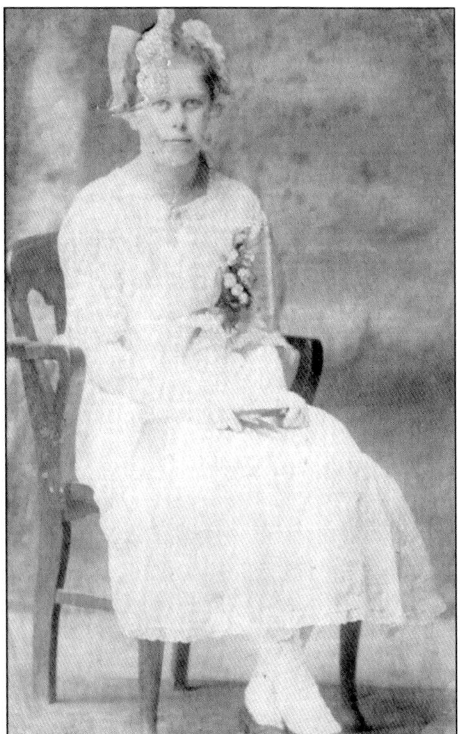

Laura Klann sits for her 1916 confirmation photograph. Laura was born in Troy, Michigan, in 1904 to William and Louise Klann, who bought a 66-acre farm at the southwest corner of 26 Mile and Mound Roads in Shelby Township around 1920. Laura and Gust Strouse's son Donald was born in 1923 and their youngest daughter, Delores, was born in the Wilcox house in 1941. (Delores Strouse Metro.)

Here Gust Strouse drives his Farmall tractor at the farm around 1945. He was a truck farmer raising large quantities of vegetables and driving them down to a market stall at Detroit's Eastern Market. The Strouse family's cash crops were carrots, squash, potatoes, and cucumbers. They also raised pigs for meat, chickens for eggs, and a few cows for milk. (Delores Strouse Metro.)

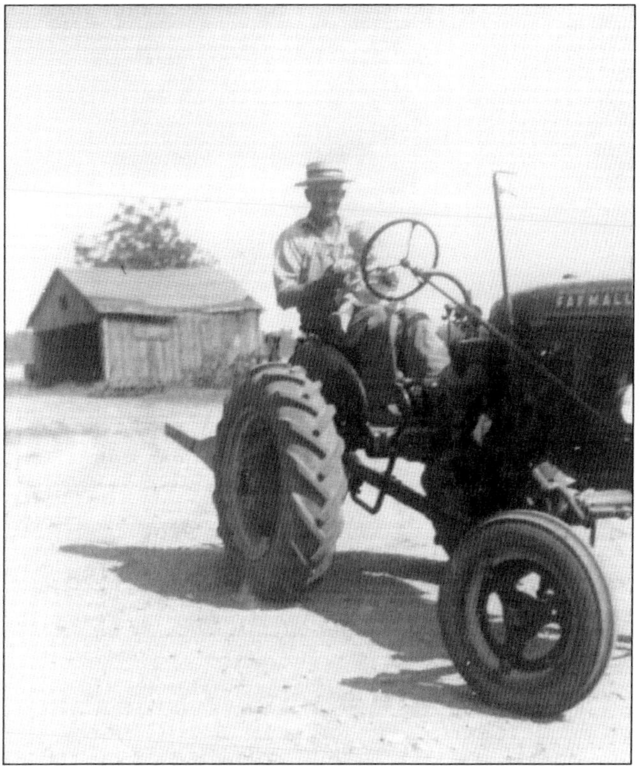


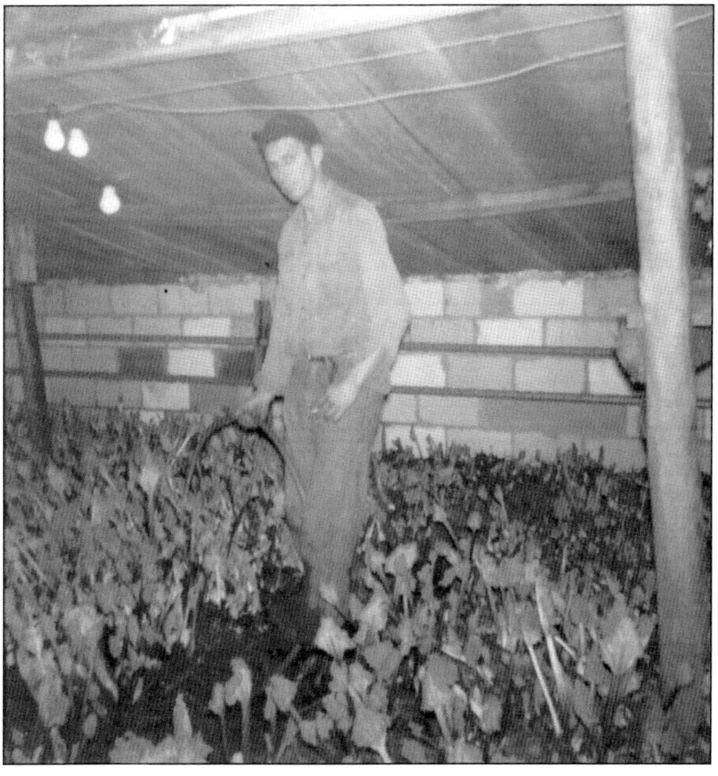

Donald Strouse waters rhubarb plants in the mid-1950s in the family's hothouse. Rhubarb had become an important crop for Shelby Township farmers by this time. Grown in hothouses, rhubarb generated income during the slow winter months. And there was a large market for the juice, which made a popular tonic. Hothouse rhubarb was also sweeter, more tender, and better for cooking. (Delores Strouse Metro.)

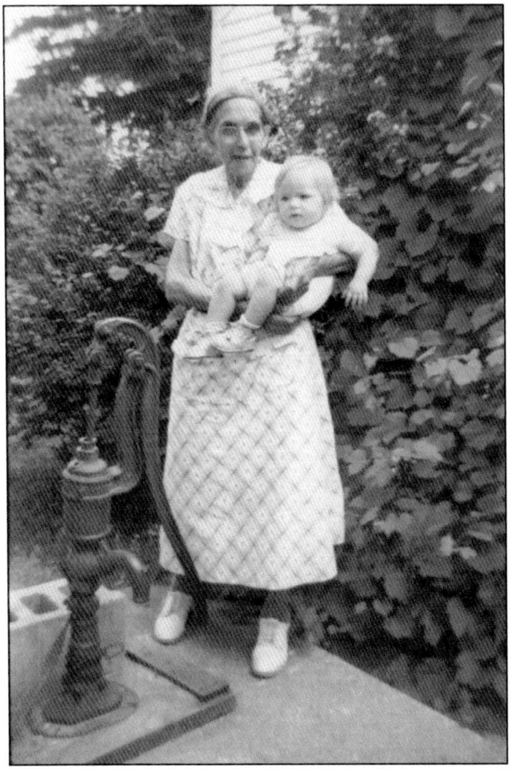

At left, Louise Klann holds her granddaughter Delores Strouse next to the water pump at the Strouse farm. This well with its hand pump was the only source of water for the Strouse family until indoor plumbing was installed in the late 1950s. Until then, water for cooking, drinking, and bathing had to be drawn and carried into the kitchen. Below, Delores Strouse (right) plays outside in 1945 while Laura Strouse, seated on the kitchen steps near an unidentified child, watches. The tubs hanging on the wall were for washing laundry and bathing in the kitchen. The house had electricity, which came to Shelby Township in the 1930s, but it did not have central heating. Two potbelly coal-burning stoves and a wood-burning kitchen stove heated the house in winter. (Both, Delores Strouse Metro.)

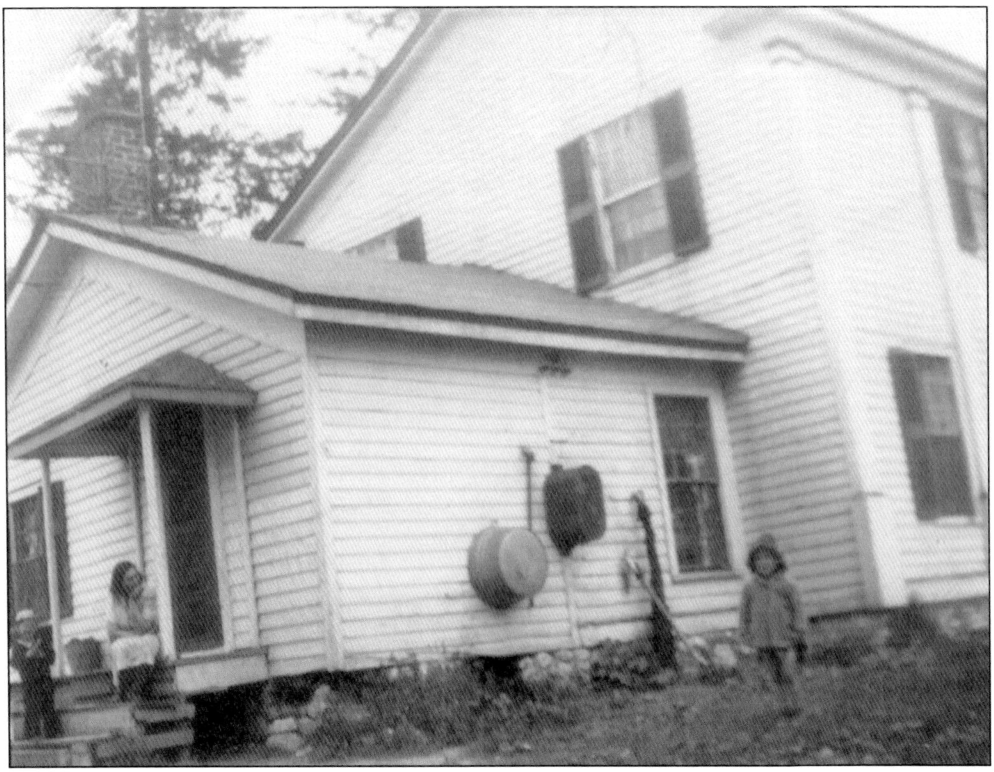

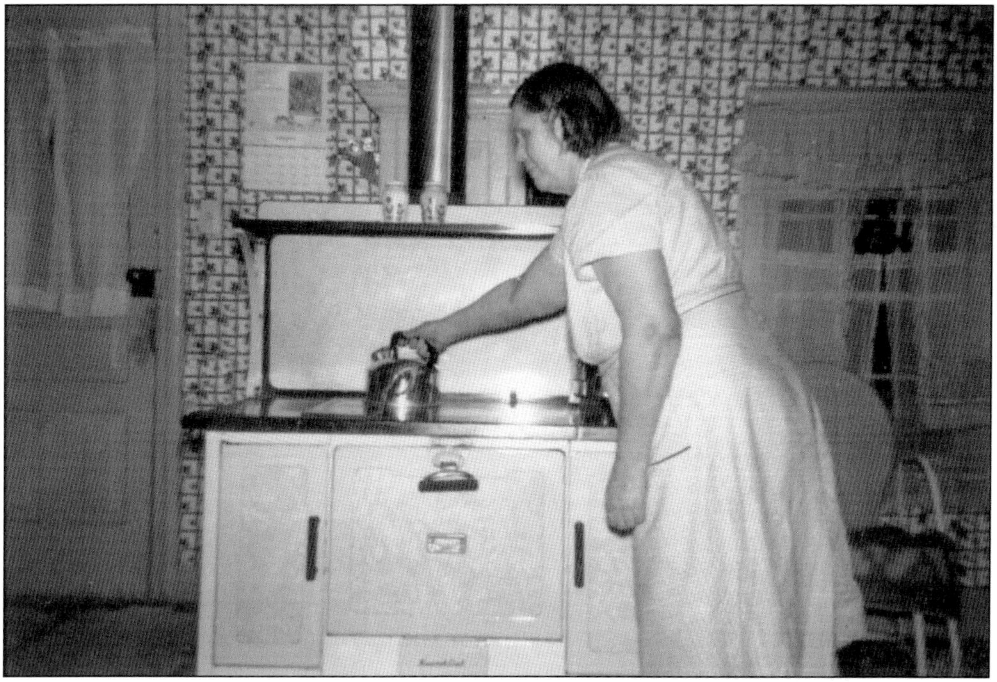

Laura Strouse heats water on her wood-burning kitchen stove in 1958. While electric stoves were available, Laura had cooked on a wood-burning stove all her adult life and preferred using this Round Oak model (manufactured in Dowagiac, Michigan). Laura lived on the farm until her death in 1991. Eight years later, the property was sold to a real estate developer. (Delores Strouse Metro.)

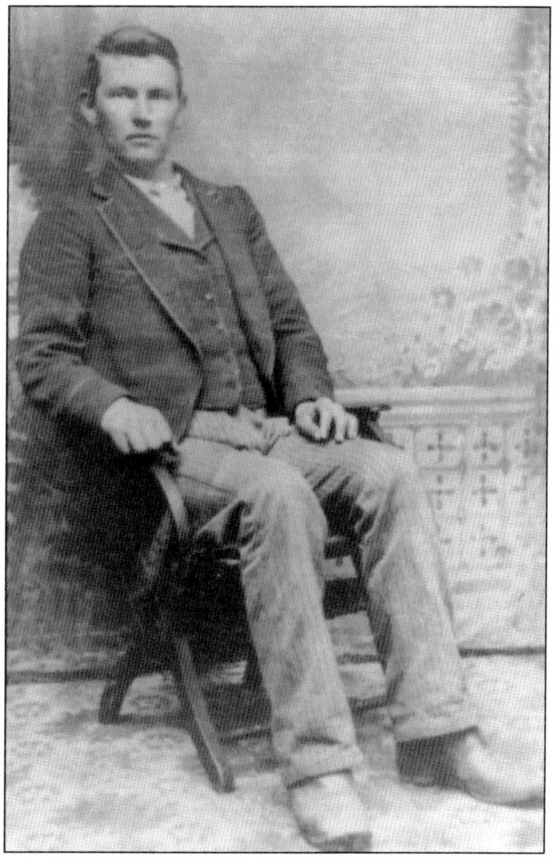

Pictured here around 1895 is George Smith, grandson of Andrew Jackson Smith. George Smith was born in 1876 on or near his grandfather's farm in Shelby Township. He was a truck farmer who also owned a meat market on Cass Avenue in Utica and was active in local politics. (Gayle Jocks.)

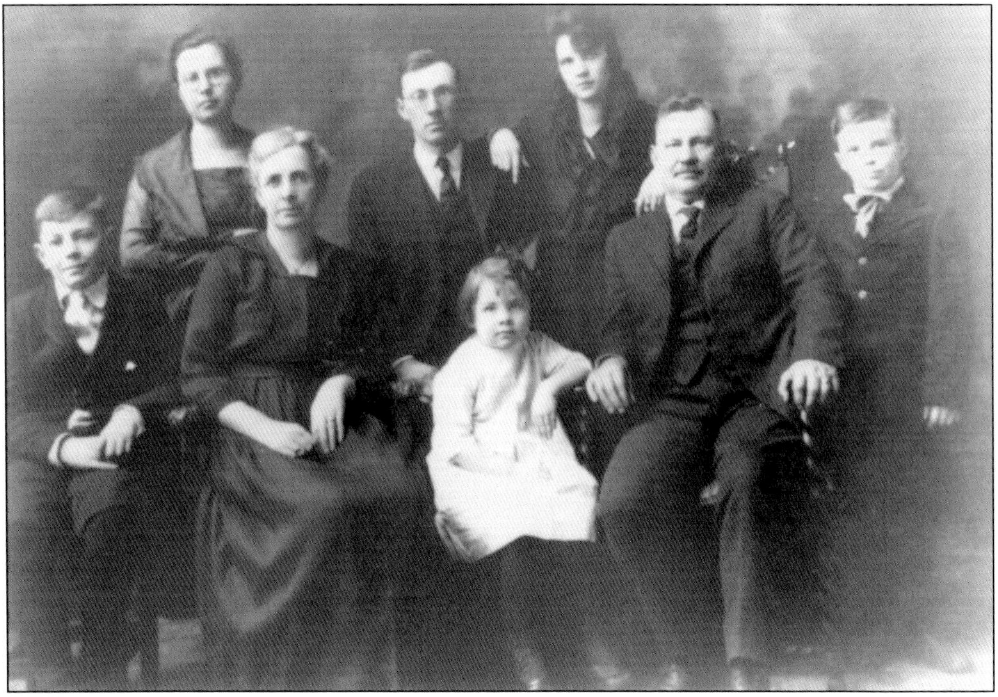

George Smith married Elizabeth Valentine in 1895, and they had six children. Pictured here around 1921, the Smith family members are, from left to right, (first row) Orville, Elizabeth, Georgia, George, and Vernon; (second row) Myrtle Eugenia, Leon, and Kathryn. Many of George and Elizabeth's descendants still live in and around Shelby Township. (Gary and Mary Miller Bradt.)

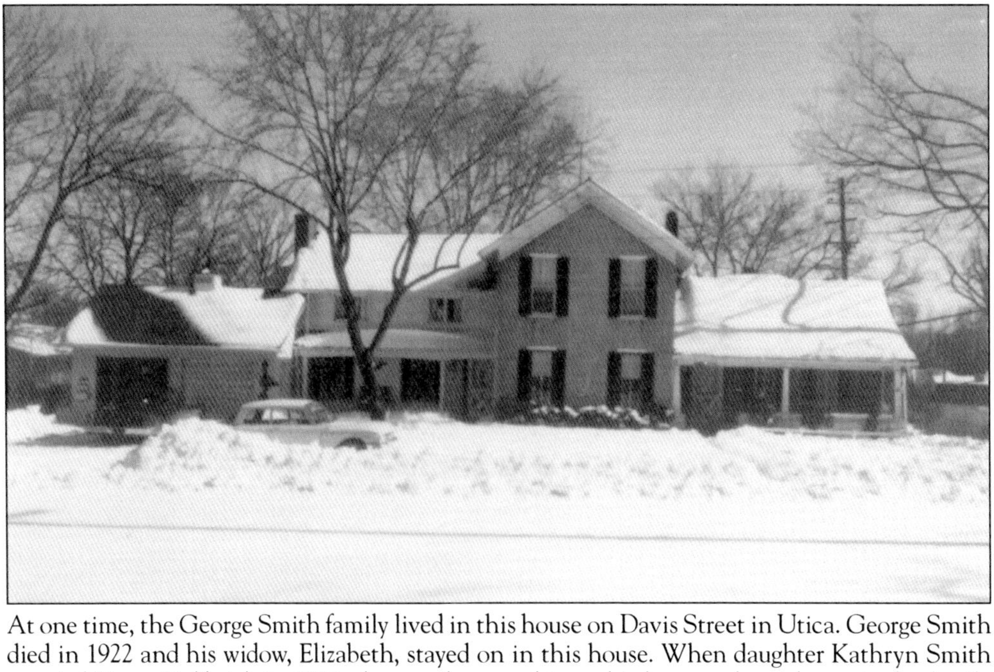

At one time, the George Smith family lived in this house on Davis Street in Utica. George Smith died in 1922 and his widow, Elizabeth, stayed on in this house. When daughter Kathryn Smith married Omar Helferich in 1926, the couple moved into this house, where they raised a family of their own. (Joyce K. Clark.)

Omar Helferich (right) is shown here with two of his brothers, Elmer (left) and DeWitt, around 1930. He was one of six children raised by Wallace and Myrtilla Helferich on a farm in Shelby Township. The boys attended the primary school in Disco. DeWitt Helferich served as township treasurer for nearly 20 years. (Joyce K. Clark.)

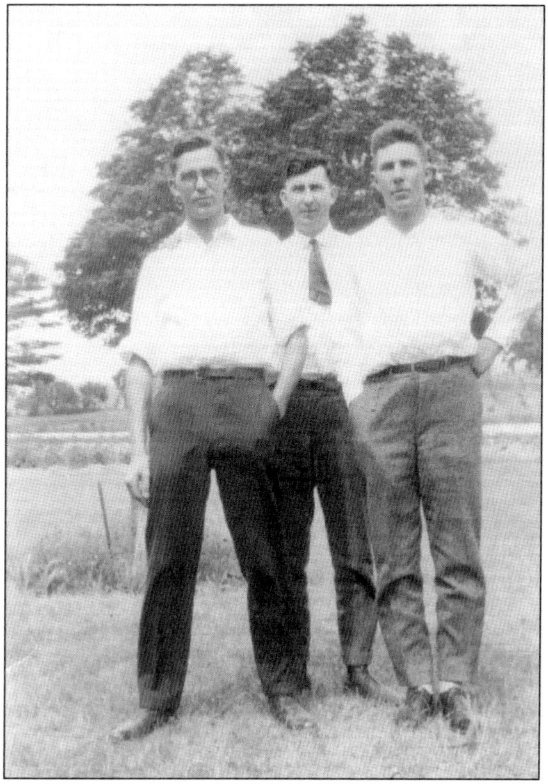

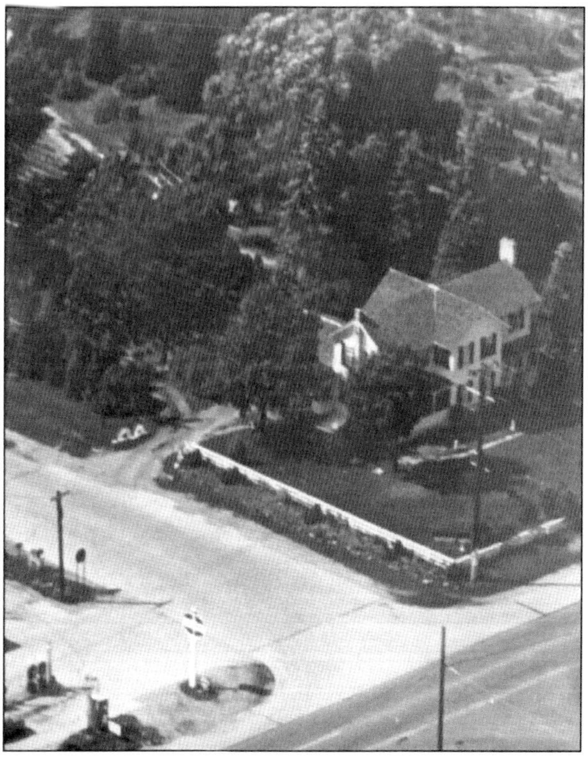

This is the Wallace Helferich house at the northwest corner of 23 Mile Road and Van Dyke Avenue around 1950. George Helferich, Wallace's father, came to Shelby Township in the late 1800s and bought over 100 acres of farmland around this intersection. By 1930, this part of the Helferich property belonged to the John Tear family, who established a nursery. (Nightingale family.)

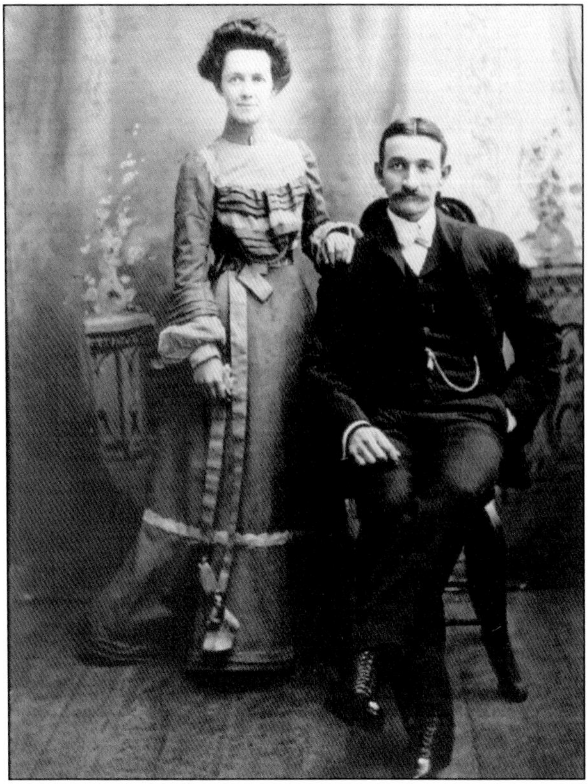

Melvina and Orville Fogelsonger pose for their wedding portrait around 1905. Melvina was from the McLellan family, early settlers of Shelby Township who farmed near 22 Mile and Schoenherr Roads. Orville was born in 1873 and was the son of John Fogelsonger, who came to the township from New York between 1860 and 1870. The elder Fogelsonger bought 160 acres on Van Dyke Avenue between 23 Mile and 24 Mile Roads and raised his family in the house pictured below. The Fogelsongers were Mennonites, a Protestant sect with beliefs similar to those of the Amish, including pacifism and a simple lifestyle. Like the Amish, Mennonites in the United States were predominantly Swiss and German immigrants. Orville, a farmer and brick maker, lived with his family in a house across the street from his father's. (Both, STHC.)

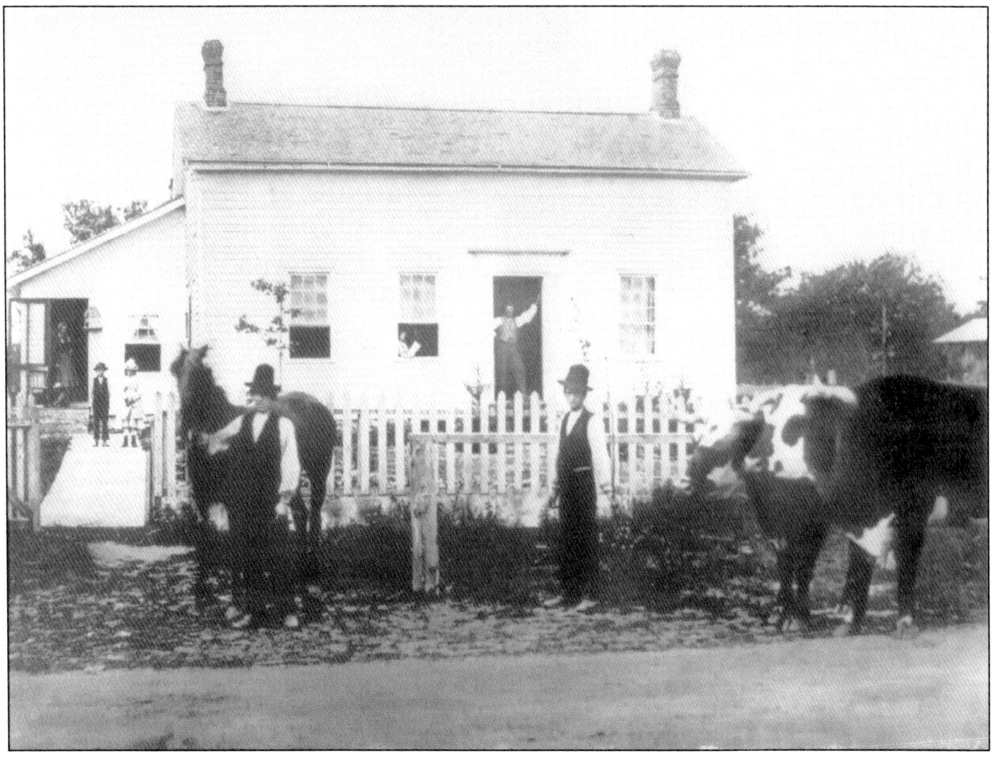

In 1901, Frank Powierski started a successful hardware store and plumbing business in Detroit. Around 1905, he bought the John Fogelsonger farm, which included the old house, farm buildings, and 160 acres. In this c. 1940 photograph, he stands beside the house he built just north of the old Fogelsonger house on Van Dyke Avenue in 1909. (Ronald A. Powerski family.)

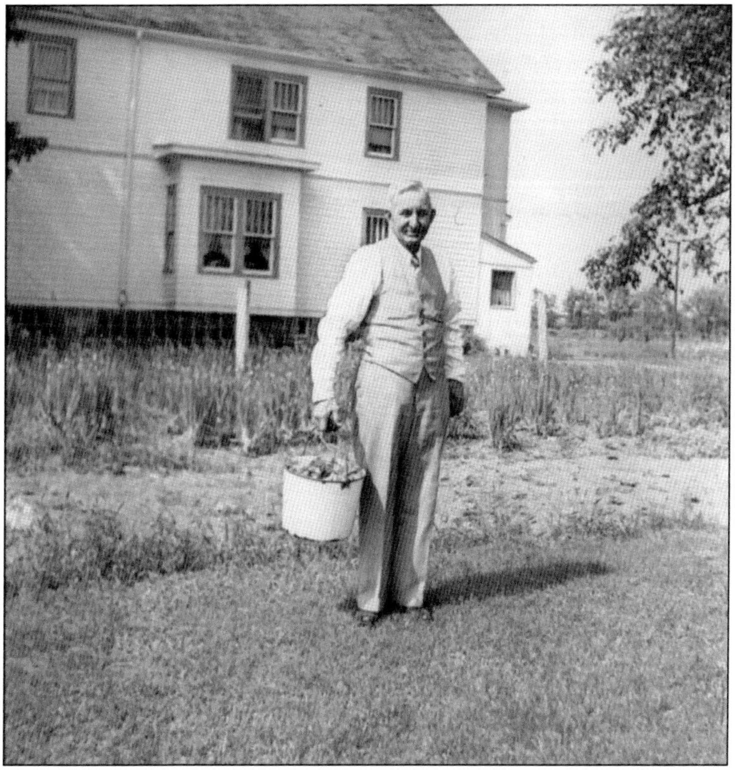

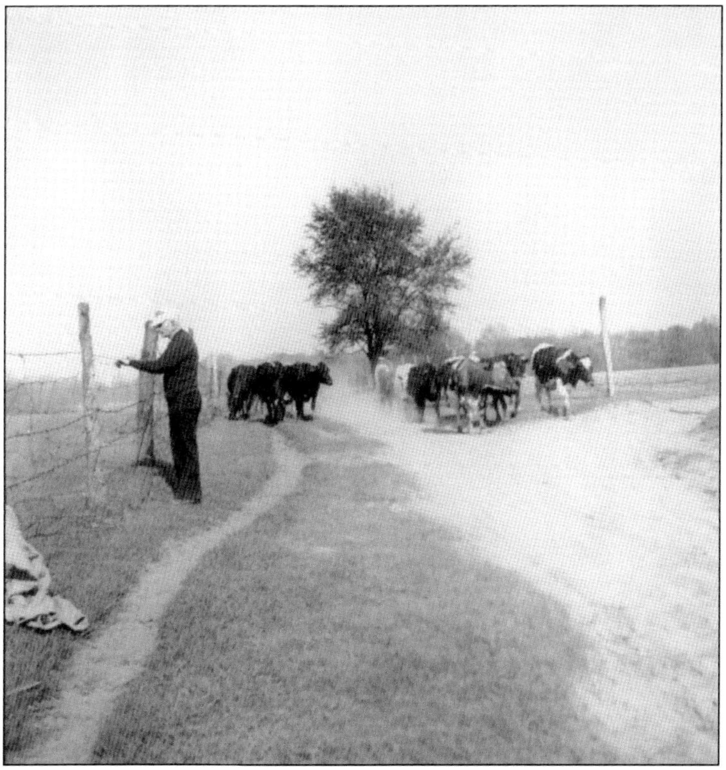

Frank Powierski checks the fence on his farm while driving his cows back from pasture around 1940. Until he retired, Powierski split his time between his businesses in Detroit and his farm in Shelby Township. His wife, Mary, lived on the farm while the three Powierski children, Bernice, Aloysius, and Casimir, attended the primary school in Disco beginning in 1916. (Ronald A. Powerski family.)

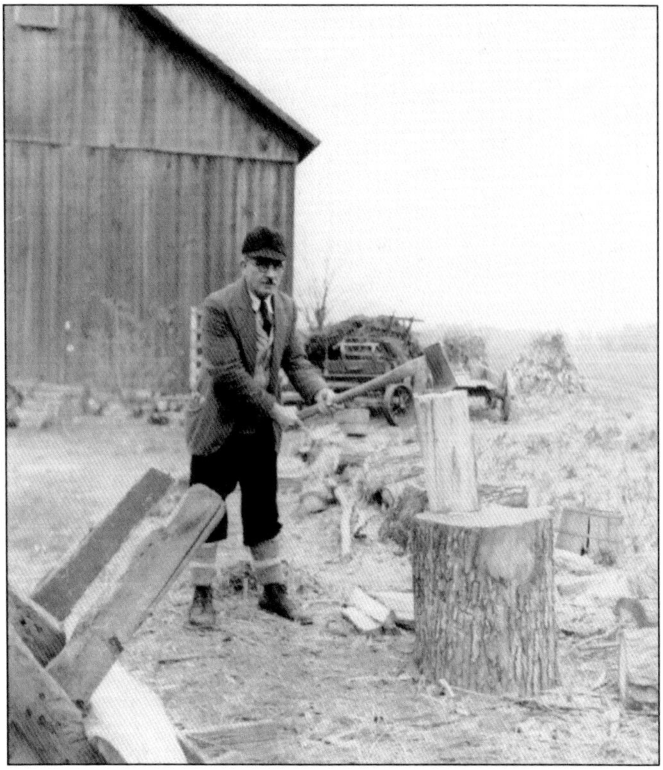

Family members and friends frequently visited the Powierski farm in Shelby Township to enjoy recreation and relaxation in the country away from the noise and congestion of Detroit. They even helped out with the many chores around the farm like this unidentified visitor (left) chopping firewood behind the barn in the late 1930s. Wild game, such as deer, ducks, turkeys, and pheasants, were abundant in the farm's open fields and along the stream that cut through the property. In spite of this abundance, these two unidentified hunters (below) appear to have only bagged a pumpkin during their outing on the Powierski farm around 1940. (Both, Ronald A. Powerski family.)

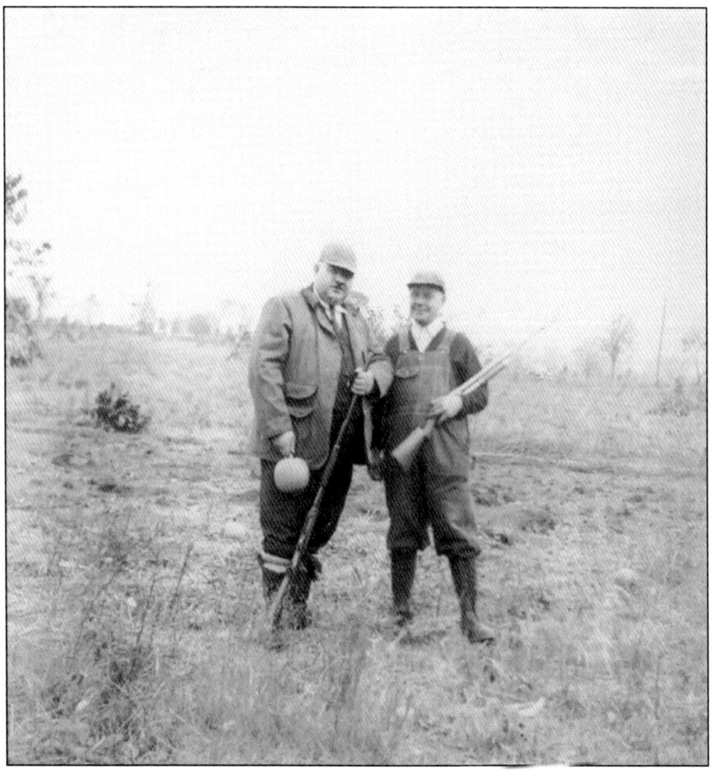

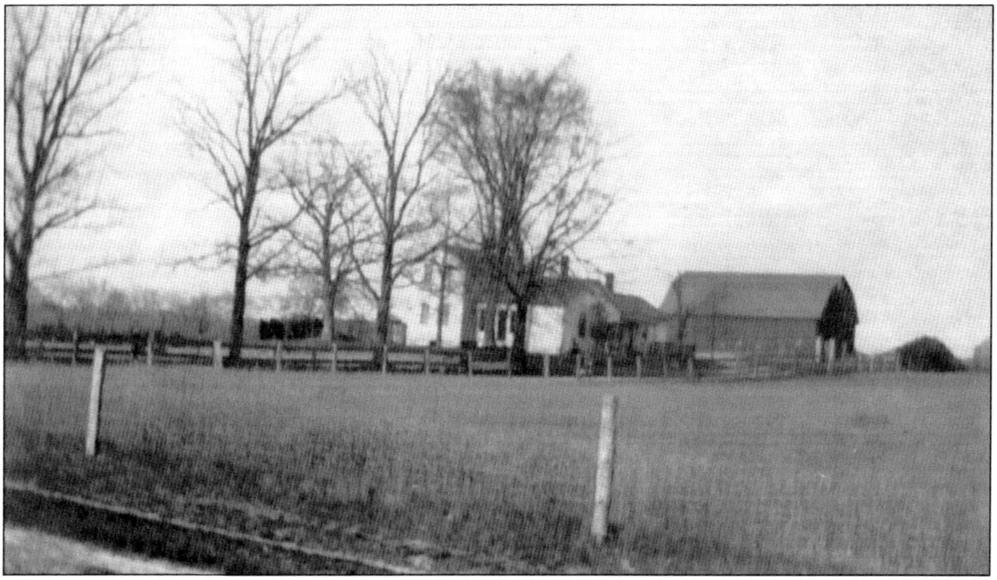

This is the farmstead that once belonged to James Parish, a New York farmer who came to Shelby Township between 1840 and 1850. Located on the east side of Van Dyke Avenue just north of 21 Mile Road, the 125-acre farm was purchased by Joachim Remer in 1888. Joachim had emigrated from Germany in 1872 and settled in Sterling Township. (Maynard W. Remer family.)

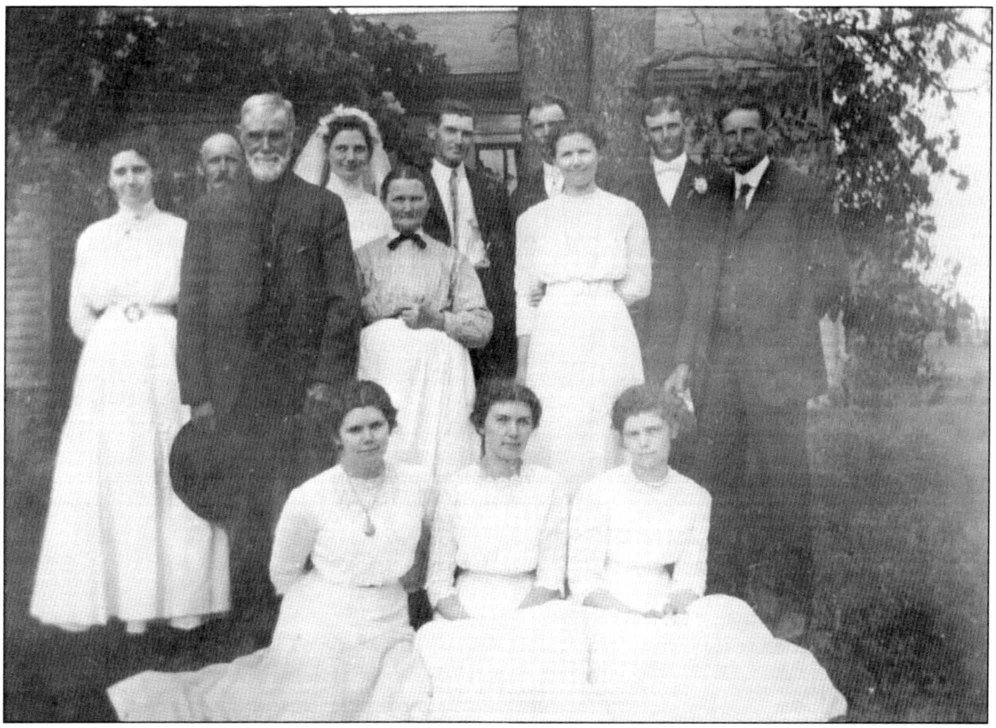

Joachim and Marie Remer pose with their 11 sons and daughters in front of their farmhouse in 1912. The family members are, from left to right, (first row) Emma, Louise, and Mary; (second row) Joachim, Marie, Sophia, and Charles; (third row) Minnie, John, Fredericka, George, Theodore, and William. (Maynard W. Remer family.)

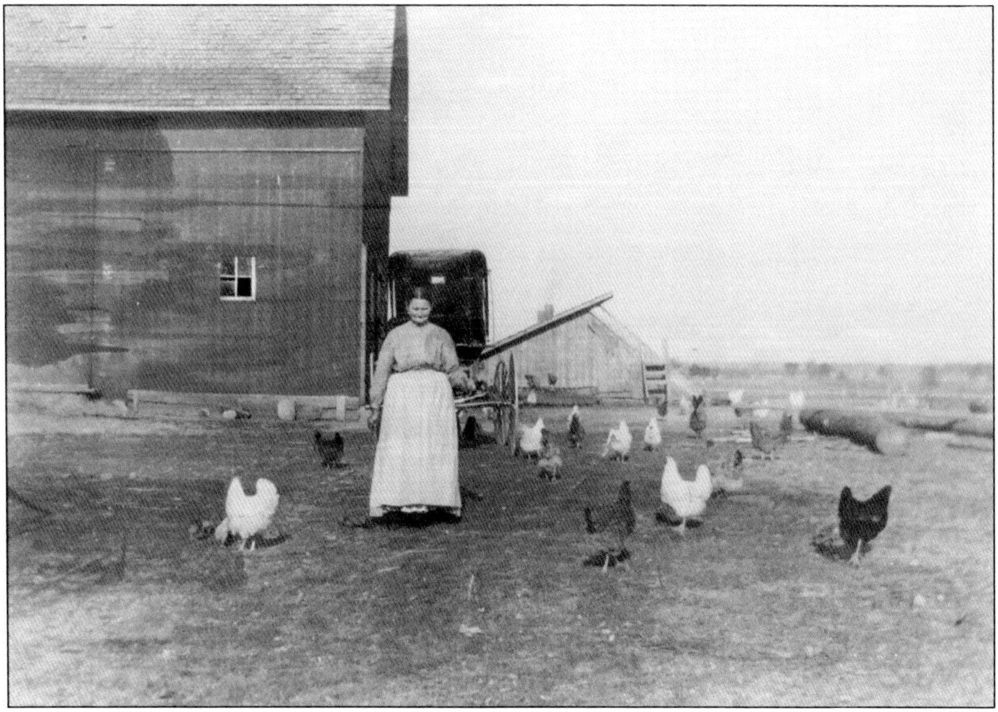

Marie Remer feeds chickens at the farm around 1905. Joachim and Marie Remer bought farms in Shelby Township for some of their sons, who paid back the money once their own farms were established. Most of the Remer's daughters married and moved out of the area. William Remer acquired his parents' farm where he lived with his older sister Minnie. (Maynard W. Remer family.)

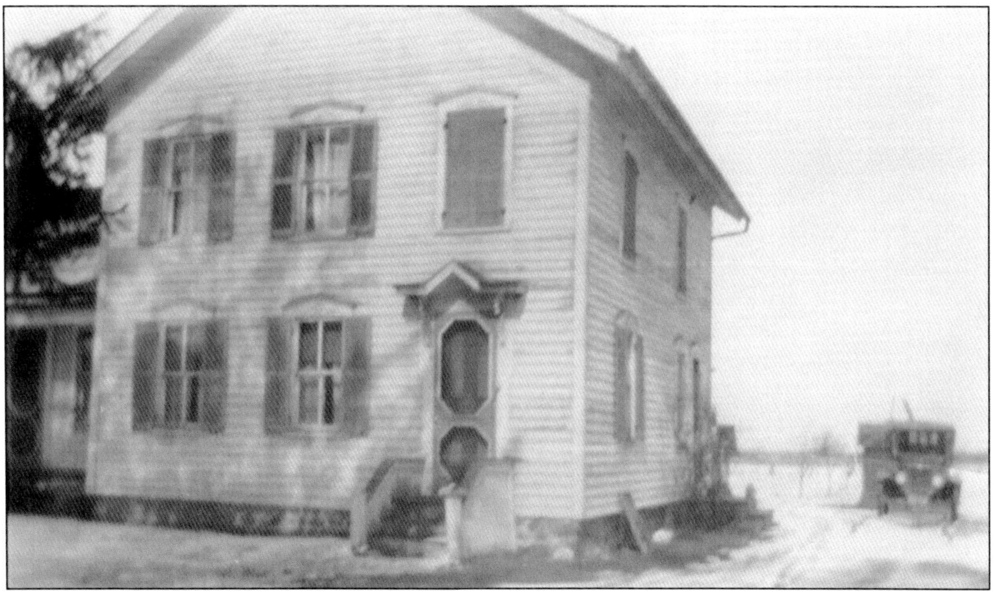

Joachim Remer bought the George Sweitzer farm on Shelby Road south of 23 Mile Road for his son Theodore Remer in 1893. The 130-acre farm included this house with farm buildings behind it plus two barns and a milk house across the street. This photograph of the farmhouse was taken around 1925 before it was remodeled in 1929. (Maynard W. Remer family.)

Theodore Remer sits with his wife, Lydia, for their wedding day portrait in 1907. The photograph was taken by Smith's Studio in Saginaw, Michigan. They had two sons, Elmer and Maynard, who were born in Shelby Township. Both boys attended nearby Ewell School and Utica High School. (Maynard W. Remer family.)

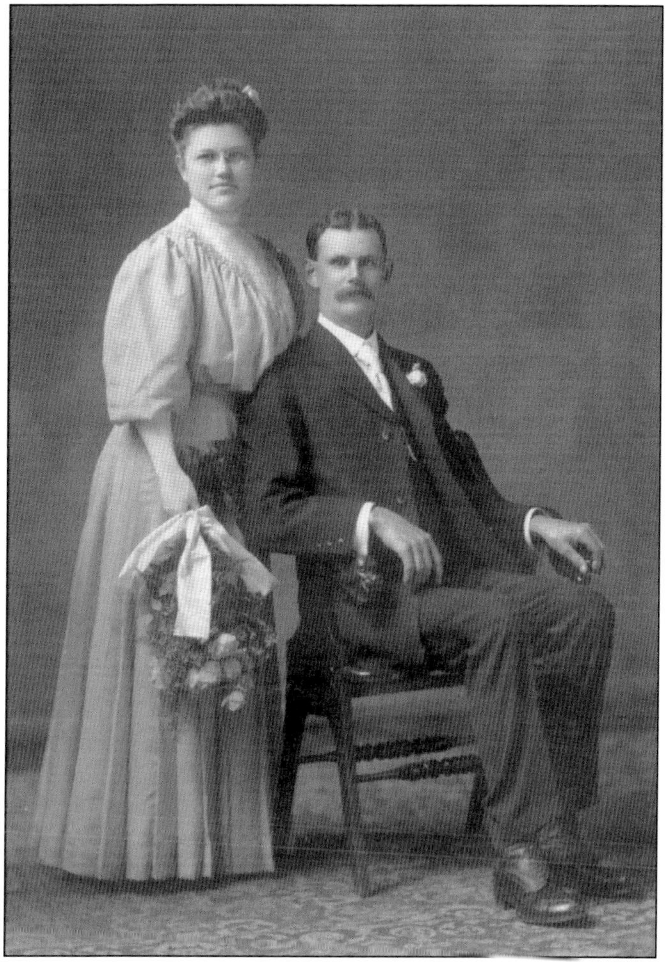

Pictured here around 1928 are Theodore Remer's farm fields with the barns on Shelby Road in the distance. While Remer (right) stacks harvested grain, young Maynard Remer helps. The Remers also grew watermelons and muskmelons, which were trucked down to the market in Royal Oak. A herd of dairy cows provided milk, which was picked up at a nearby railroad siding. (Maynard W. Remer family.)

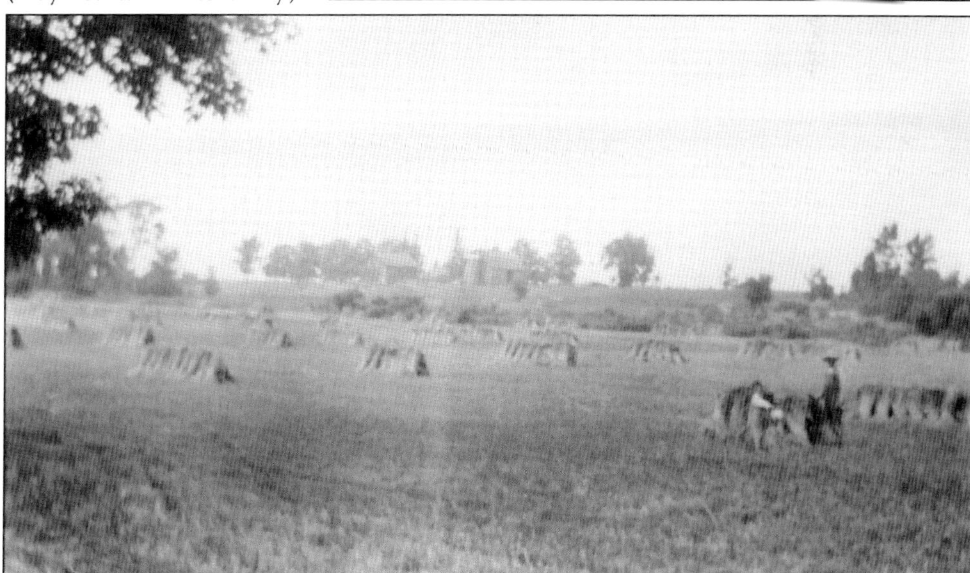

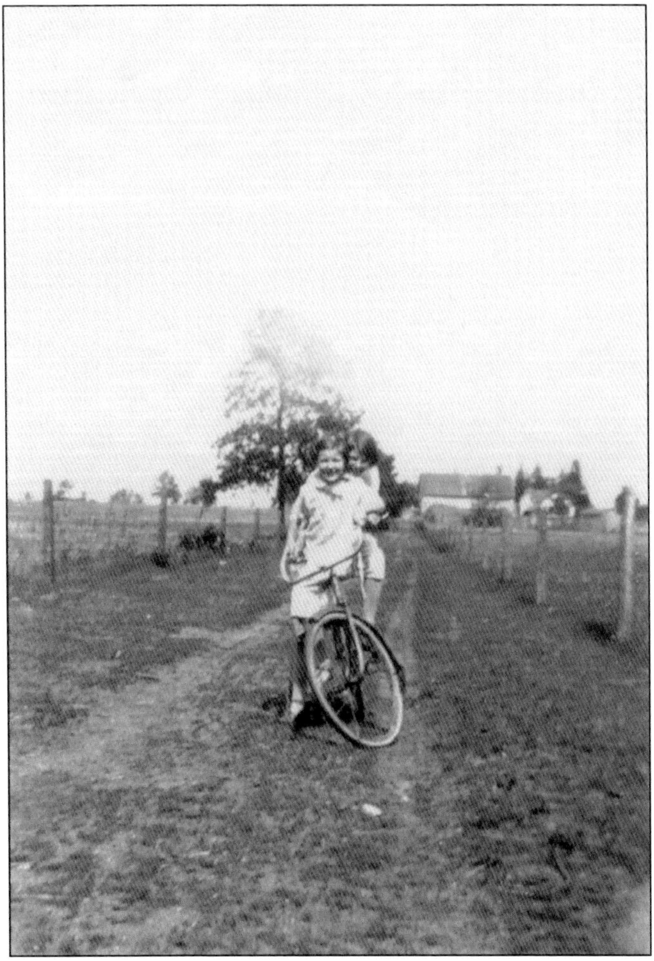

Charles Remer acquired the George Wright farm on Shelby Road north of 21 Mile Road. Here daughter Esther Remer (left) rides a bicycle behind the barn around 1925. Cousin Marie Kreutzfeldt from Saginaw, Michigan, sits behind her. The children were charged with guiding the herd of cattle back and forth across the railroad tracks that ran through the property. (Maynard W. Remer family.)

By the second quarter of the 20th century, some of the large 19th century farms had been carved into smaller farms. Around 1930, the Summers farm at 21 Mile Road and Van Dyke Avenue was subdivided and platted as Burton Van Dyke Farms. Frank Ewert (left), with his son Gerald, takes a break from building his house on his small farm on Burton Street around 1940. (Ronald Ewert.)

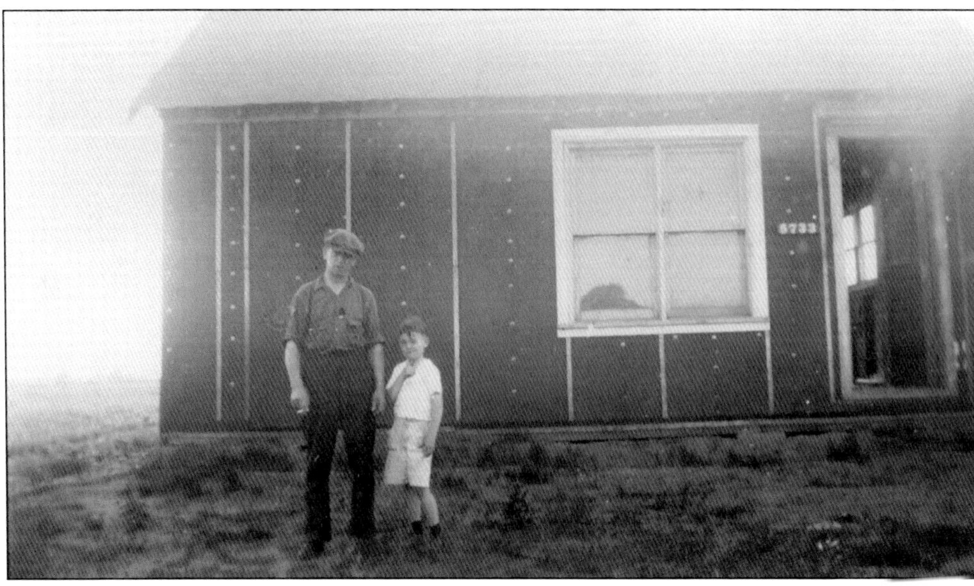

George Miller (right) and Paula Hafner became engaged in Emmett, Michigan, in 1932. They married in 1934 and a year later purchased a portion of the Runyan farmstead on 23 Mile Road in Shelby Township. There they built a small house and started a farm. George Miller tended the farm mornings and worked afternoons at a truck manufacturing plant near Detroit. (Gary and Mary Miller Bradt.)

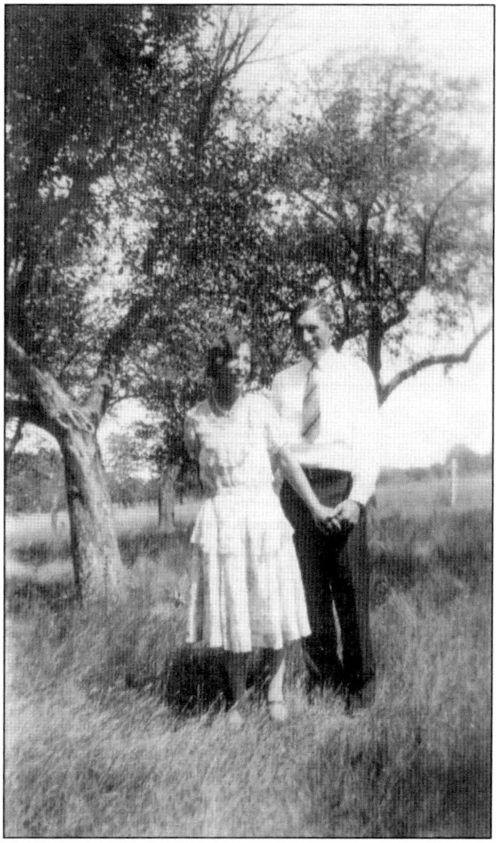

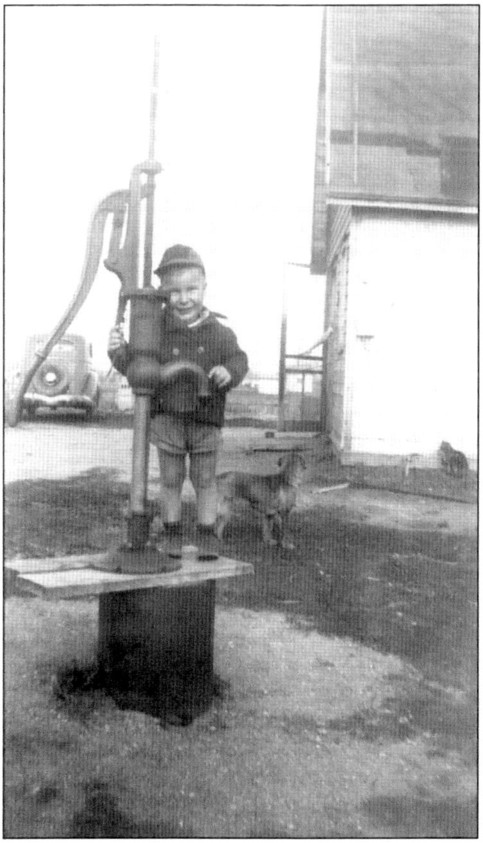

Here in 1939, one-year-old David Miller stands at the pump that supplied the family's household water. George and Paula Miller raised six children on their farm. For his growing family, George built a larger house on the farm in 1948. The new house had improvements such as indoor plumbing and central heat, which were lacking in the first house. (Gary and Mary Miller Bradt.)

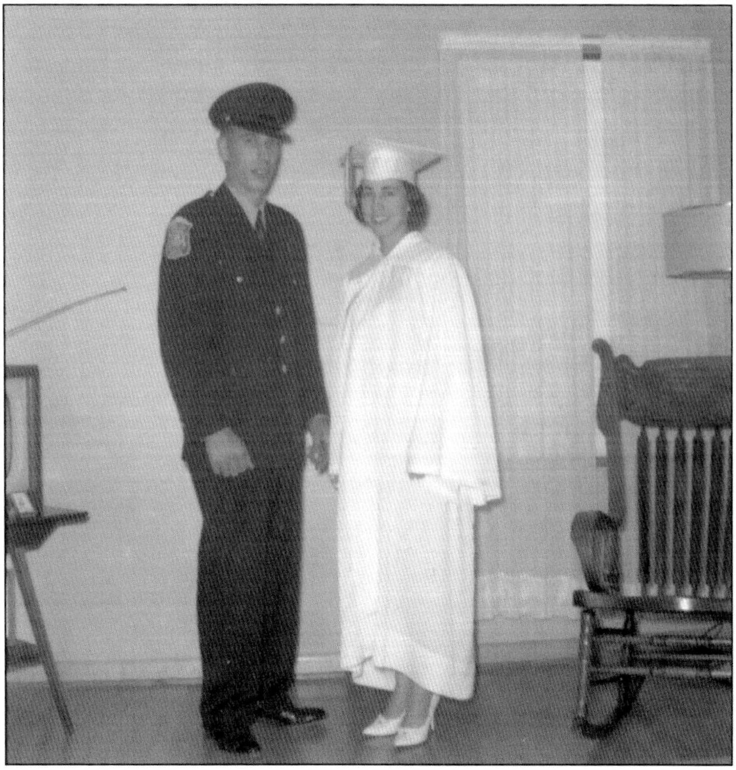

The Miller children attended the elementary school in Disco and the secondary school in Utica. David Miller (left) served in the navy before joining the Shelby Township Police Department in 1961. That same year, his sister Mary Miller (right) graduated from Utica High School. David Miller worked traffic control for his sister's graduation ceremony. (Gary and Mary Miller Bradt.)

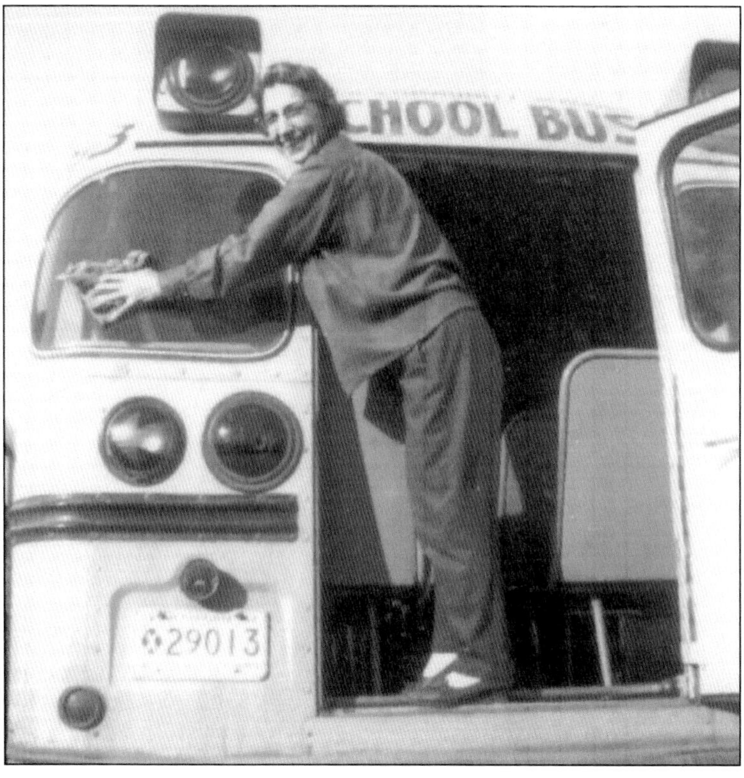


After George Miller died in 1955, Paula Miller worked a number of jobs to help make ends meet, including driving a bus for the Utica Community School District. Here she is in 1962 cleaning the windows of her bus. She died in 2005 and is buried in the Utica Cemetery next to her husband. A housing development occupies the former Miller farm. (Gary and Mary Miller Bradt.)

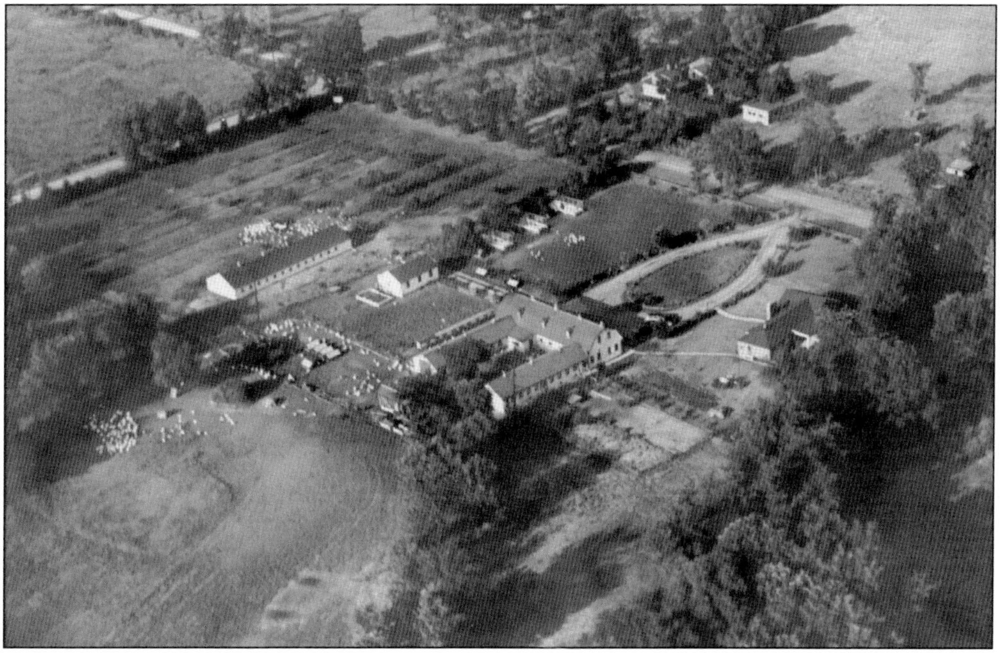

This 1950 photograph shows the Odilon Houtekier poultry farm located at the southwest corner of 24 Mile and Mound Roads. The large, U-shaped barn near the center of the photograph was used to house the birds, which can be seen as small white dots scattered around the property. (Gary and Barbara Churchill.)

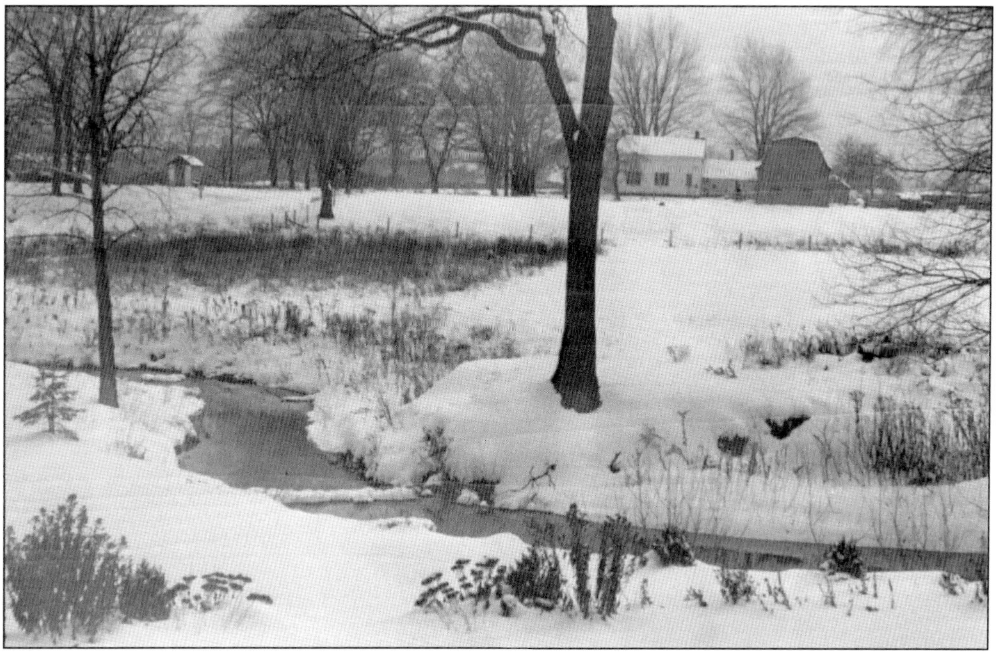

The Houtekier farm was a piece of the 19th-century farm once owned by the Wales family, which had been split into 10-, 15-, and 30-acre parcels. The Wales had settled in Shelby Township around 1823. Their farmstead, which still stands on Mound Road, is visible in this photograph taken from the Houtekier property around 1945. (Dolores Schmidt.)

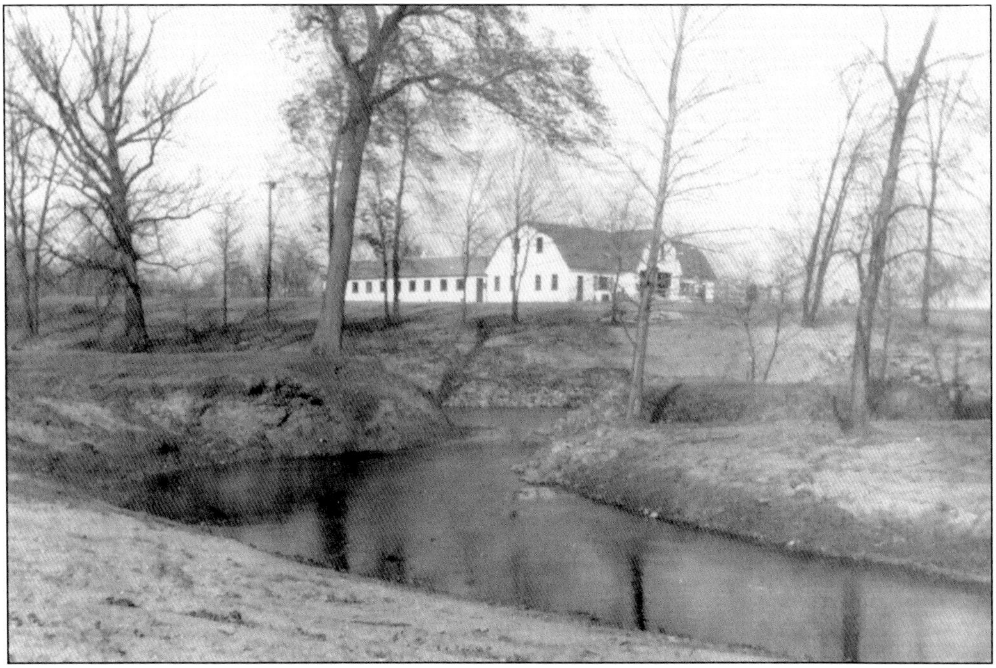

Odilon Houtekier came to Shelby Township with his family around 1945. The first structure he built on his property was the U-shaped barn (above). Then he added the ranch-style house (below) along with more farm buildings. Houtekier delivered eggs around the township from his poultry farm. He ran a hardware store on Van Dyke Avenue south of 22 Mile Roads, and he built and sold homes around the 24 Mile Road area. Houtekier also managed to find time to be active in the community, heading a residents' group called the Citizen Association of Shelby Township that worked to establish a fire department for the township. His son-in-law Clyde Schmidt was the first chief of the township's full-time fire department. Houtekier also served a term as township trustee in 1965. (Both, Dolores Schmidt.)

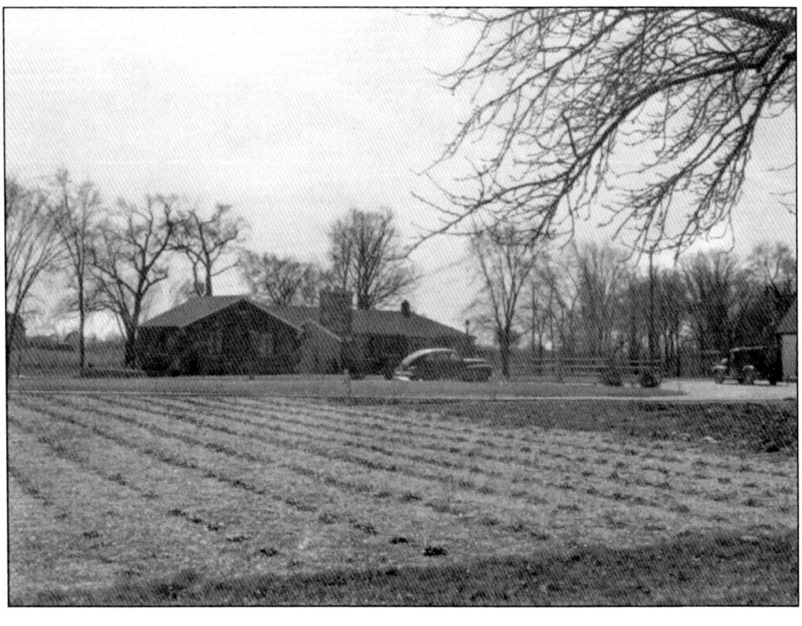

# *Four*

# Schools

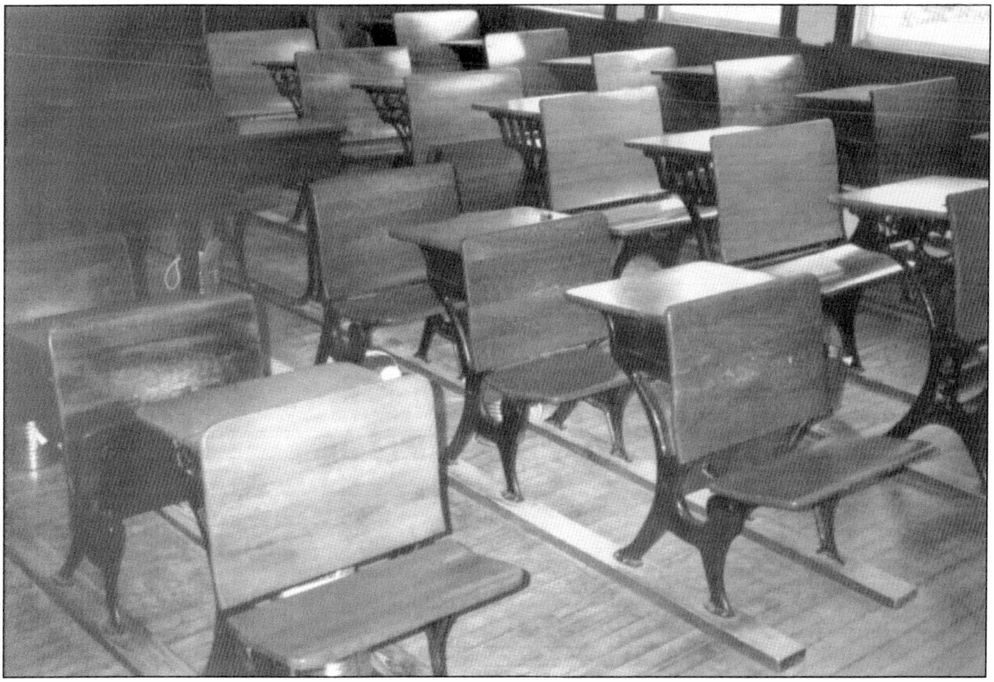

Empty desks await students in a one-room schoolhouse in Shelby Township. For over 100 years, such schools were where most of the township's children completed their primary education. Beginning in 1818, classes were taught in homes or rough log structures. By 1860, children could attend one of seven grade schools and two higher educational facilities around the township. (STHC.)

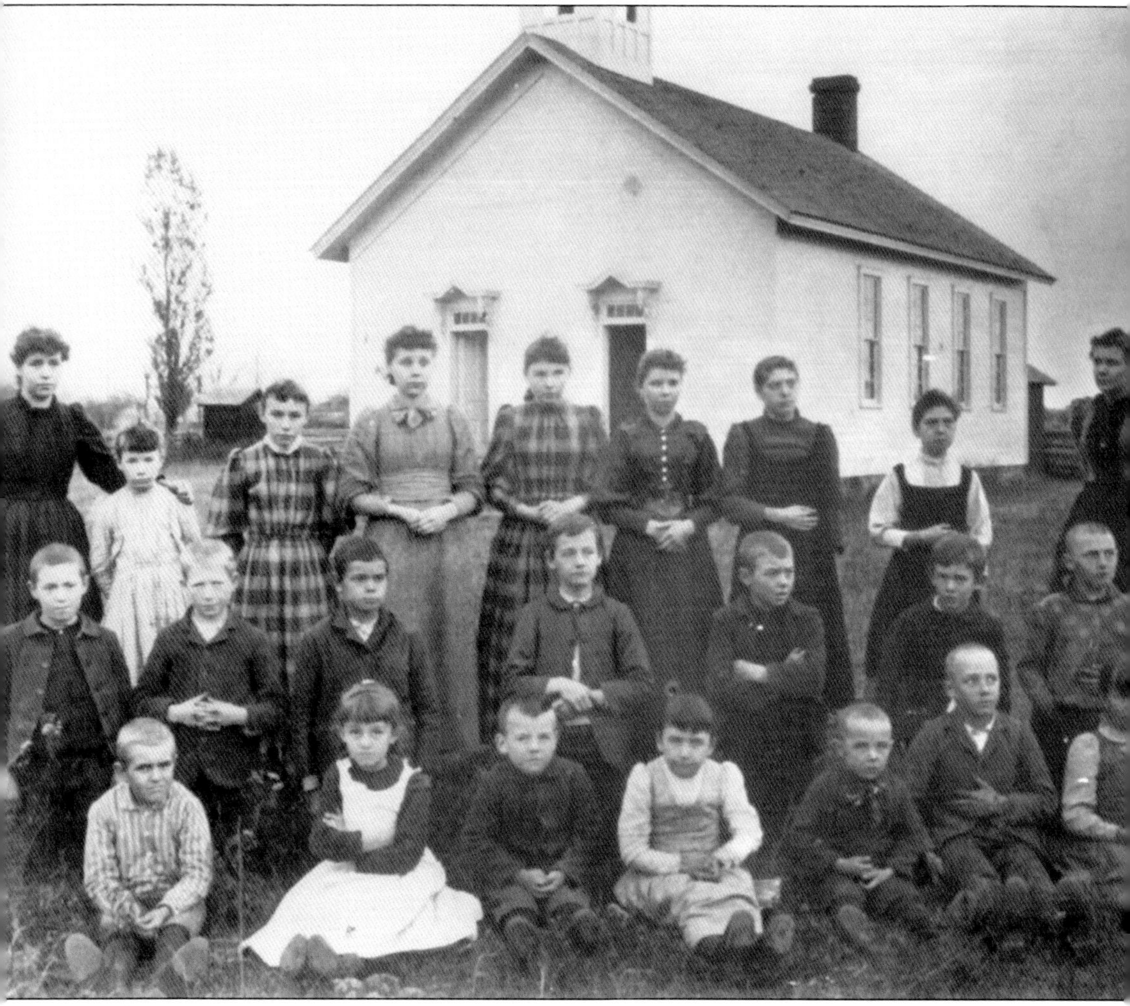

This is a portrait of the Prestonville School in 1893. Note the two entry doors, one for girls and one for boys, which led into separate cloakrooms. Typical of these schools, one teacher taught all primary grade levels in one room. Shelby Township was divided into school districts with usually one schoolhouse per district; Prestonville was in District Number Three. The original schoolhouse was located on 25 Mile Road just west of Schoenherr Road on the Preston family farm. A larger schoolhouse (pictured) was built around 1880 on Preston land to the south on Schoenherr Road. The schoolchildren are, from left to right, (first row) John Boldt, Bessie Warren, Lyle Warren, Alta Phillips, Martin Dopp, Henry Dopp, and Vena Boldt; (second row) Martin Preston, Robert Jean, Andrew Robertoy, Neil Van Horn, Ray Preston, William Phillips, and Paul Stoltz; (third row) Maude Preston, Jessie Phillips, Etta Phillips, Fanny Rowley, Flora Phillips, Elizabeth Dopp, Winifred Wolvin, and Pearl Wolvin; Jennie Jean, the teacher, is standing on the far right. (STHC.)

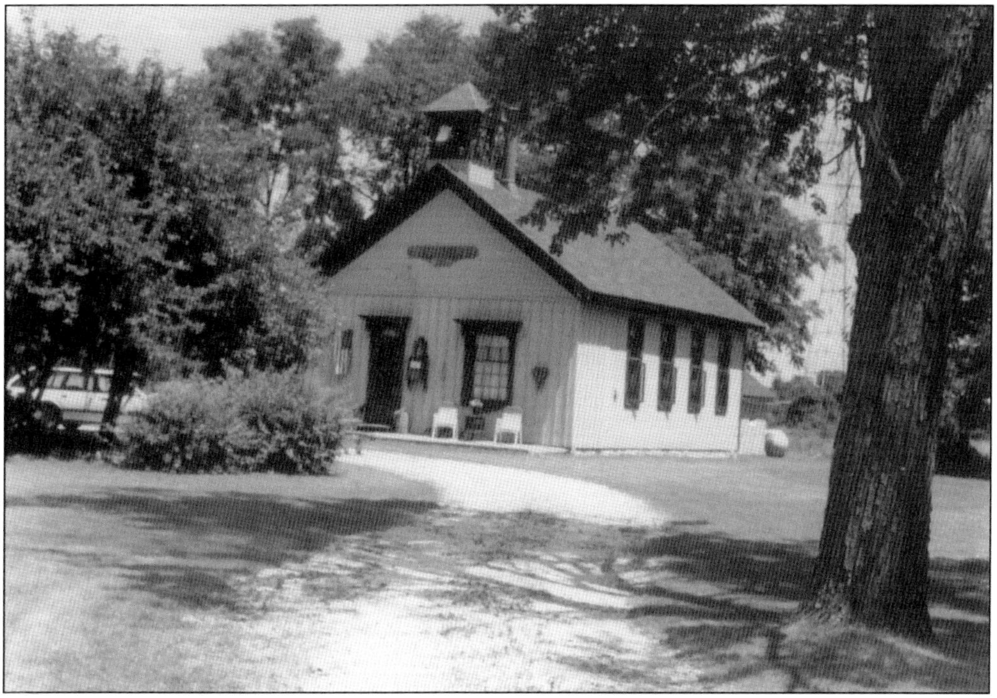

The Prestonville schoolhouse on Schoenherr Road, shown here around 1975, became a private residence after the school closed in 1954. In the 1940s and 1950s, Shelby Township's population increased significantly and larger schools were built. The old one-room schoolhouses had become obsolete. The former Prestonville schoolhouse was demolished in 2003 to make way for a housing subdivision. (Delores Strouse Metro.)

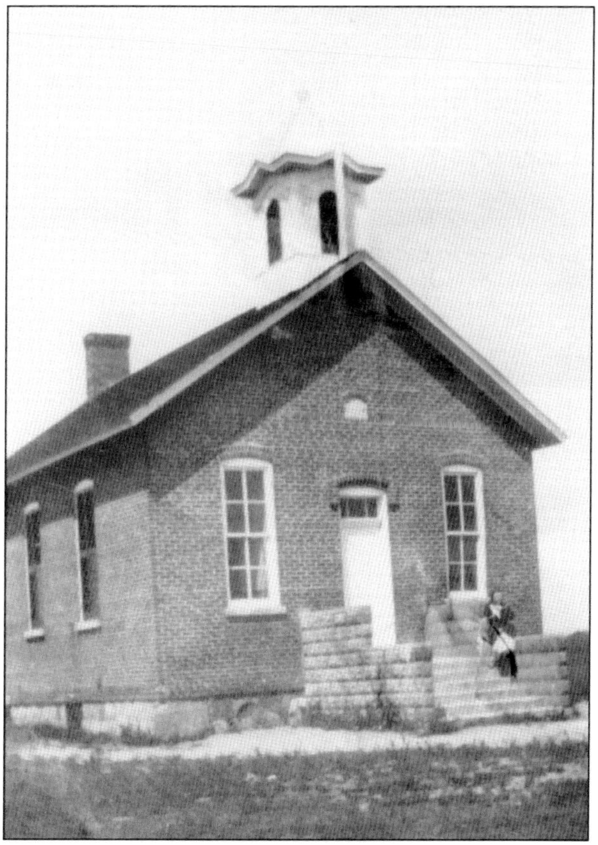

James Ewell, grandson of Shelby Township pioneer Peleg Ewell, built this brick schoolhouse in 1876 with the help of Harmon Wells. It was located on the Ewell farm at the northwest corner of 23 Mile and Shelby Roads. James Ewell remembered the hardships of the old log schoolhouse with hard slab seats and wanted a well-built, modern schoolhouse for the area children. (Maynard W. Remer family.)

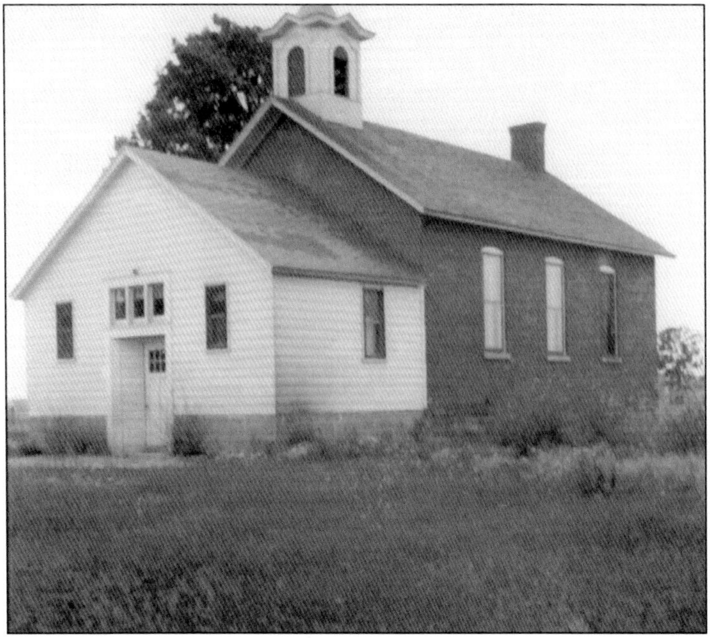

Taken around 1940, this photograph shows the 1876 Ewell schoolhouse with a 20th-century front addition. The Ewell School was in District Number Five of Shelby Township. In the 1830s, classes for the district's children were held in Peleg Ewell's house on Shelby Road. Like many of the township's early settlers, the Ewells were strong proponents of formal education. (Dorothy Peck Cummings.)

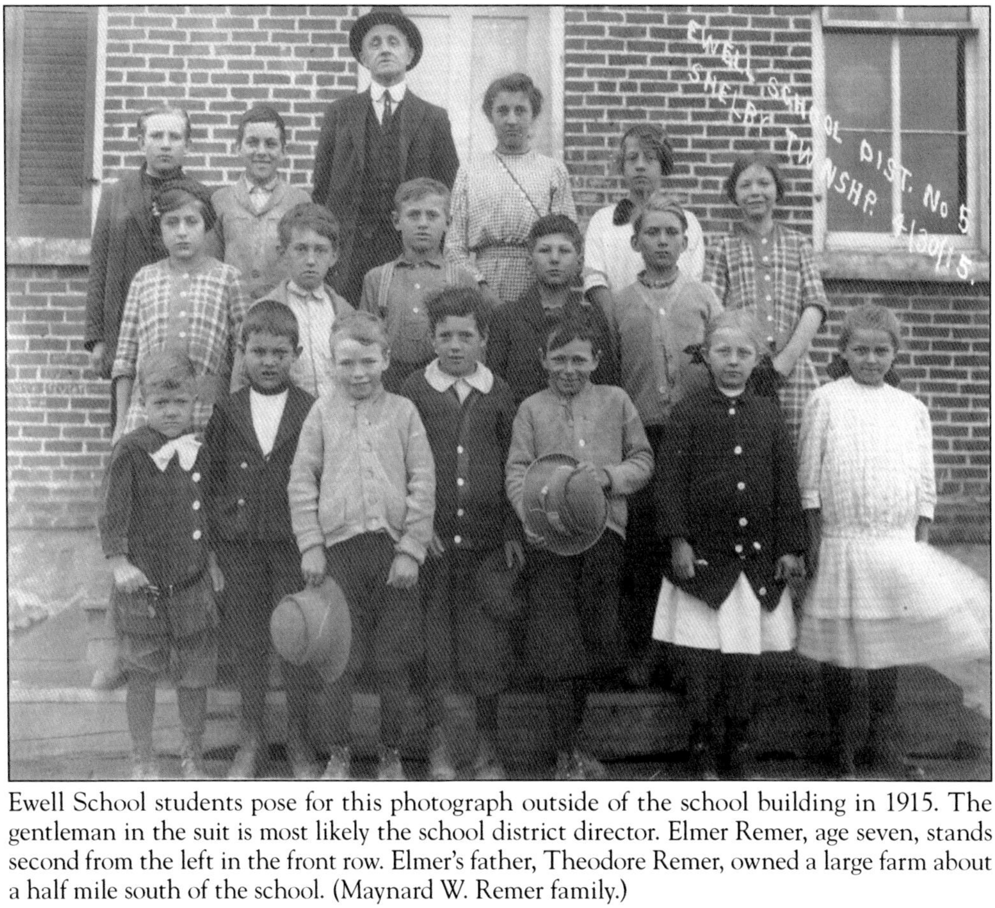


Ewell School students pose for this photograph outside of the school building in 1915. The gentleman in the suit is most likely the school district director. Elmer Remer, age seven, stands second from the left in the front row. Elmer's father, Theodore Remer, owned a large farm about a half mile south of the school. (Maynard W. Remer family.)

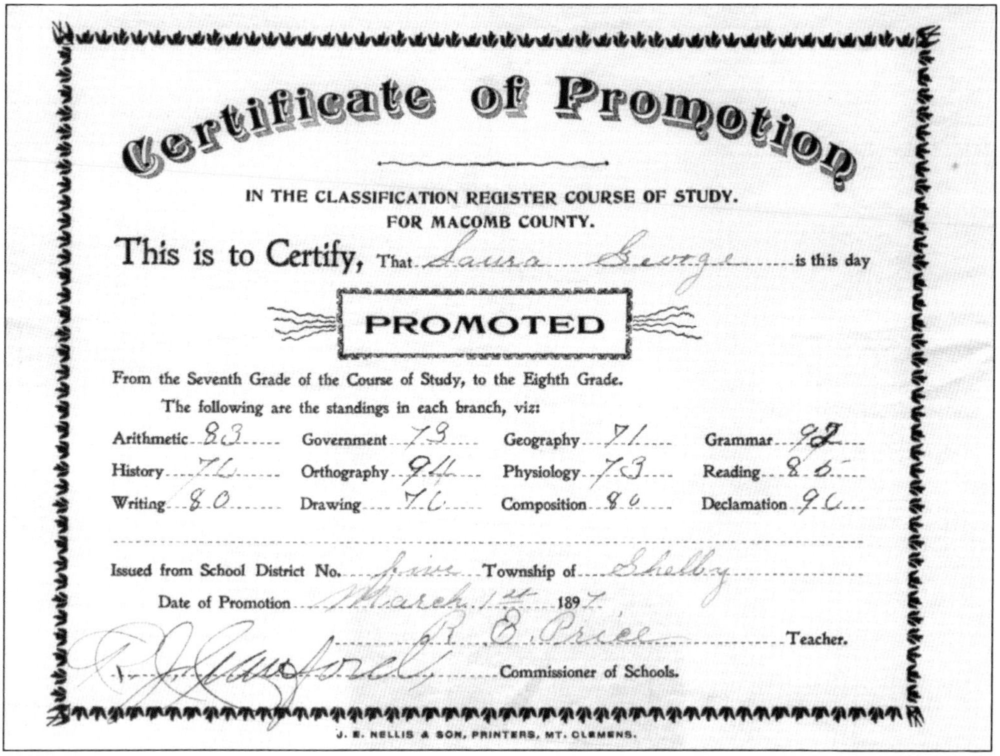

Certificate of Promotion

IN THE CLASSIFICATION REGISTER COURSE OF STUDY.
FOR MACOMB COUNTY.

This is to Certify, That Laura George is this day

PROMOTED

From the Seventh Grade of the Course of Study, to the Eighth Grade.

The following are the standings in each branch, viz:

| | | | | | | | |
|---|---|---|---|---|---|---|---|
| Arithmetic | 83 | Government | 73 | Geography | 71 | Grammar | 92 |
| History | 76 | Orthography | 94 | Physiology | 73 | Reading | 86 |
| Writing | 80 | Drawing | 76 | Composition | 80 | Declamation | 96 |

Issued from School District No. five Township of Shelby

Date of Promotion March 1st 1897

R. E. Price Teacher.

Commissioner of Schools.

J. E. NELLIS & SON, PRINTERS, MT. CLEMENS.

Students were required to pass examinations in several subjects in order to move from one grade to the next. This certificate shows that Ewell School student Laura George passed all her seventh-grade subjects in 1897. Laura went on to complete the eighth grade and graduate from Ewell School in 1898. (STHC.)

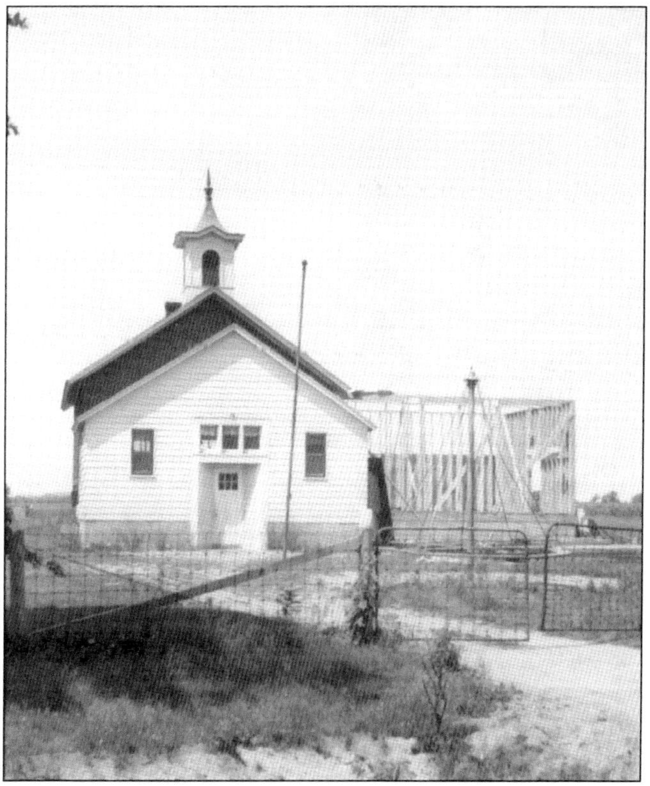

Between 1940 and 1950, as the population of Shelby Township was growing, classroom overcrowding was becoming a problem. Here the Ewell School building gets a much-needed addition in the early 1940s. Most of the one-room schools in the township were becoming overcrowded during this time, and the system of one teacher in one room for all primary grades was being challenged. (Dorothy Peck Cummings.)

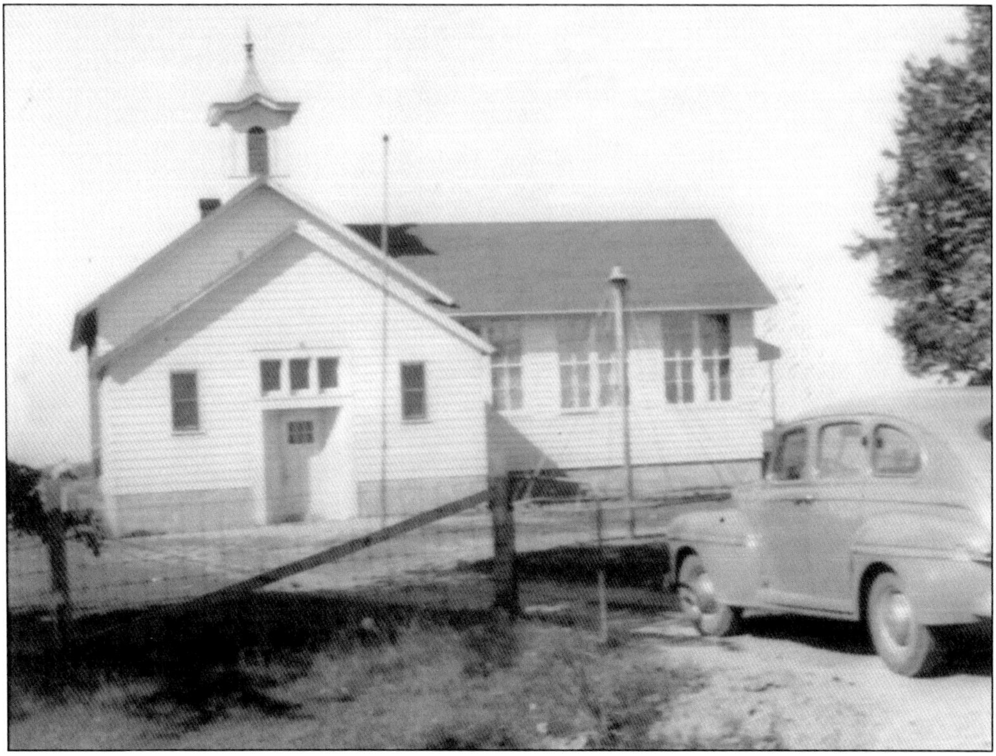

The Ewell schoolhouse expansion was completed by the mid-1940s. By 1950, the building was again bursting at its seams and unable to accommodate the growing population, as seen by the number of students in the photograph below. One teacher, Myrtle Peck, stands to the far right with possibly one or two more teachers in the second to last row. The last class was held in this building in the mid-1950s before it was torn down in 1957. A larger, modern building was erected on the same site, and school opened there in 1958. It was the first all-electric school in southeast Michigan. The 1958 building still stands, having been expanded over the years, and operates as the Ewell Elementary School. (Both, Dorothy Peck Cummings.)

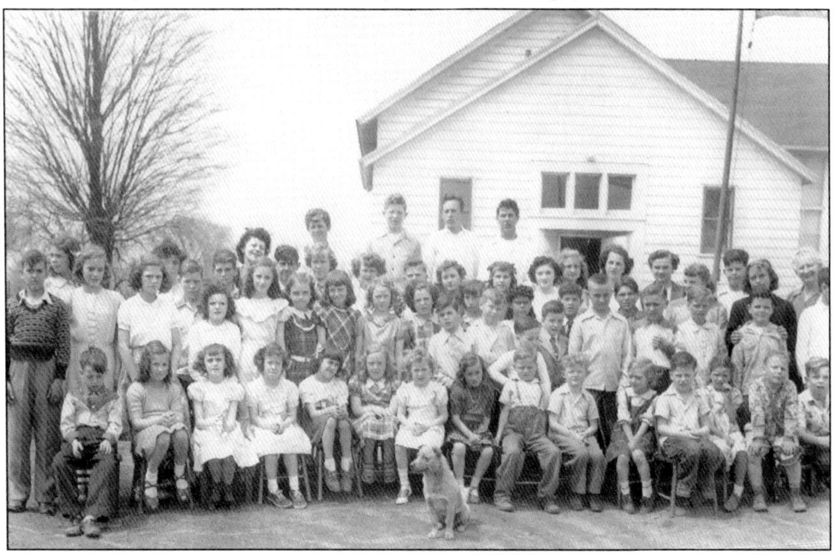

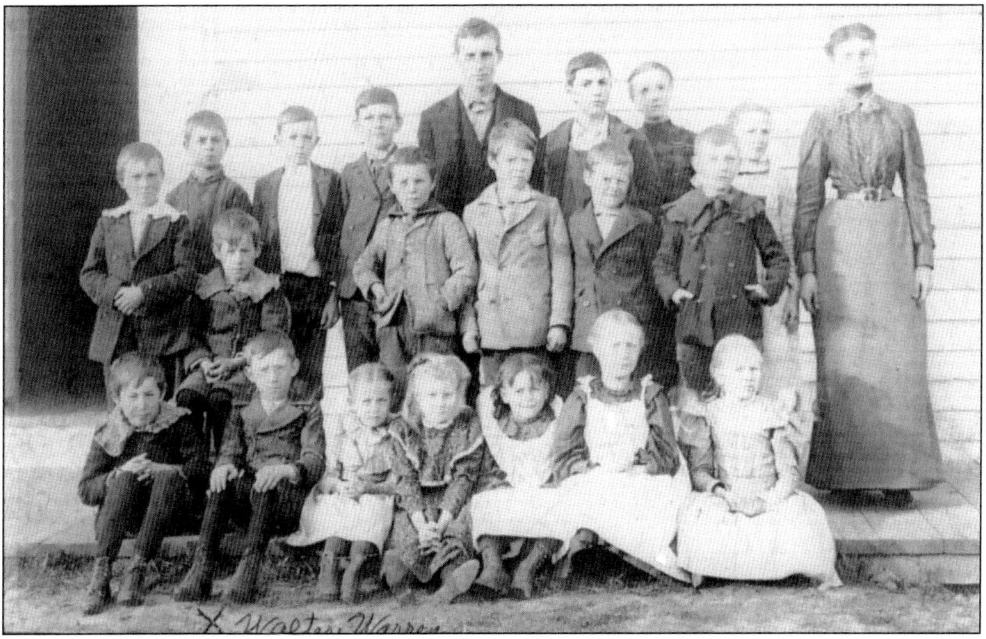

Andrews School students and their teacher (right) pose outside the one-room schoolhouse around 1906. The Andrews School, in District Number Four, was located at the northeast corner of 25 Mile and Mound Roads on the Andrews farm. The school closed in the 1950s. The building was moved in 1976 to the Shelby Township municipal grounds and is the only one-room schoolhouse remaining in the township. (STHC.)

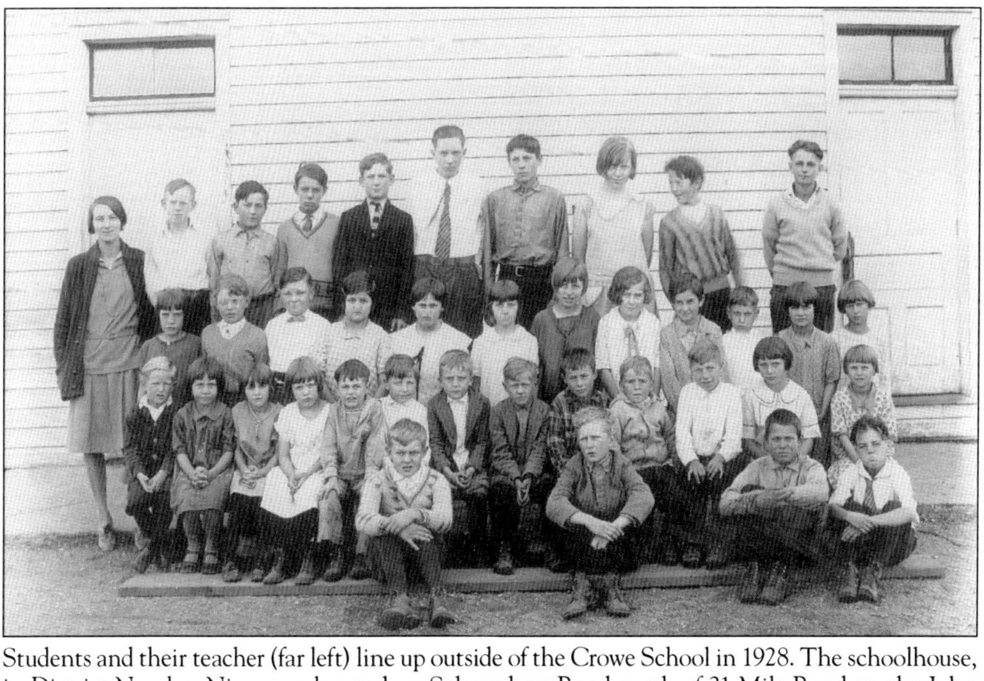

Students and their teacher (far left) line up outside of the Crowe School in 1928. The schoolhouse, in District Number Nine, was located on Schoenherr Road north of 21 Mile Road on the John Crow farm. It was established sometime before 1859. Carl Lagodna is seated in front (left). His brother Ralph is standing in the third row, second from the left. (Lynn and Grace Drake.)

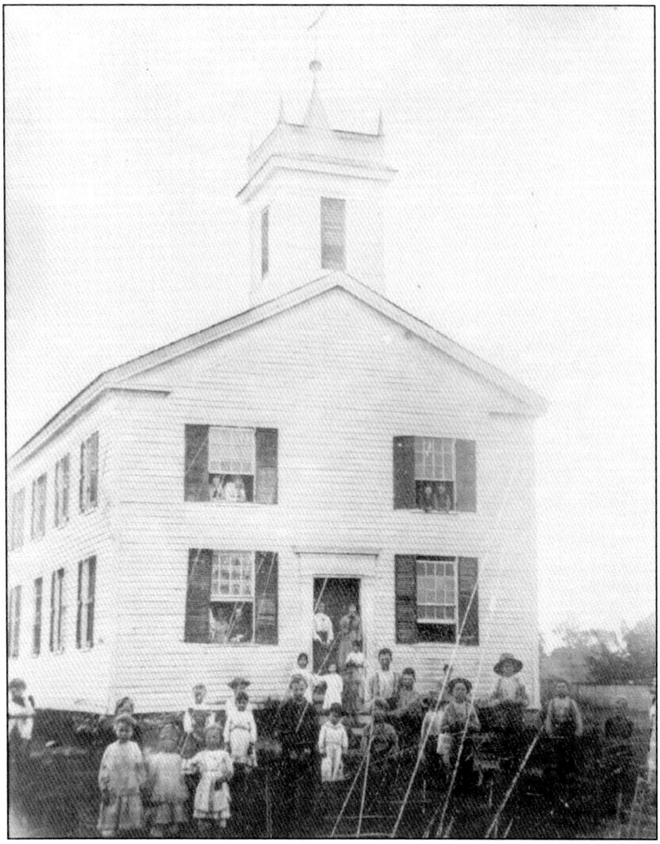

In 1850, the Mutual Literary Institute, later renamed Disco Academy, opened at the southwest corner of 24 Mile Road and Van Dyke Avenue. The residents of Disco wanted a teaching academy and a place of higher learning in the village. The two-story building housed the private academy and high school plus the primary school for District Number Six. (Hugh Switzer and George Roberts family.)

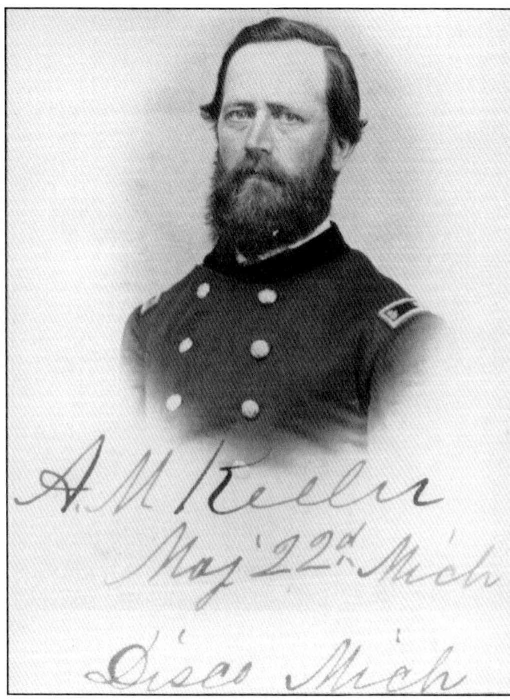


Alonzo Keeler was hired to build and run the academy. Alonzo had attended Oberlin College in Ohio and was teaching school in nearby Washington Township when approached by the residents of Disco. The school flourished under his leadership. In 1861, Alonzo helped organize Company B of the 22nd Michigan Volunteer Infantry and left Shelby Township to fight in the Civil War. (Archives of Michigan.)

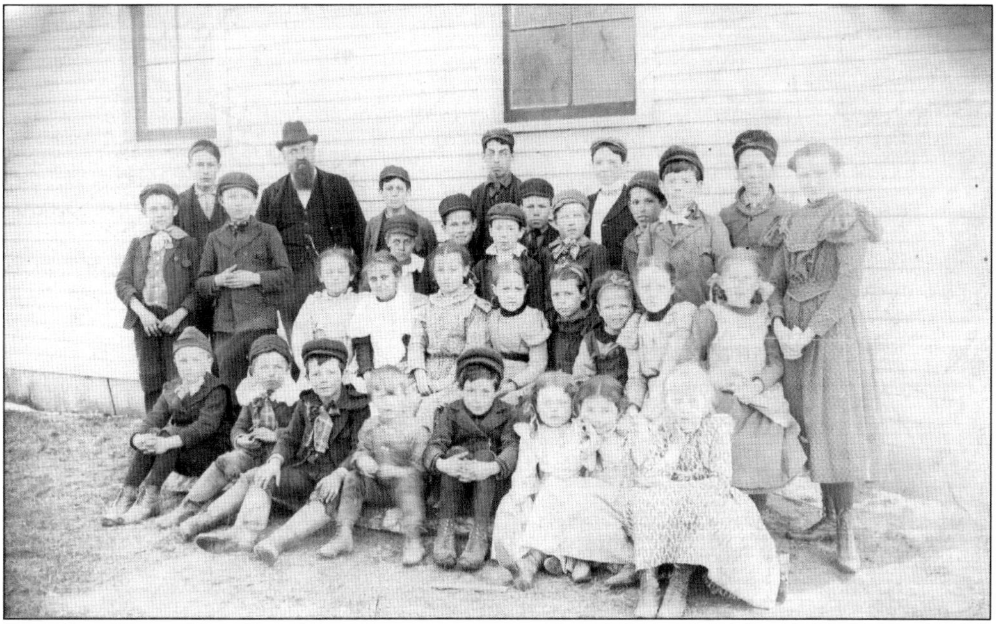

Here Disco School students pose beside the schoolhouse in an undated photograph. The man in the suit is probably the school district director. In 1865, the academy closed due to competition from the new union school in Utica. The grade school remained in the lower floor of the building, while the top floor was used for meetings and church services. (Hugh Switzer and George Roberts family.)

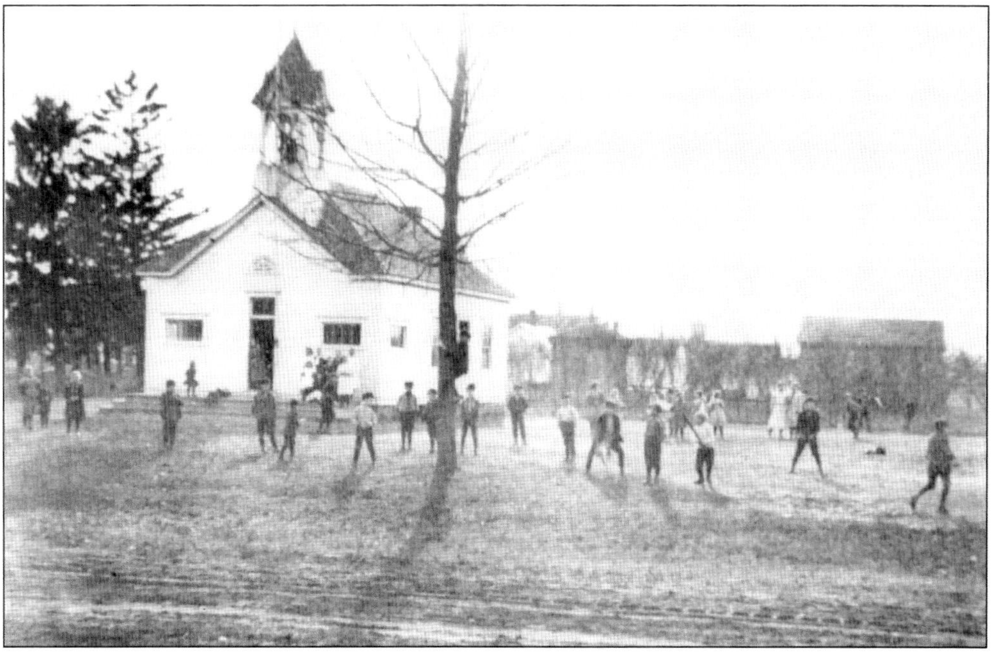

Around 1903, a new two-room schoolhouse for the primary grades of District Number Six was constructed next to the old academy building. The academy building was later moved to a nearby farm on Van Dyke Avenue, where it was used as a polling station, a tavern, and for offices until it burned down in 1945. (Hugh Switzer and George Roberts family.)

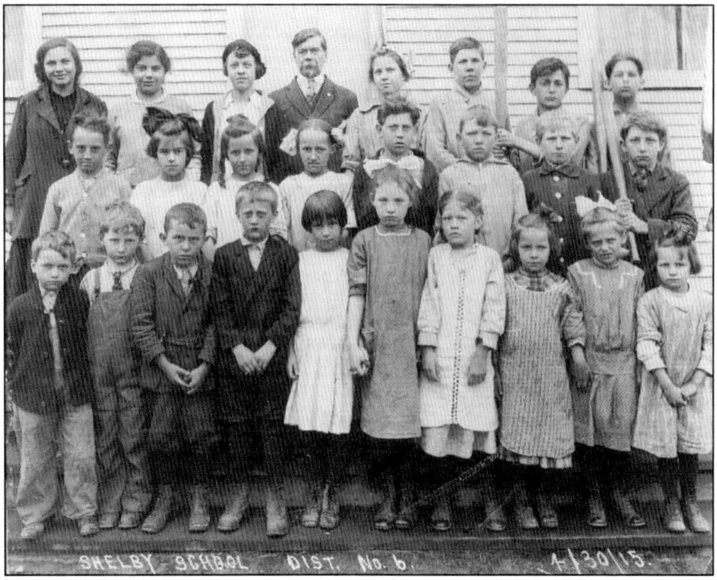


Here Disco School students pose in front of the school in 1915. Records from this time show that the director of District Number Six was Edward Millar, who could be the gentleman standing in back. The woman on the left may be the teacher. The teachers in these schools were often not much older than the oldest children in their classes. (STHC.)

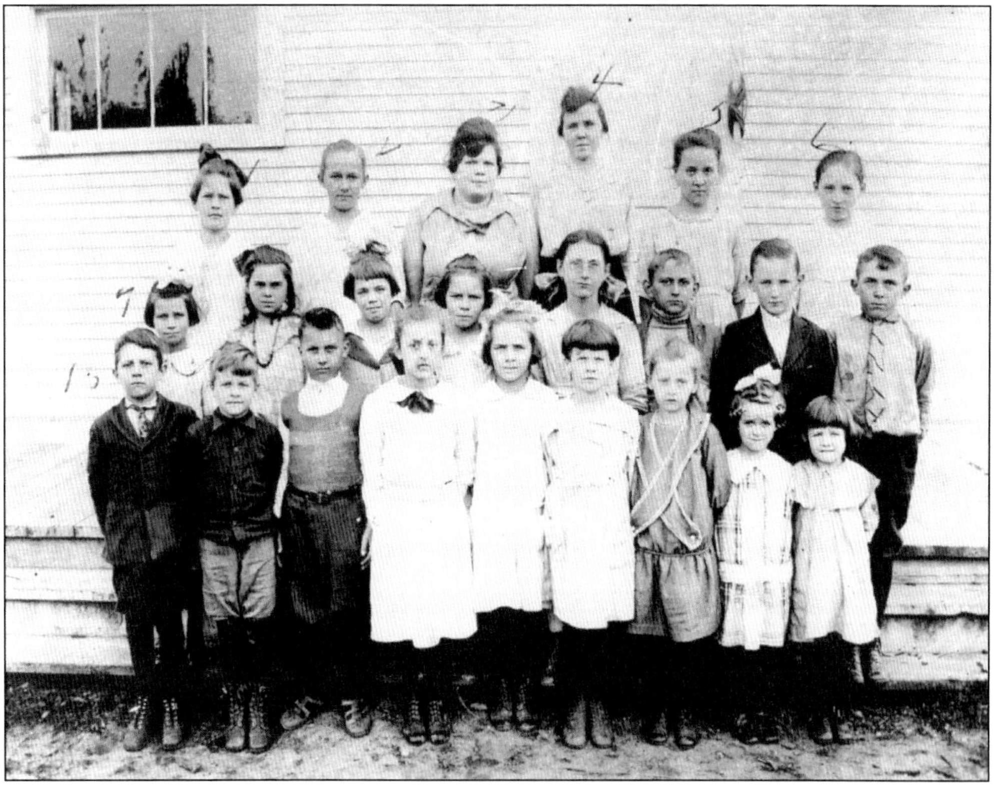

From 1919, the class members of Disco School are, from left to right, (first row) Albert Ward, Melvin Smith, Almond Rowley, Bernice Rowley, Mary Ann Miller, Gladys Smith, Elizabeth Rowley, Loraine Smith, and unidentified; (second row) Mabel Fogelsonger, Marion Metz, Maud Fogelsonger, unidentified, Bernice Powierski, Alfred Burgess, Aloysius Powierski, and Edward Miller; (third row) Martina Herrington, Ruth Fogelsonger, Aleen Fields, Mattie Rosso (teacher), Corine Fogelsonger, and Edith Burgess. (STHC.)

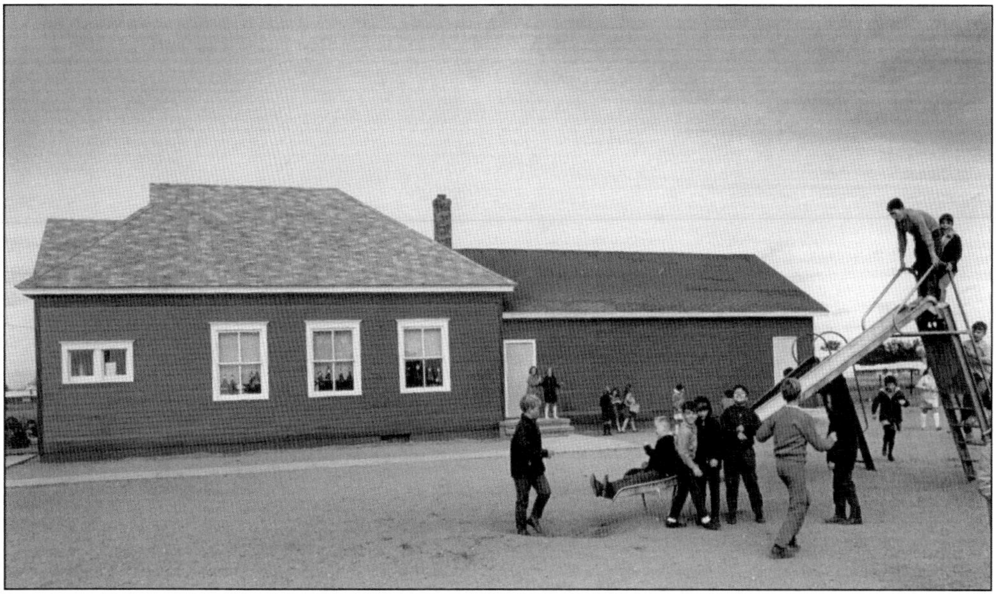

By 1946, there were 143 students attending classes in the two-room Disco schoolhouse. The school district voted to build a new school on Van Dyke Avenue a half mile south of 24 Mile Road. The Disco schoolhouse was moved, minus its belfry, and placed behind the new school around 1950. It was used as an annex for classrooms until it burned in 1973. (MD.)

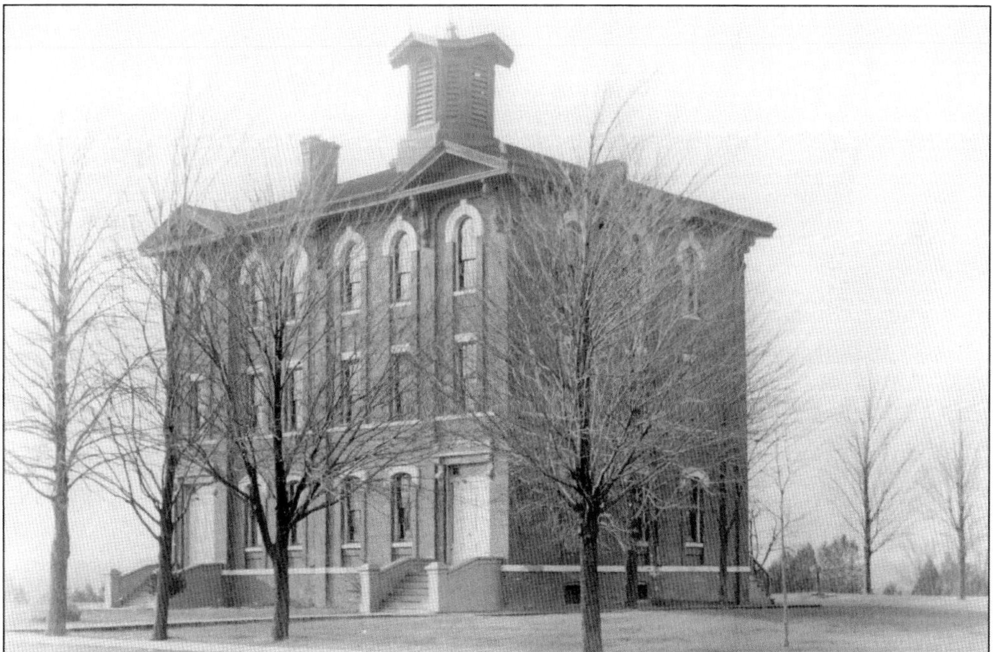


The Utica Union School, shown here around 1900, opened on Brownell Street in Utica in 1860. It was a three-story brick building with a primary school (first through sixth grades), a grammar school (seventh and eighth grades), and a high school. Students had to pay tuition to attend the school, but it was less expensive than tuition for the private academy in Disco. (Sterling Heights Historical Commission.)

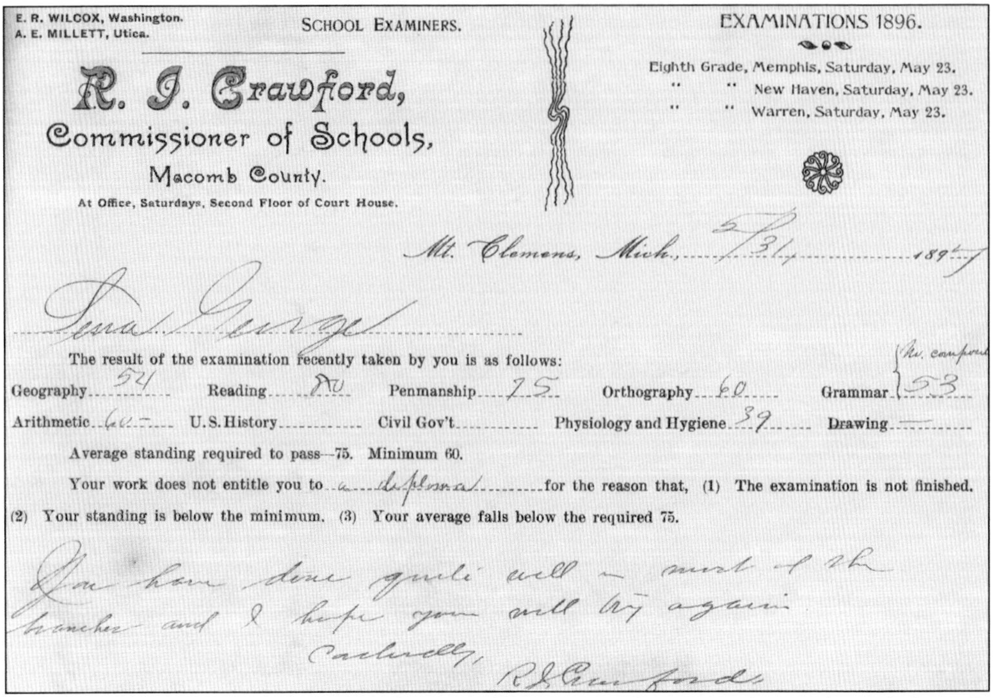

E. R. WILCOX, Washington.
A. E. MILLETT, Utica.

SCHOOL EXAMINERS.

EXAMINATIONS 1896.

Eighth Grade, Memphis, Saturday, May 23.
" " New Haven, Saturday, May 23.
" " Warren, Saturday, May 23.

R. J. Crawford,
Commissioner of Schools,
Macomb County.

At Office, Saturdays, Second Floor of Court House.

Mt. Clemens, Mich., 5/31, 1897

Lena George

The result of the examination recently taken by you is as follows:

Geography 54 Reading 80 Penmanship 75 Orthography 60 Grammar 53
Arithmetic 60 U.S. History Civil Gov't Physiology and Hygiene 39 Drawing

Average standing required to pass—75. Minimum 60.

Your work does not entitle you to a diploma for the reason that, (1) The examination is not finished. (2) Your standing is below the minimum. (3) Your average falls below the required 75.

You have done quite well — most of the teacher and I hope you will try again.
Cordially,
R. J. Crawford.

To get into high school, students had to travel to Mount Clemens and pass the eighth-grade examinations. As shown here, Ewell School student Lena George failed several of her subject tests in 1897. She repeated the eighth grade, passed her examinations in 1898, and went on to attend the Utica Union School. (STHC.)

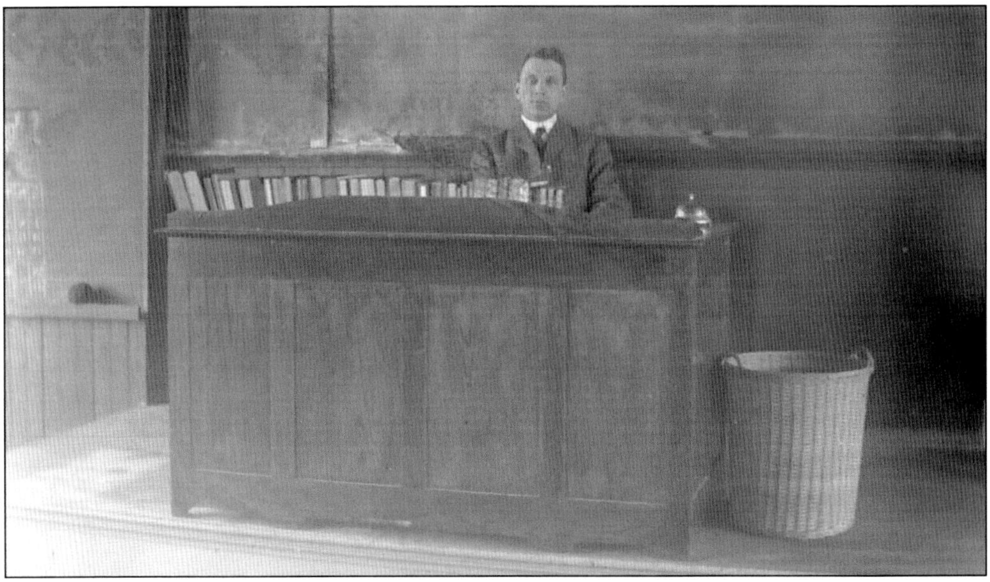

The Utica Union School was renamed Utica High School in 1900. Here an unidentified teacher sits behind his desk at the school around 1907. The school curriculum featured courses in mathematics, science, English, history, the classics, art, and music. It had a high reputation for excellence and was the school of choice for many area students. (Douglas Harvey; photograph by Burt Harvey.)

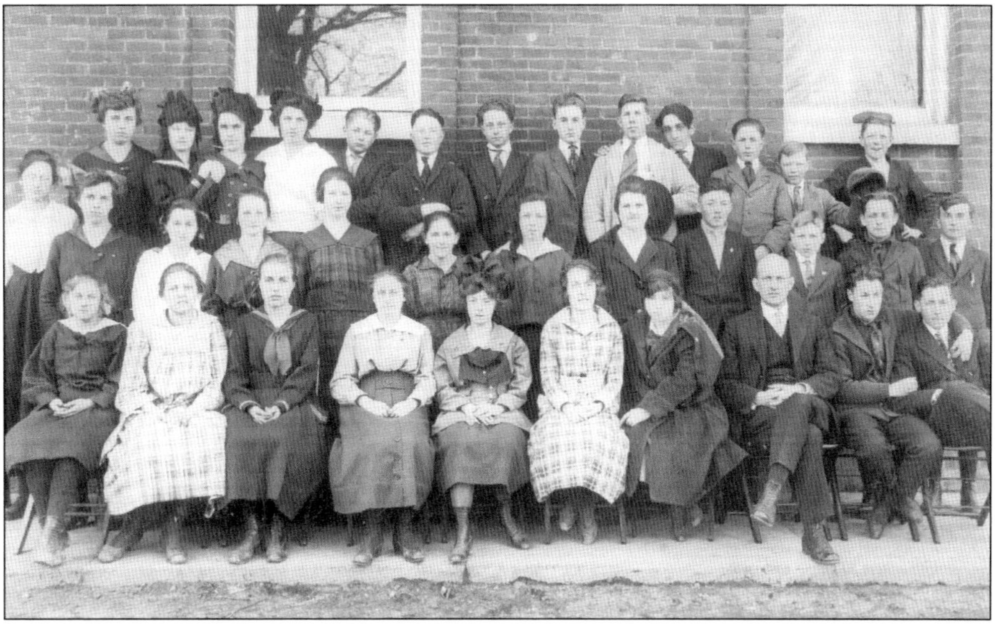

The students of Utica High School pose outside the school around 1917. School superintendent Roy Lunger sits in the front row, third from the right. He held this post from 1916 to 1929 and oversaw many improvements to the school curriculum, such as adding standardized textbooks and business courses. (STHC.)

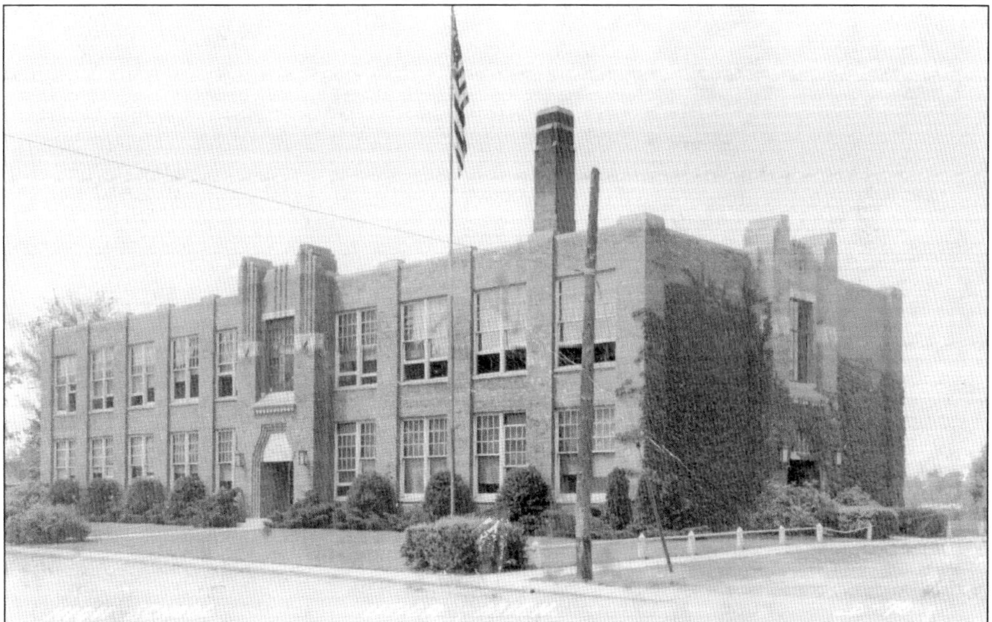

Due to overcrowding in the 1860 school building, a new Utica High School was built next door in 1929. The old building became an annex for the district primary school and was torn down around 1960. The 1929 building still stands on Brownell Street in Utica and is now the home of Eppler Junior High School. (Gary and Mary Miller Bradt.)

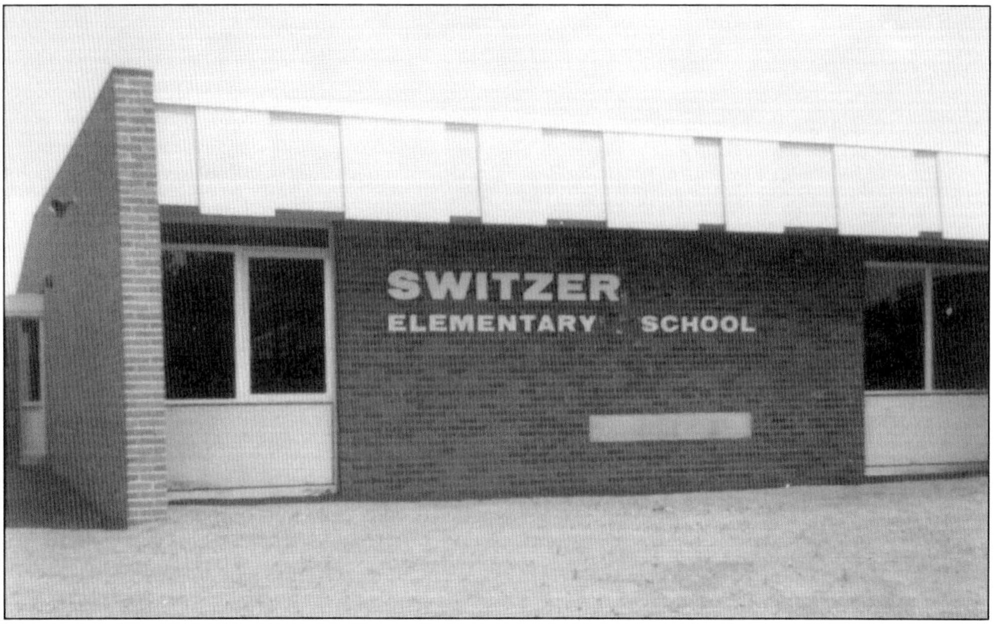


Around 1949, the many school districts in Shelby Township began consolidating under the single Utica Community Schools District. Several new elementary, junior, and senior high schools were built in the township, including the Switzer Elementary School on Shelby Road. Built in 1963, it was named for longtime resident and teacher Josephine Switzer. (Hugh Switzer and George Roberts family.)

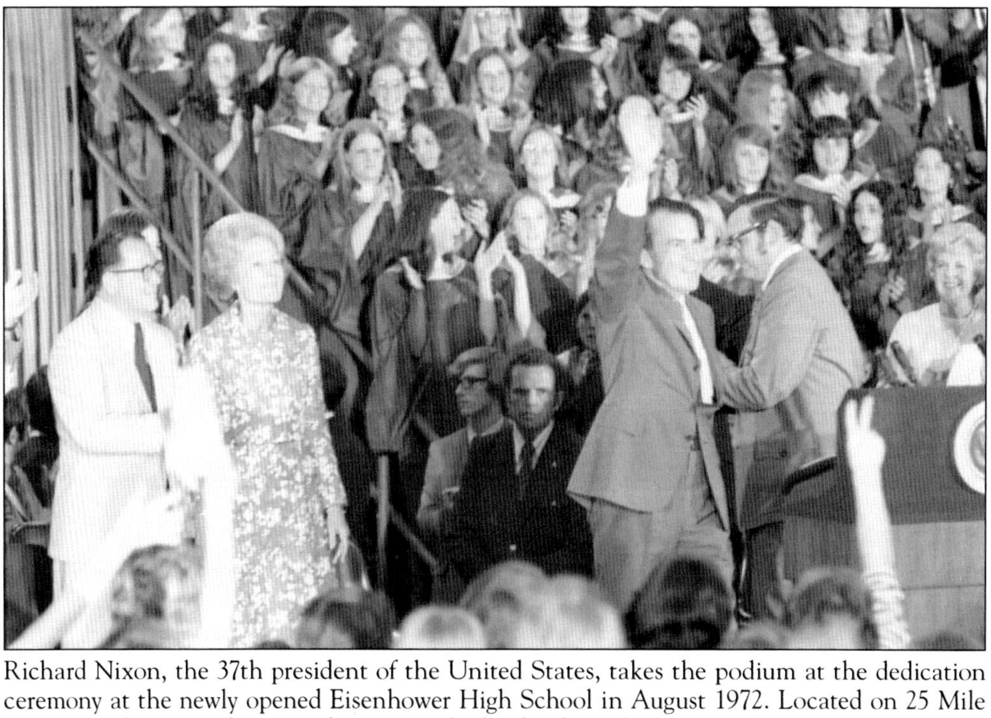

Richard Nixon, the 37th president of the United States, takes the podium at the dedication ceremony at the newly opened Eisenhower High School in August 1972. Located on 25 Mile Road, Eisenhower High is one of two senior high schools in Shelby Township. The other is Utica High School, which was built on Shelby Road in 1955. (WPRL.)

*Five*

# Planes, Trains, Automobiles, Buggies, and a Barge

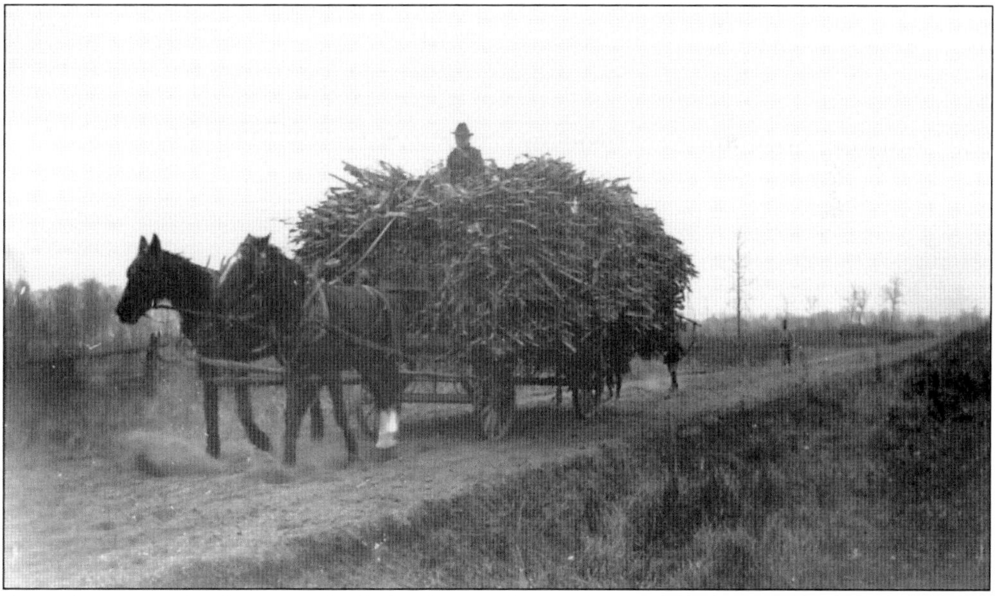

A two-horse team hauls a wagon loaded with twigs down a dusty road around 1907. The contribution of the horse as a means of transportation in the settlement and growth of Shelby Township is immeasurable. The animal pulled pioneers' wagons, farmers' plows, workers' carts, and villagers' buggies. Horses pulled canal barges and even the first trains. (Douglas Harvey; photograph by Burt Harvey.)

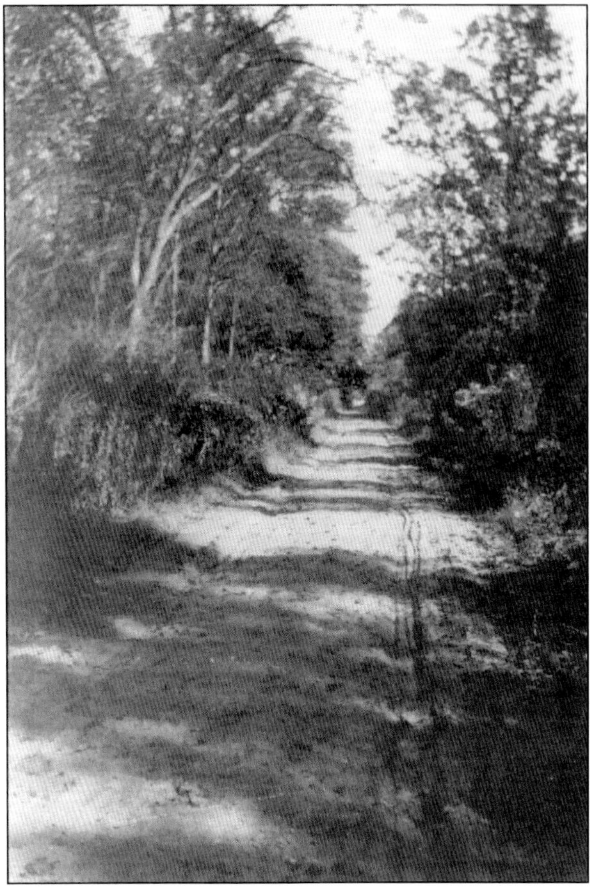

The first roads in Shelby Township were dirt tracks, like this stretch of 22 Mile Road around 1918, which became deeply rutted by wagon wheels and all but impassible in wet weather. In the early 1830s, plank roads, where wooden boards were used as pavers, were sometimes built rendering the roads passable in most weather. (STHC.)

Plank roads proved difficult to maintain, and the technique was only used for major connector roads, such as Utica Road, up until around 1850. Most roads in Shelby Township remained unpaved for 100 years or more, like this stretch of 25 Mile Road (looking west between Shelby Road and Dequindre Road) shown in 1943. (Michael and Christy Meyer.)

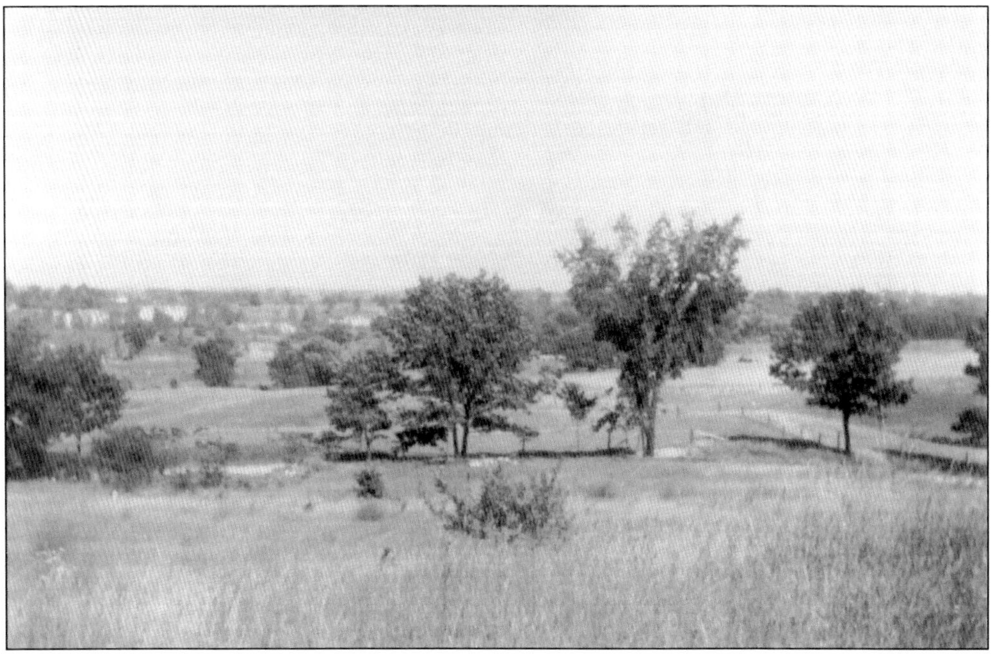

In 1837, the Michigan State Legislature passed an act to improve internal transportation by building canals, turnpikes, and railroads. The first of these projects was the Clinton and Kalamazoo Canal, which was designed to cut across Michigan from Mount Clemens through Shelby Township to Lake Michigan. Here a section of the canal runs along 22 Mile Road in Shelby Township around 1940. (Maynard W. Remer family.)

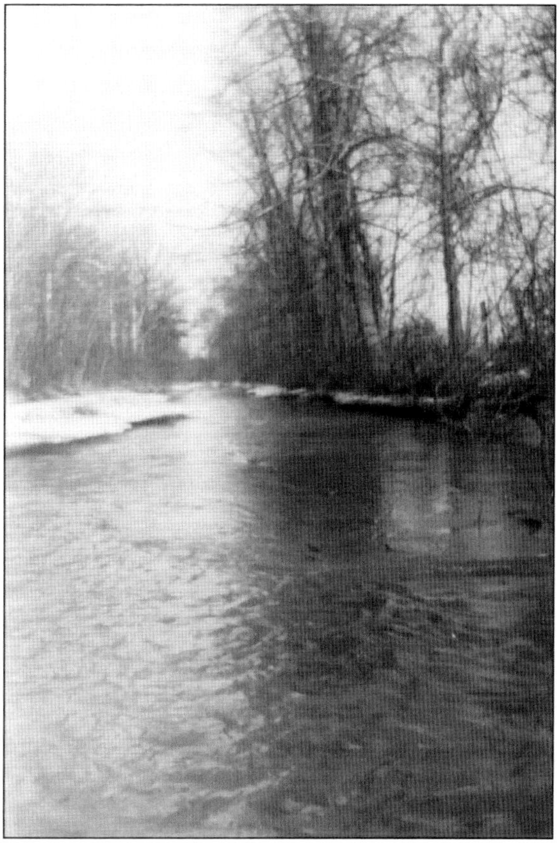

The Clinton and Kalamazoo Canal closely followed the Clinton River as it passed through Shelby Township. Just east of the township, at Yates Mill in Rochester, the canal was carried over the river via an aqueduct. The wooden structure developed leaks soon after it was built around 1840, which can be seen in this photograph from 1915. The aqueduct finally rotted away in the 1970s. (MD.)

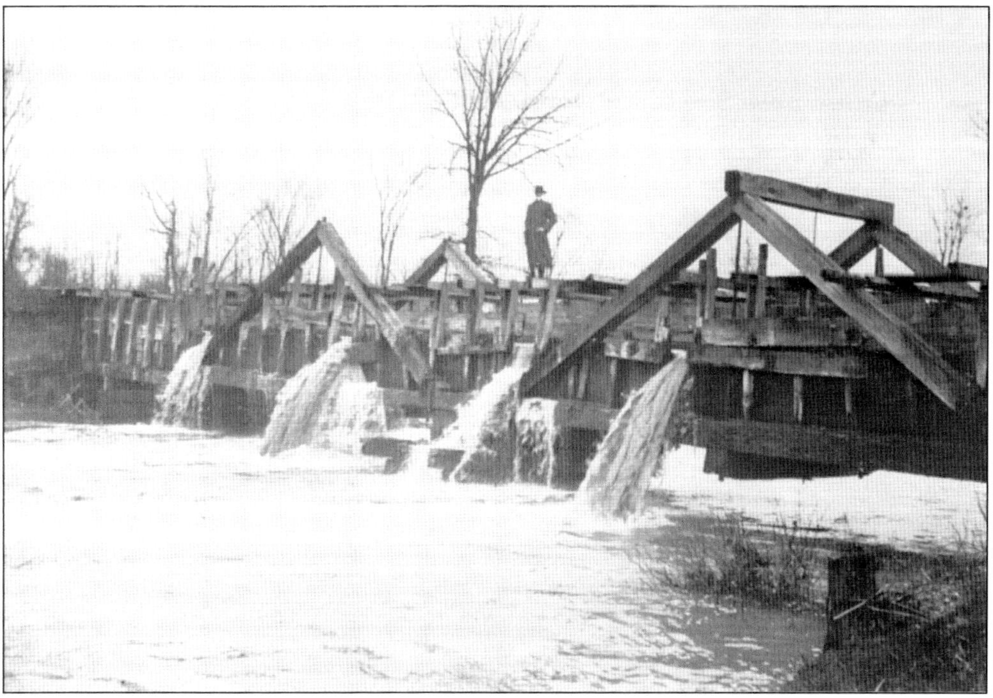

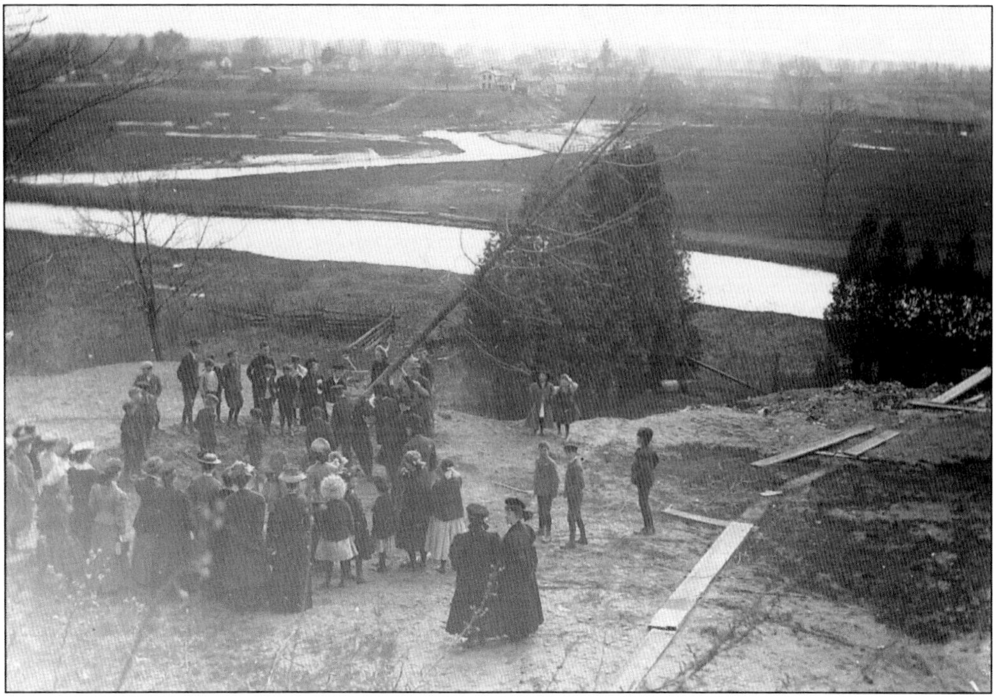

Taken from the top floor of the Utica High School building around 1907, these two photographs show the Clinton and Kalamazoo Canal in the foreground with the Clinton River in the background. From 1839 to 1843, the state spent nearly $400,000 building the canal of which only 16 miles were completed from Mount Clemens to Rochester. A national economic depression and the failure of the funding corporations spelled doom for the canal project. Workers went unpaid, work stopped, and parts of the canal fell into ruin. In 1844, the State Board of Internal Improvements reported that the canal was a failure. The section that ran through Shelby Township was subsequently used as a millrace. Below, the canal and the river head into Utica to power the mills seen in the distance. (Both, Douglas Harvey; photographs by Burt Harvey.)

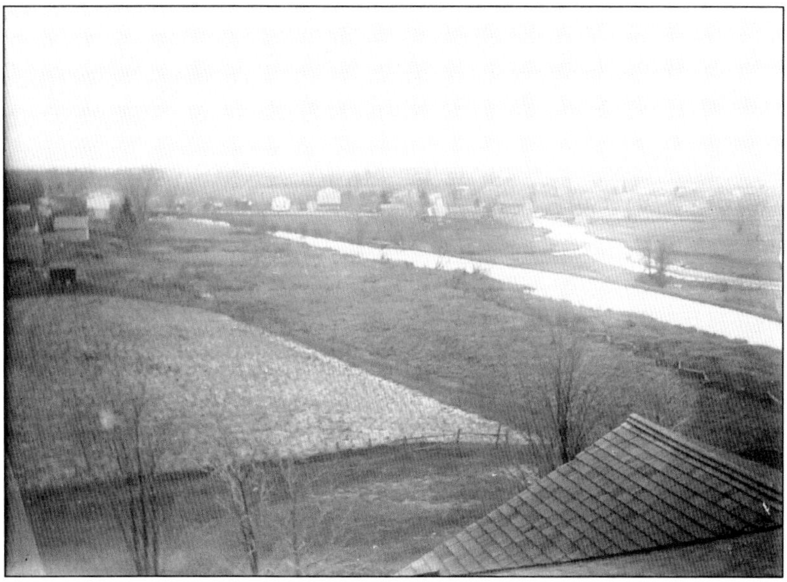

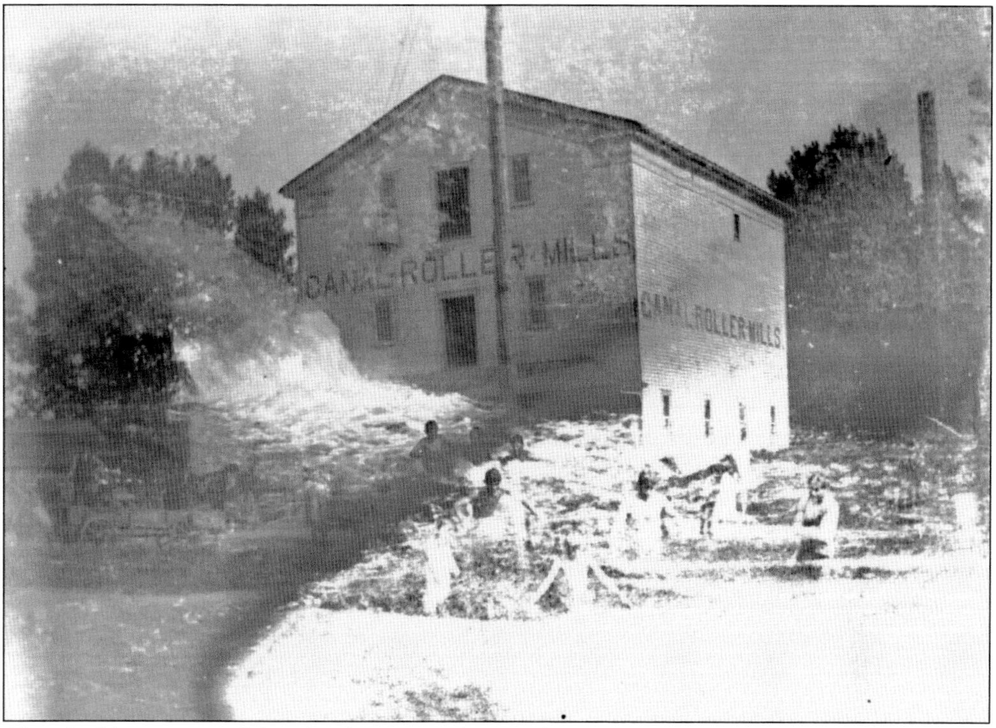


This double exposure (above) taken around 1907 shows children bathing in the Clinton and Kalamazoo Canal millrace along with a gristmill in Utica that was powered by the canal waters running through Shelby Township. David Price and Charles Chapel built the Canal Roller Mills in 1846 on the south side of Main Street near Davis Street. Water from the canal was supplied to the mill by a wooden trough. The Crissman family of Utica acquired the Canal Roller Mills along with the title to the canal and its right-of-way from the state in 1880. The mill became part of the Utica Milling Company founded by the Crissman family. Below, the canal empties into the Mill Pond in Utica. (Both, Douglas Harvey; photographs by Burt Harvey)

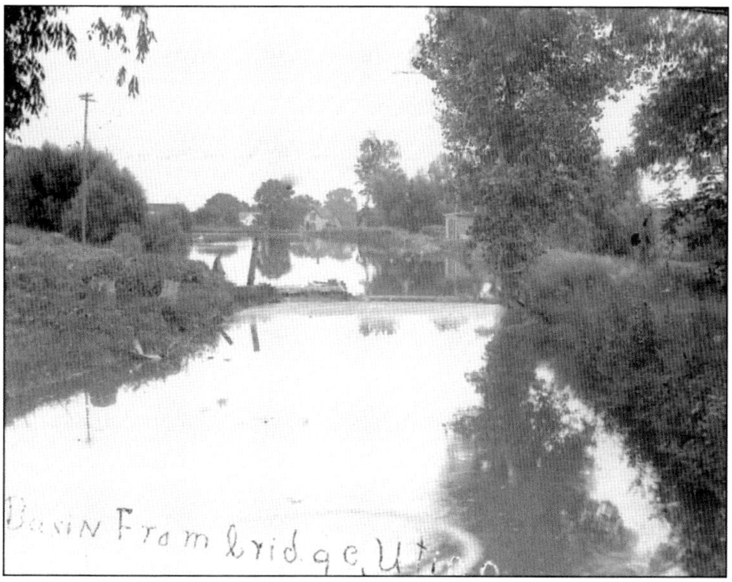

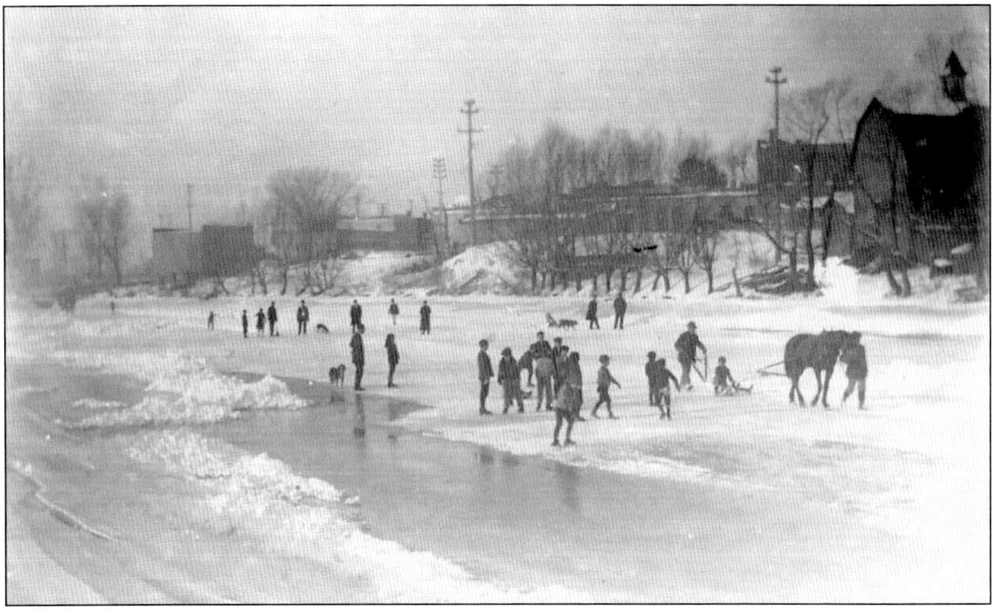

The Mill Pond, also known as the Basin, was a widened section of the Clinton and Kalamazoo Canal designed for turning and docking horse-drawn canal barges. But only one barge ever used the canal to ferry goods from Mount Clemens to Utica. In two years, only $96 in tolls was collected from this activity. After the barge run ceased, the basin was used for recreation, for generating electricity, and as a source of ice. In these *c.* 1907 photographs, townsfolk enjoy some fun on the frozen basin while a cutting team harvests ice. One man guides the horse, another steers the ice cutter, and a boy provides the weight. The buildings in the background are on the south side of Main Street in Utica. (Both, Douglas Harvey; photographs by Burt Harvey.)

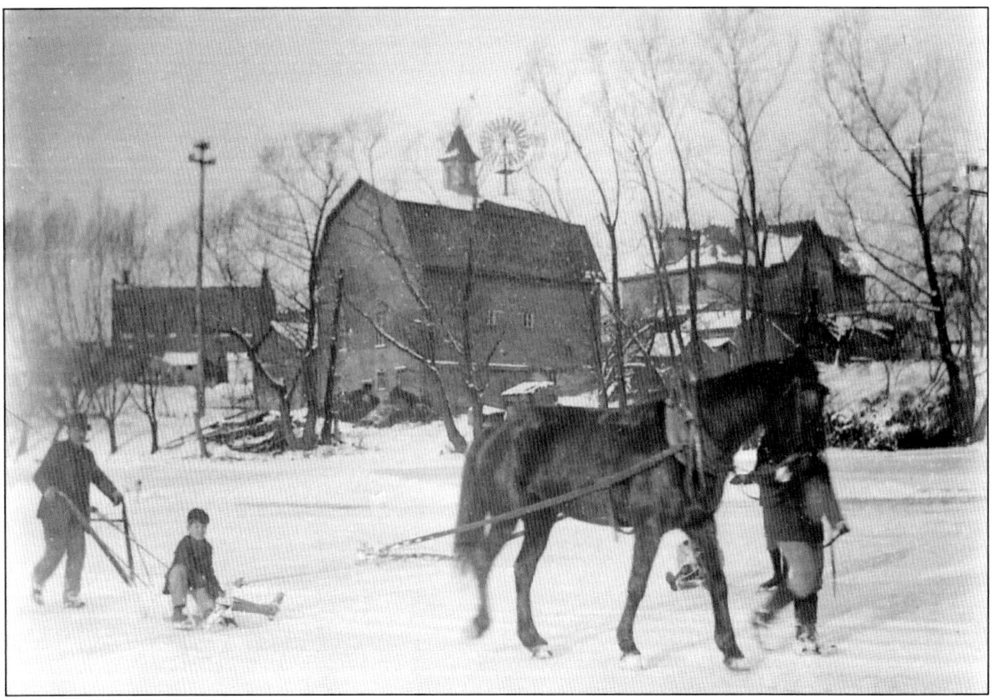

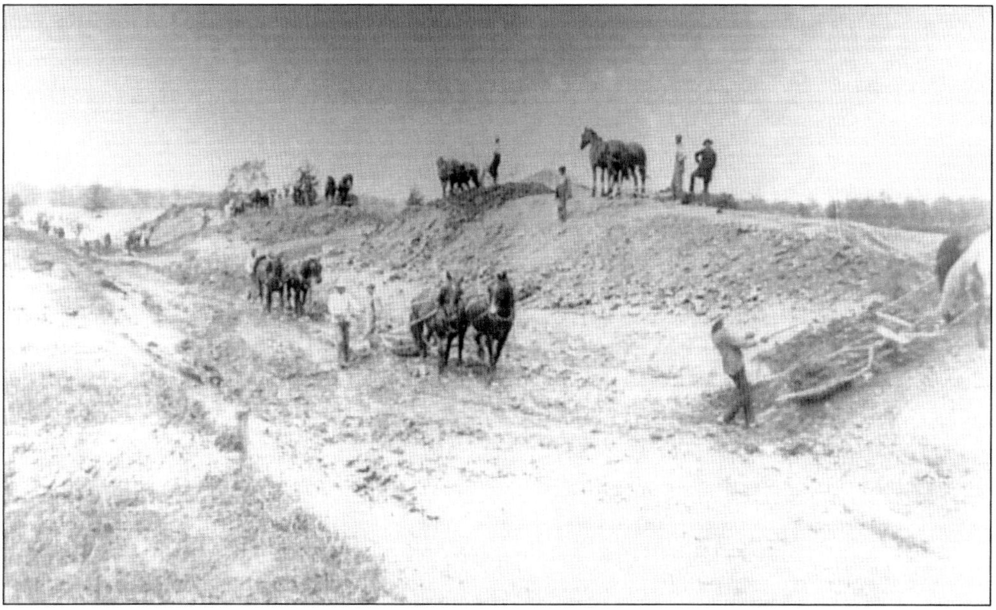

In these two photographs from the late 1800s, workers level the ground for a rail bed alongside the Clinton and Kalamazoo Canal. Building began on the Shelby and Detroit Railroad, another Michigan internal improvements project, around 1835. The plan was to connect Shelby Township farmers via the canal to the markets of Detroit. It was an early form of railroad, known as a strap railroad, where horses pulled carriages on wooden rails faced with thin iron straps. It was an effective mode of transportation but often dangerous as the straps could come loose and spring through the floor of a passing carriage. The railroad ceased operations in 1844 due to the state's money problems and the inability of the tracks to support the newest development in railroad technology, the steam locomotive. (Both, STHC.)

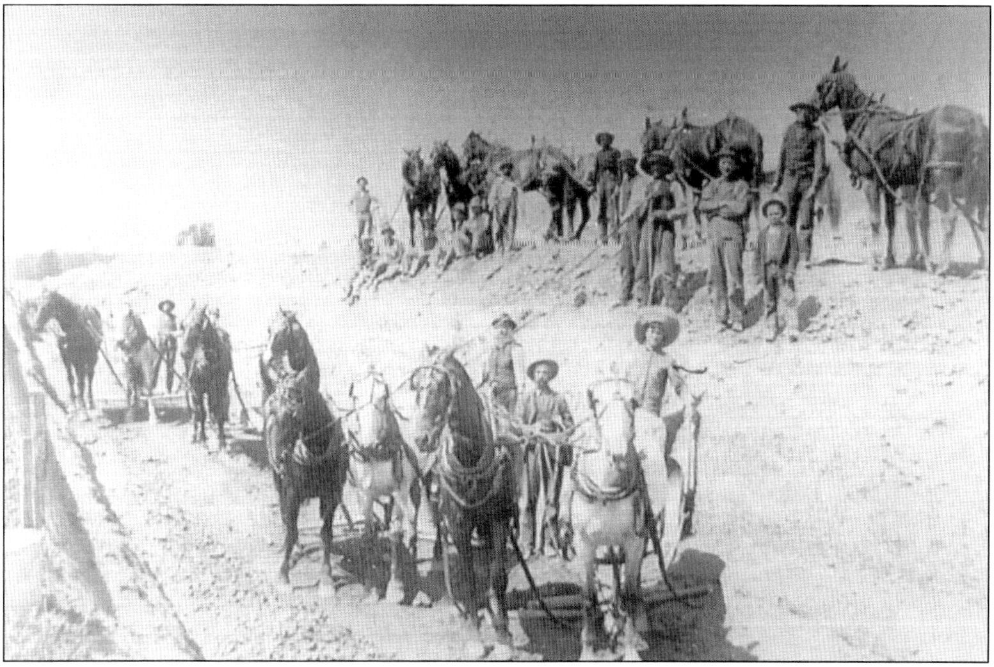

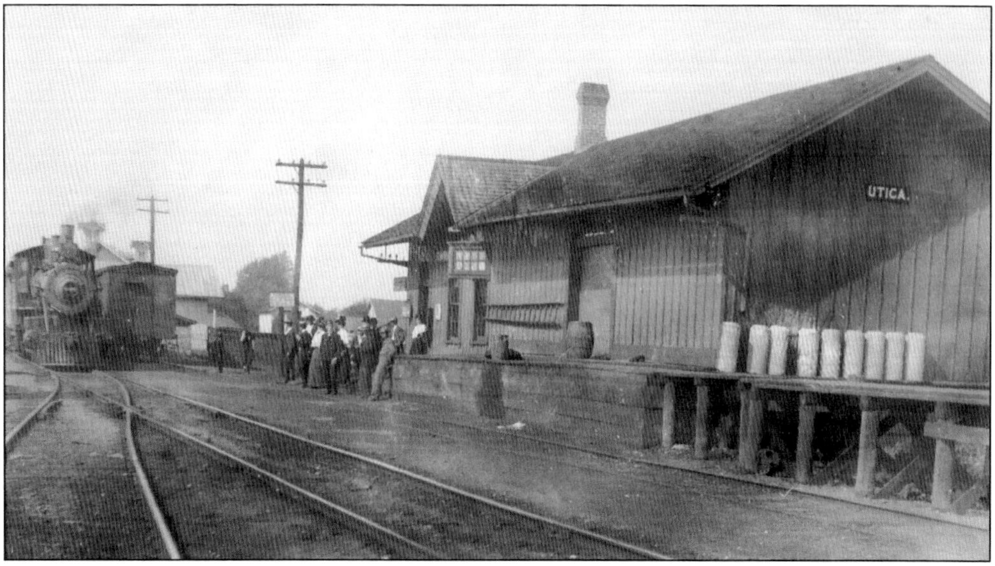


In 1872, the Detroit and Bay City Railroad opened for service from Detroit through Utica on to Rochester and Bay City. The tracks were laid on the old strap railroad bed, passing through Shelby Township close to the old canal. The depot on Greeley Street in Utica, shown in this 1905 postcard, was built in 1872. The Michigan Central Railroad took over operations around 1900. (Louis Resner.)

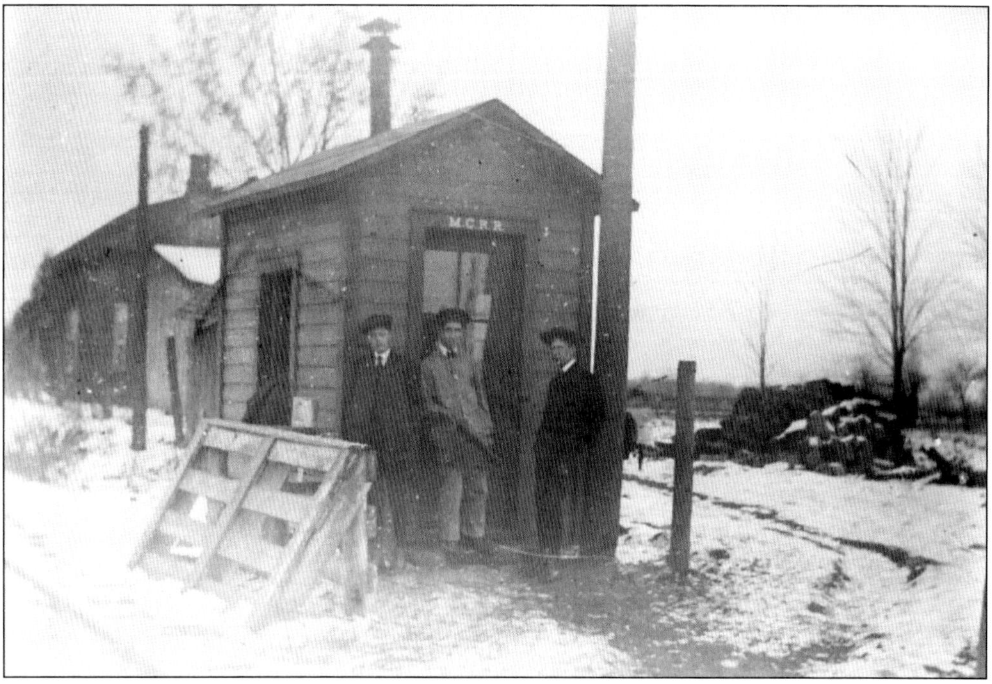


To reduce accidents at vehicle crossings and sidings, the railroad companies built flagman's shacks along the tracks. Here a flagman stands between two lads at a local shack around 1907. The flagman's job was to direct rail, vehicle, and foot traffic safely over the tracks. Wooden gates, like the one in this photograph, helped keep livestock off the tracks. (Douglas Harvey; photograph by Burt Harvey.)

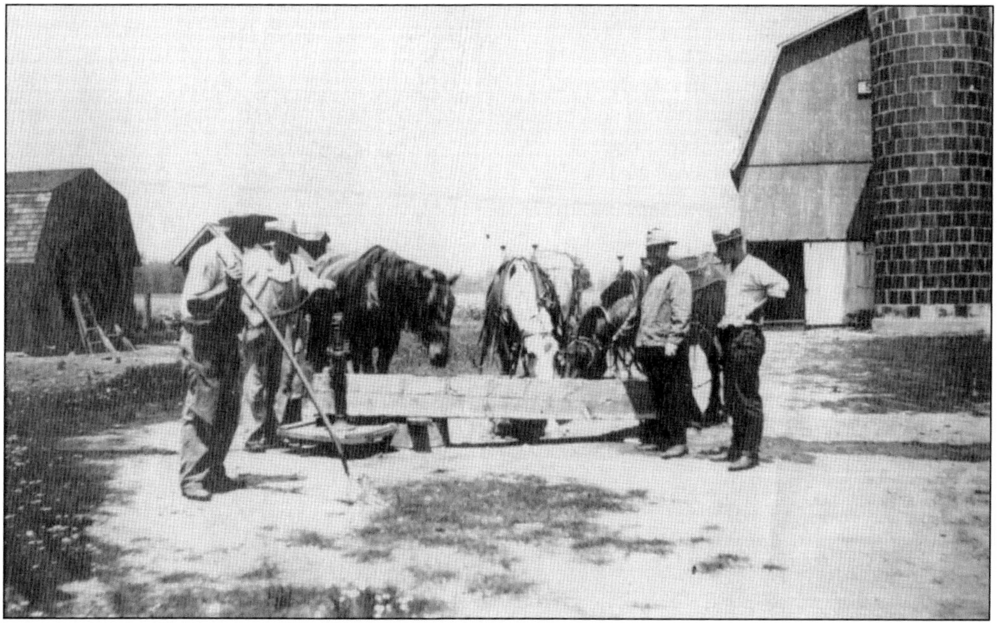

Men working the fields at Fred Lagodna's farm take a break around 1920 to water the team of horses. For over 100 years since the first settlers arrived, farmers throughout Shelby Township used horses to work their land and to take them to church, to market, or for a Sunday drive. (Lynn and Grace Drake.)

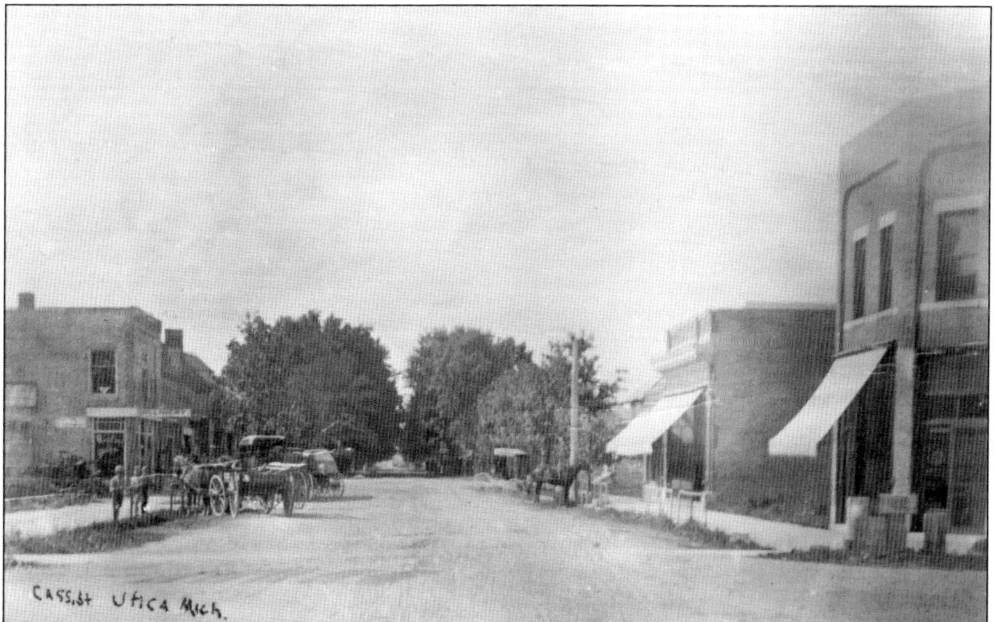


This is Cass Avenue looking north from Main Street in Utica around 1905. Note the buggies parked along the street and the numerous hitching rails in front of each store. In a few years, these carriages would disappear from the streets of Shelby Township and be replaced by automobiles. (Louis Resner.)

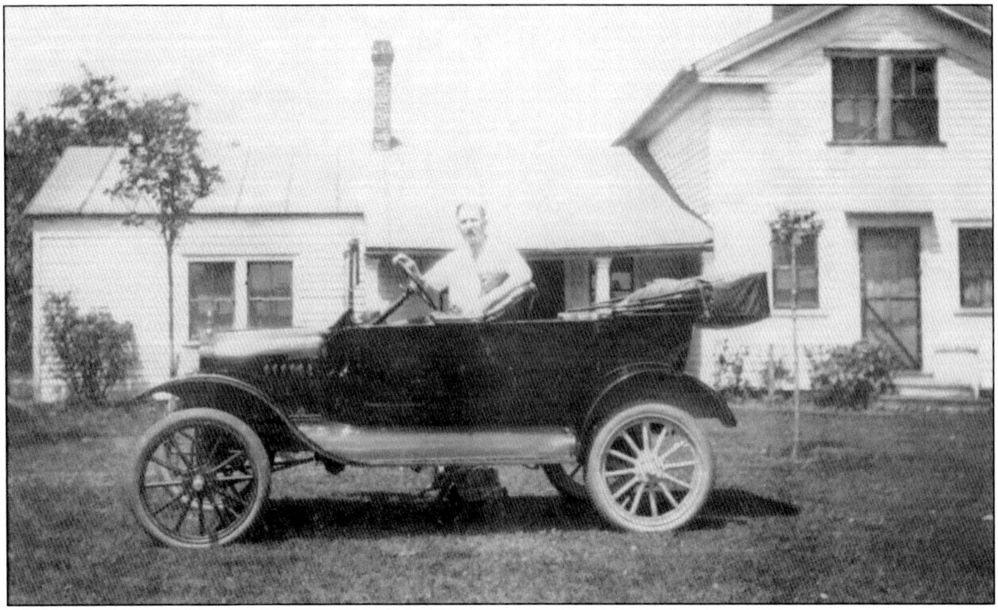

By 1919, when this photograph was taken, many residents of Shelby Township had invested in an automobile while keeping a horse and buggy ready in the wings. Here, in front of the Lagodna home on 22 Mile Road, family friend Herman Stuehmer sits behind the wheel of his motorcar, possibly a 1917 Ford Model T Tourer, with young Carl Lagodna on his lap. (Lynn and Grace Drake.)

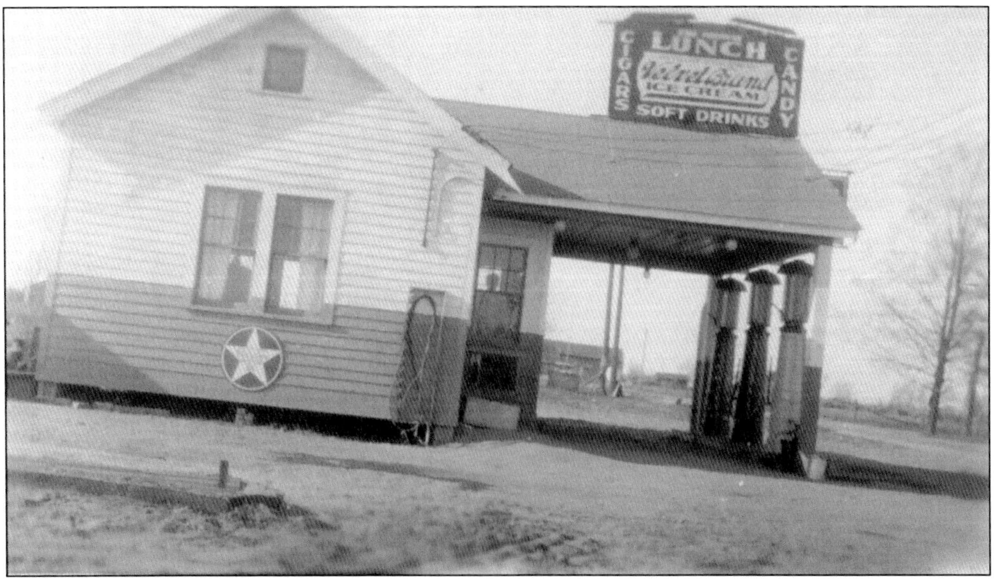


Between 1922 and 1926, Van Dyke Avenue was paved between Utica and Disco. Filling stations, cafes, and convenience stores sprang up along these newly paved corridors, catering to the newest consumer—the motorist. This is the Midway Café at 22 Mile Road and Van Dyke Avenue in the late 1920s. Note the gravity-feed fuel pumps and the Staroline motor oil advertisement. (Howard Frase family.)

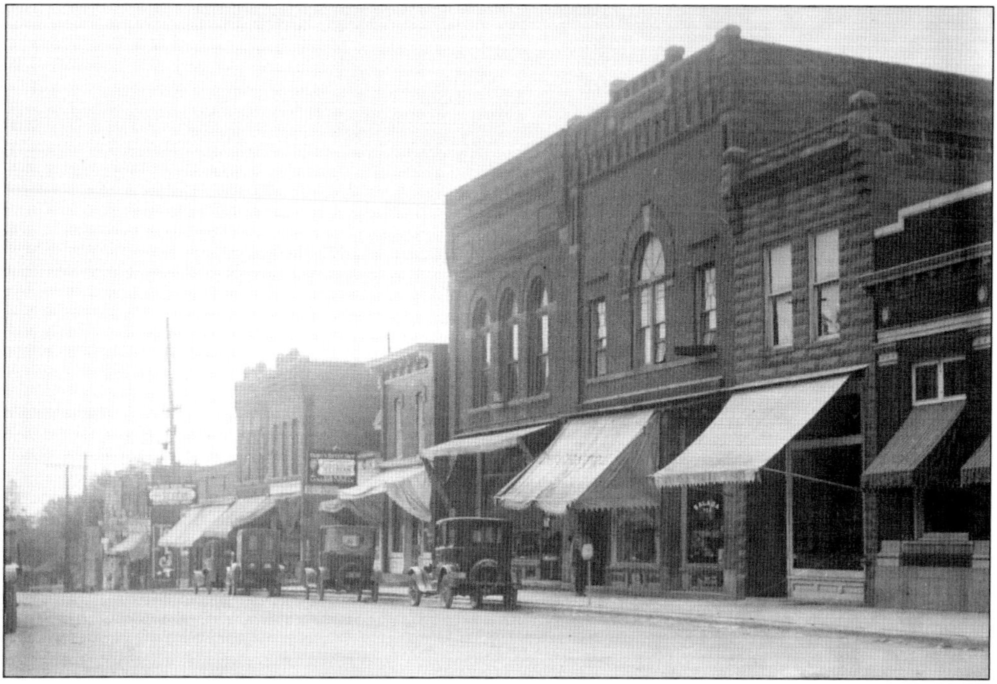

In this 1926 photograph of Main Street at Cass Avenue in Utica, the hitching rails have been removed, the road has been paved, and automobiles line the street instead of horse-drawn carriages. By 1927, residents were insisting that the traffic at this intersection was too heavy and dangerous and that a traffic-control semaphore should be installed. (WPRL.)

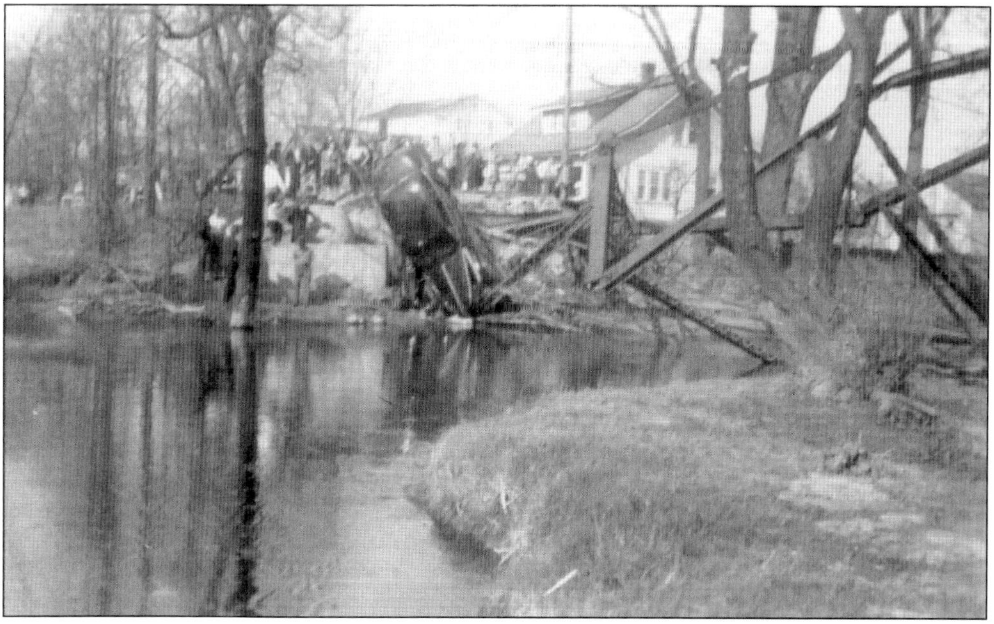

Faster, heavier automobiles and the narrow dirt roads around the area were often a dangerous mix. Here at the Davis Street Bridge, which spanned the Clinton River in Utica, a motorist lost control of his vehicle and destroyed the iron structure around 1940. Fortunately the driver was not hurt in the accident, but the automobile bridge was never rebuilt. (Maynard W. Remer family.)

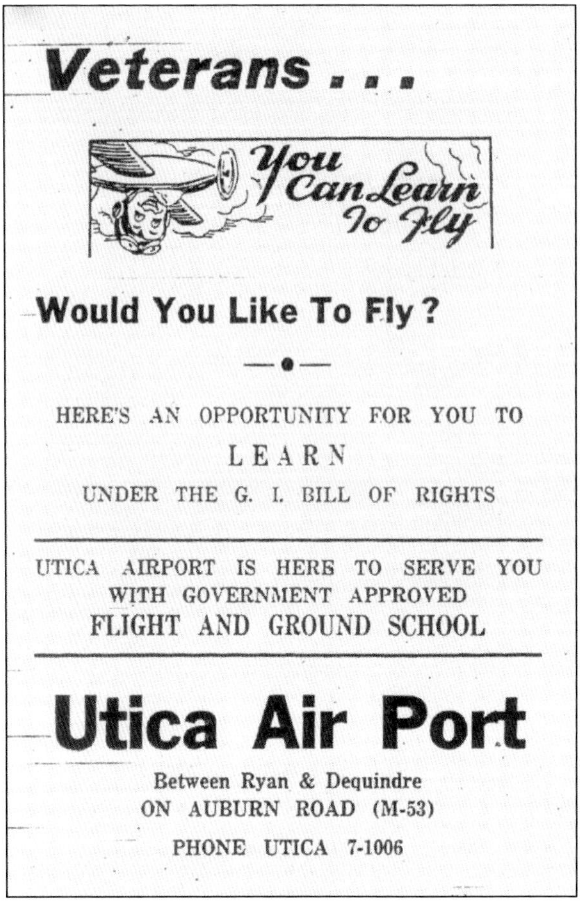
Veterans . . .

You Can Learn To Fly

Would You Like To Fly?

HERE'S AN OPPORTUNITY FOR YOU TO
LEARN
UNDER THE G. I. BILL OF RIGHTS

UTICA AIRPORT IS HERE TO SERVE YOU
WITH GOVERNMENT APPROVED
FLIGHT AND GROUND SCHOOL

Utica Air Port
Between Ryan & Dequindre
ON AUBURN ROAD (M-53)
PHONE UTICA 7-1006

The Utica Airport was located on the north side of Auburn Road east of Dequindre Road on a farm owned by the Morgan family. The airport was behind the farmhouse and consisted of a grass runway and a windsock on a pole. A few other grass-strip airports could be found in Shelby Township during the late 1930s and 1940s. (STHC.)

Here is Victor Lutzky in one of his home-built airplanes at the Utica Airport around 1941. Lutzky made the trip from Detroit to Shelby Township and back several times in this airplane. By 1952, the airport was no longer in existence. The farmland was sold to a sand and gravel company and a large water-filled quarry has since erased the grass airstrip. (Stephen and Victor Lutzky.)

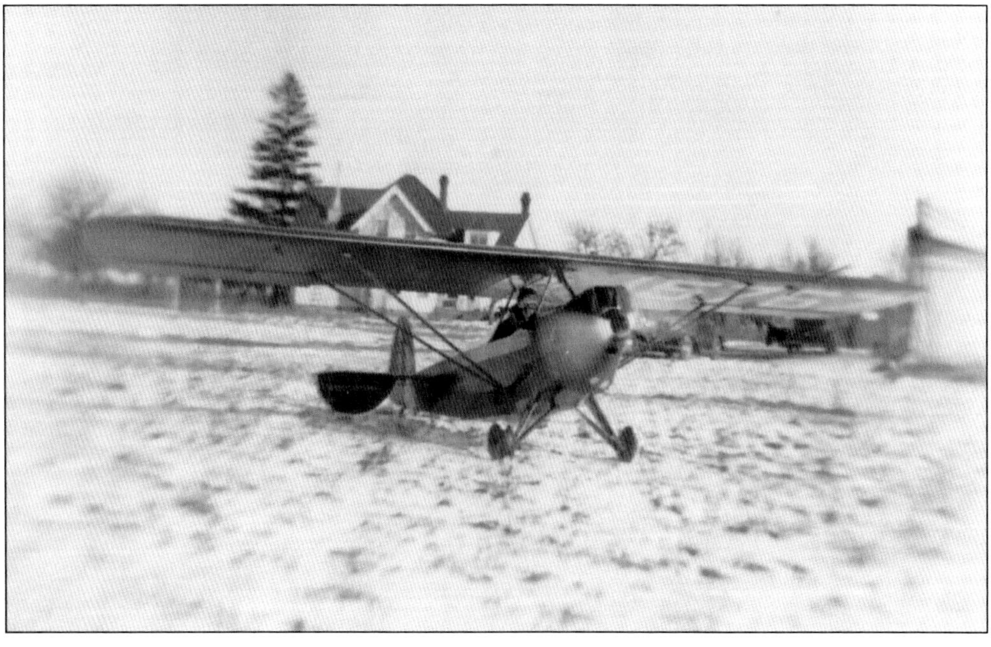

*Six*

# The Packard Proving Grounds

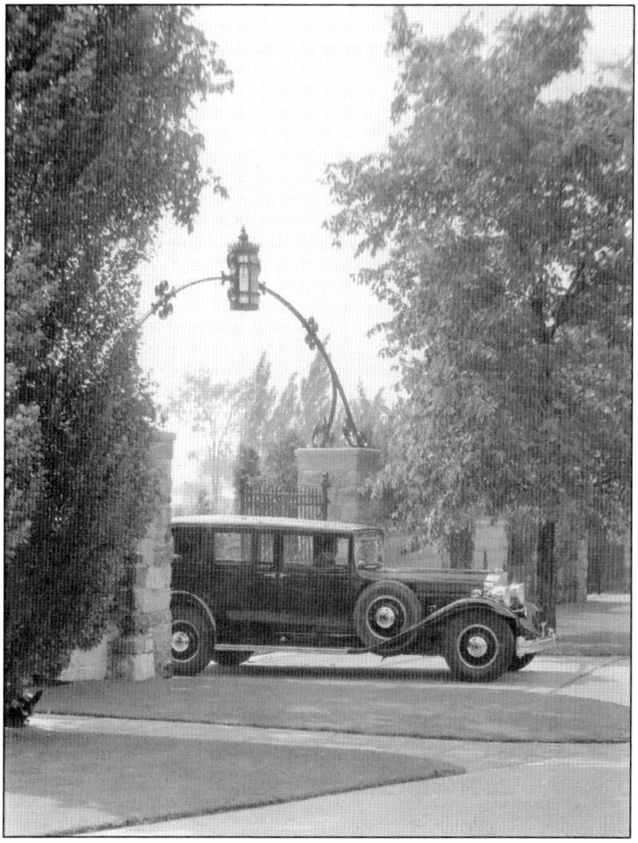

A new Packard Twin Six sedan emerges from one of the grand wrought-iron entry gates at the Packard Proving Grounds in June 1932. Beginning in 1926, the Packard Motor Car Company bought and cleared over 400 acres of farmland near the center of Shelby Township and installed a highly modern yet elegant automobile testing facility. (Roberta Vincent Mocabee.)

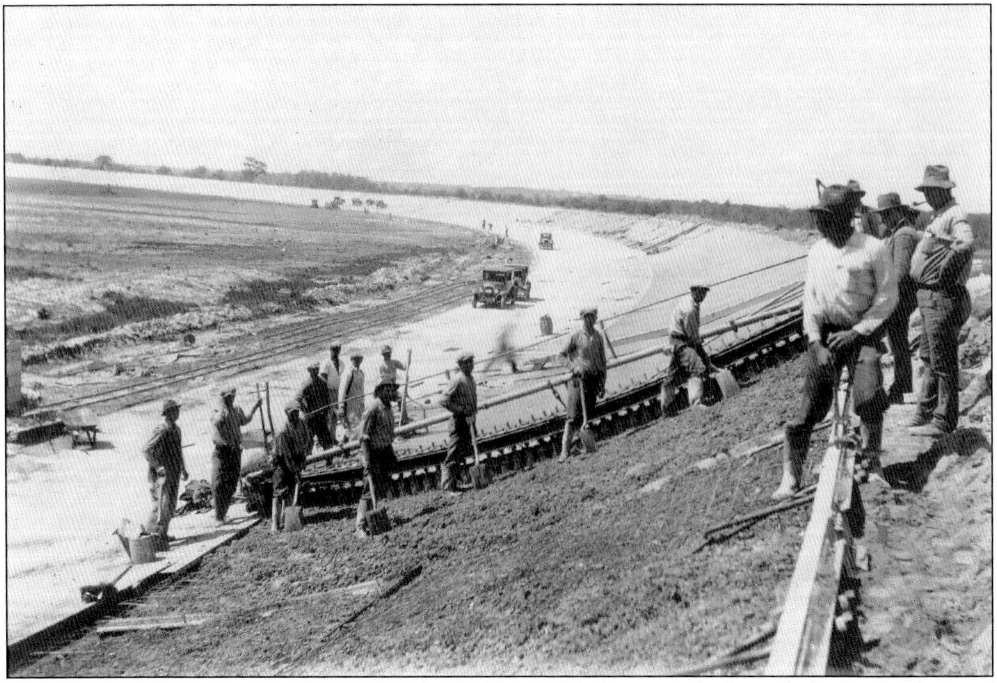

Construction began in 1927 with a 2.5-mile oval test track that stretched 1 mile from 22 Mile Road to 23 Mile Road west of Van Dyke Avenue. The track was inaugurated on June 14, 1928, when celebrated race car driver Leon Duray drove a Miller Special to a closed-circuit world speedway record of 148.7 miles per hour. (NAHC.)

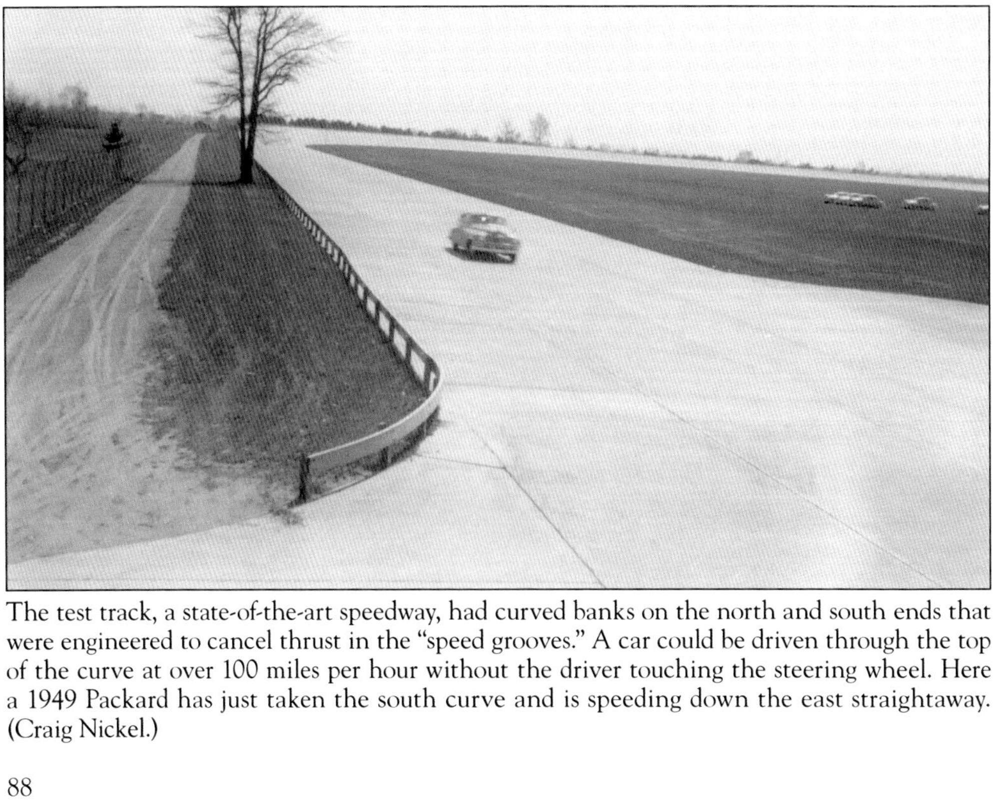

The test track, a state-of-the-art speedway, had curved banks on the north and south ends that were engineered to cancel thrust in the "speed grooves." A car could be driven through the top of the curve at over 100 miles per hour without the driver touching the steering wheel. Here a 1949 Packard has just taken the south curve and is speeding down the east straightaway. (Craig Nickel.)

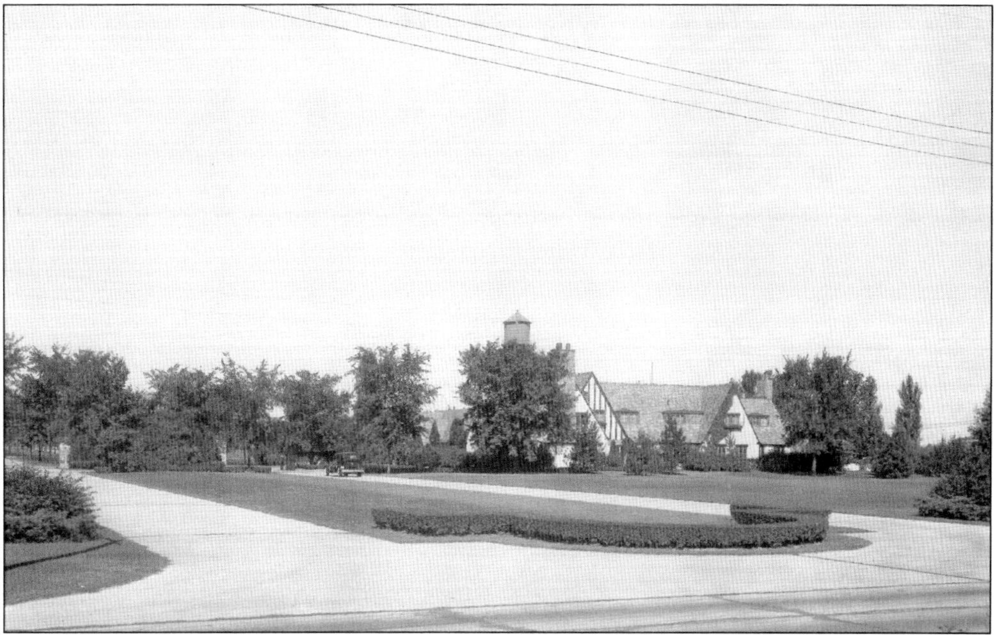

Renowned architect Albert Kahn was hired by the Packard Motor Car Company to design the principal buildings at the Packard Proving Grounds. These buildings, functional and elegant, were done in the fashionable Tudor Revival style popular with Detroit's auto barons. The gate lodge, pictured here about 1930, was set a stately distance back from Van Dyke Avenue and surrounded by lush landscaping. (Roberta Vincent Mocabee.)

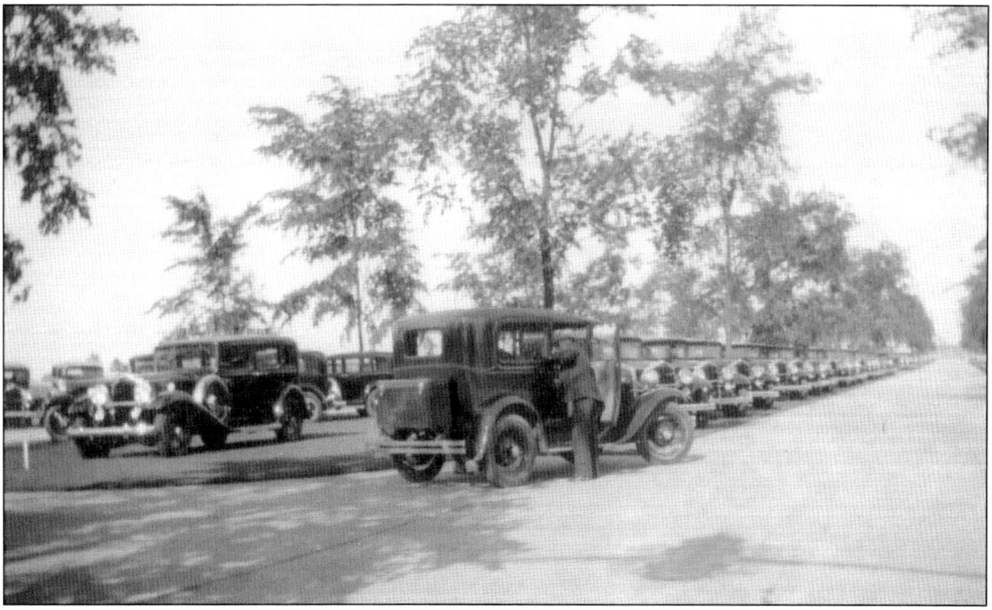

The elm-lined boulevard that stretches from inside the front gates to the test track is filled with new Packard automobiles being inspected for a show in this 1931 photograph. Visually beautiful and designed with the same standard of excellence and refinement as its automobiles, the Packard Proving Grounds was used by the Packard Motor Car Company as a backdrop for advertising its products. (Roberta Vincent Mocabee.)

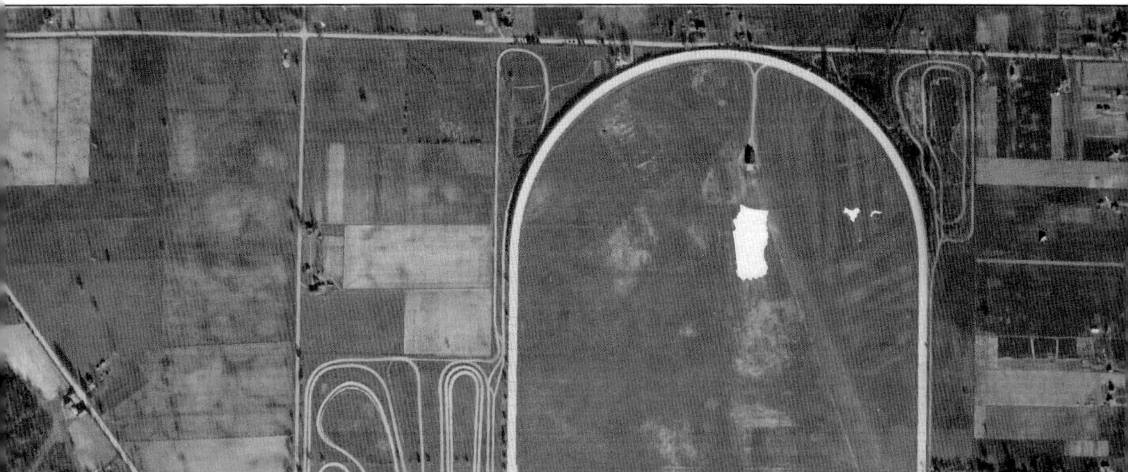

This photograph, taken from 10,000 feet in 1939, shows the complete Packard Proving Grounds test facility. By 1929, several miles of test roads had been added around the oval track where automobiles were subjected to the worst conditions Packard engineers could imagine. There was a water bath beyond the northeast curve of the test track, a sand pit to the southeast, and a complex of hazardous roads on the southwest corner of the property. Behind the gate lodge along the boulevard, a test garage, a water tower, and two storage buildings were installed. A two-story timing stand was placed at the end of the boulevard alongside the test track. An airplane hangar for housing and testing airplane engines was installed at the north end of the track infield along with a grass runway. Automobiles were transported from the factory 20 miles to the south in Detroit via a railroad spur that branched off the Michigan Central Railroad and entered the site in the southwest corner. (NAHC.)

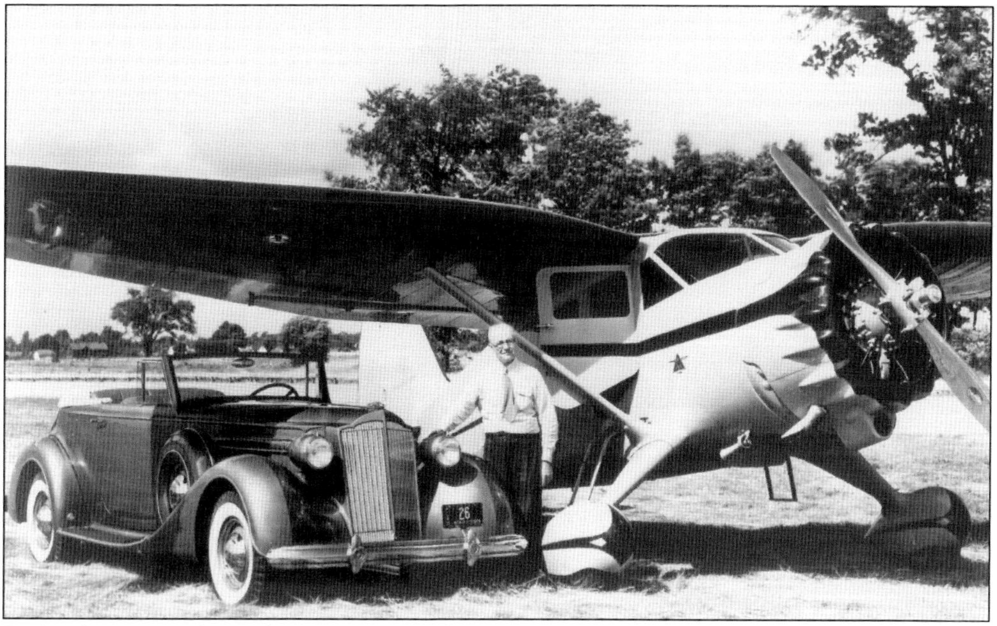

Packard vice president of engineering Col. Jesse Vincent, shown here inside the test track in 1937 with his new Packard 12 Victoria convertible and his Stinson Reliant airplane, was the driving force behind the development of the Packard Proving Grounds. Not only did he design automobile engines, he also made groundbreaking advances in marine and airplane engine design. (Robert J. Neal.)

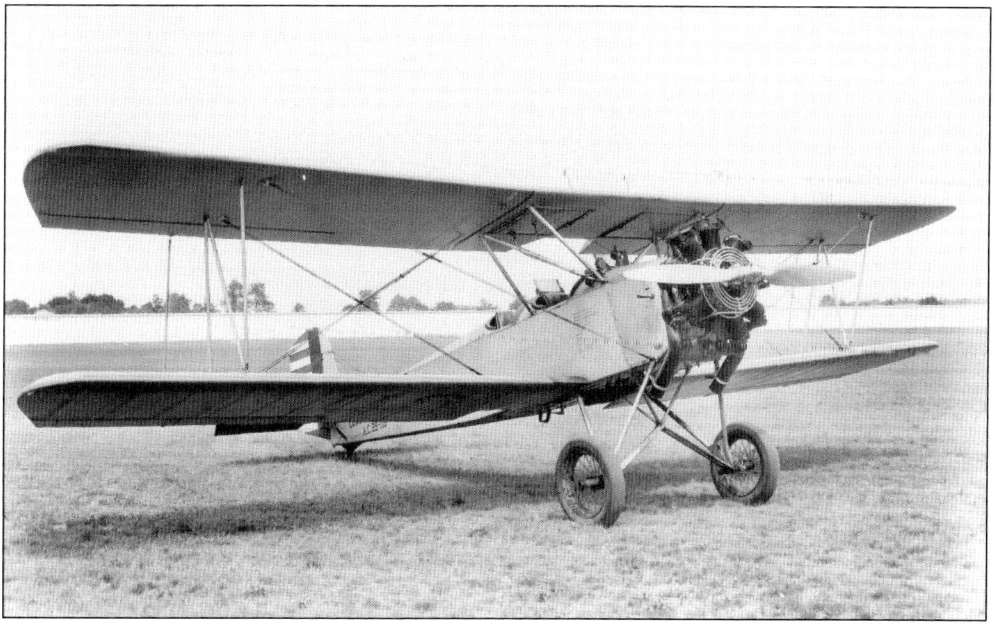

Col. Jesse Vincent saw the future possibilities for commercial aviation and recruited Capt. Lionel Woolson, a pilot and aeronautical engineer, to work for the Packard Motor Car Company in 1919. Woolson developed the DR-980, a nine-cylinder radial diesel airplane engine. It was installed in a number of airplanes such as this Army Consolidated XPT-8A photographed inside the test track in 1929. (Robert J. Neal.)

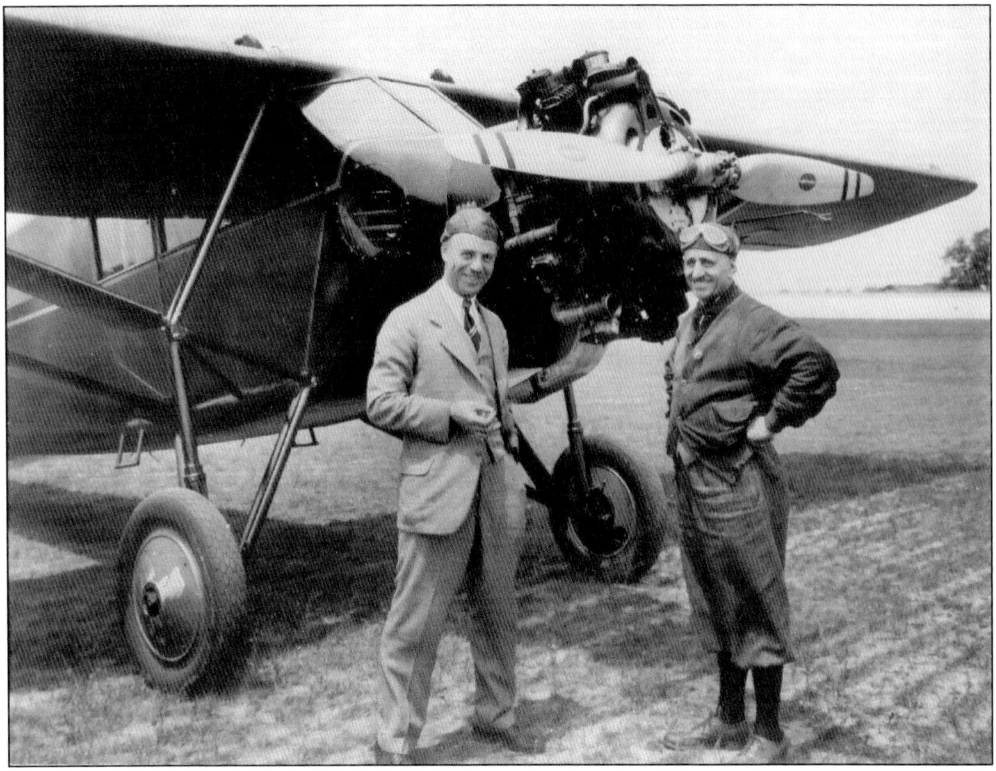

In September 1928, Capt. Lionel Woolson (left) and Packard Test Pilot Walter Lees flew this Stinson Detroiter equipped with the DR-980 diesel engine non-stop from the Packard Proving Grounds to Virginia. Accomplished in a record six hours on just $4 worth of furnace oil, this flight became the first in history of a heavier-than-air craft to be powered by a diesel engine. (Robert J. Neal.)

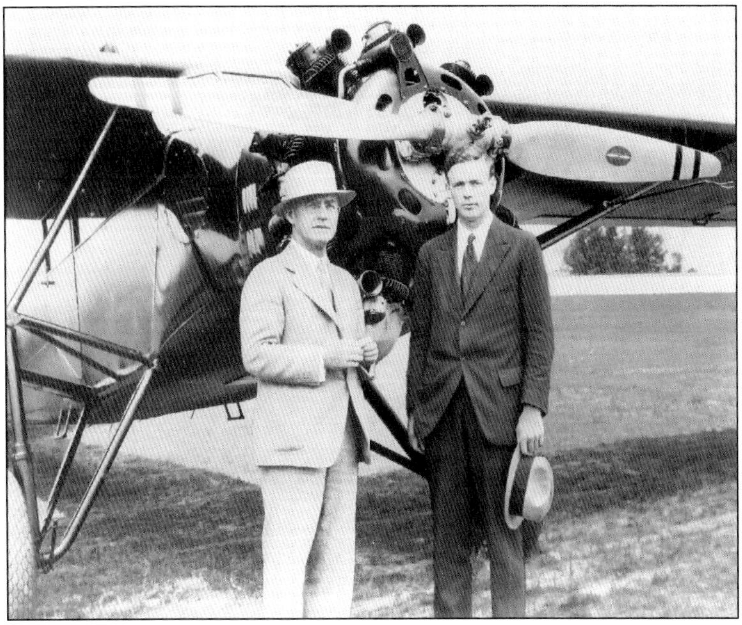

Packard Motor Car Company president Alvan Macauley (left) stands in front of the Stinson Detroiter with famed aviator Charles Lindbergh on August 15, 1929, at the Packard Proving Grounds. Lindbergh flew the plane equipped with the DR-980, expressed his pleasure with it, and then took Col. Jesse Vincent's race car for a spin around the test track at over 108 miles per hour. (Robert J. Neal.)

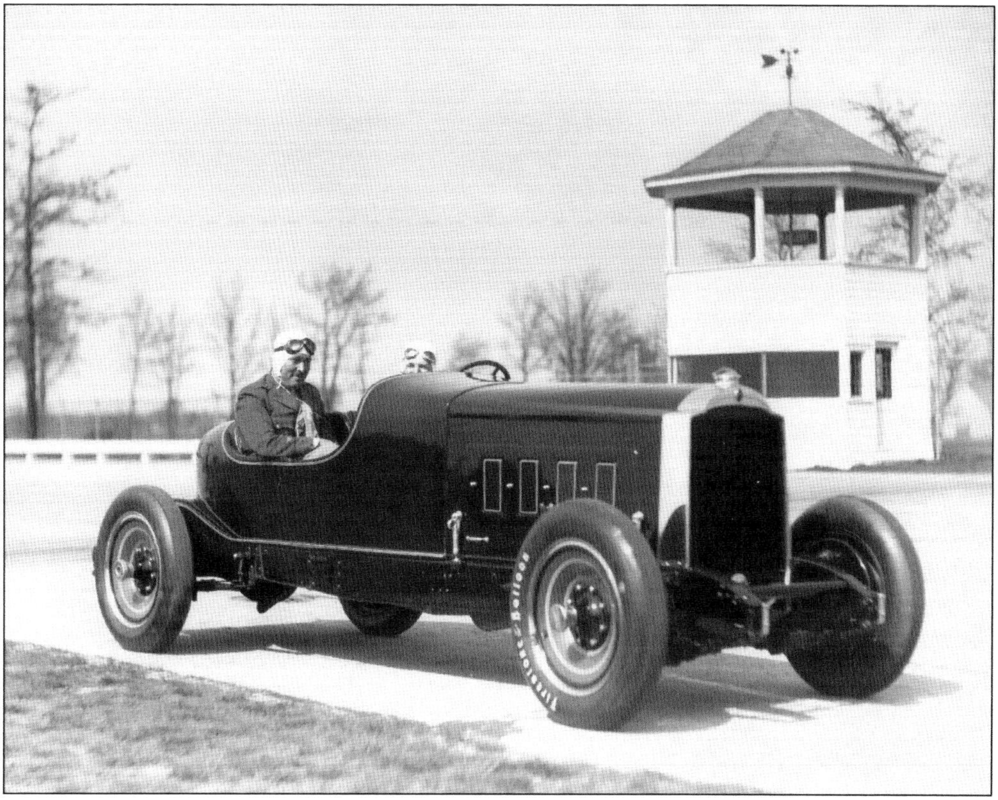

Col. Jesse Vincent was a gifted engineer who designed fast, technologically advanced engines and loved racing them in cars, boats, and planes. Here is his personal 1928 Packard Speedster in front of the timing stand on the test track around 1930. Col. Vincent's brother Charles Vincent takes the wheel while famous barnstorming pilot Roscoe Turner enjoys the ride. (Robert J. Neal.)

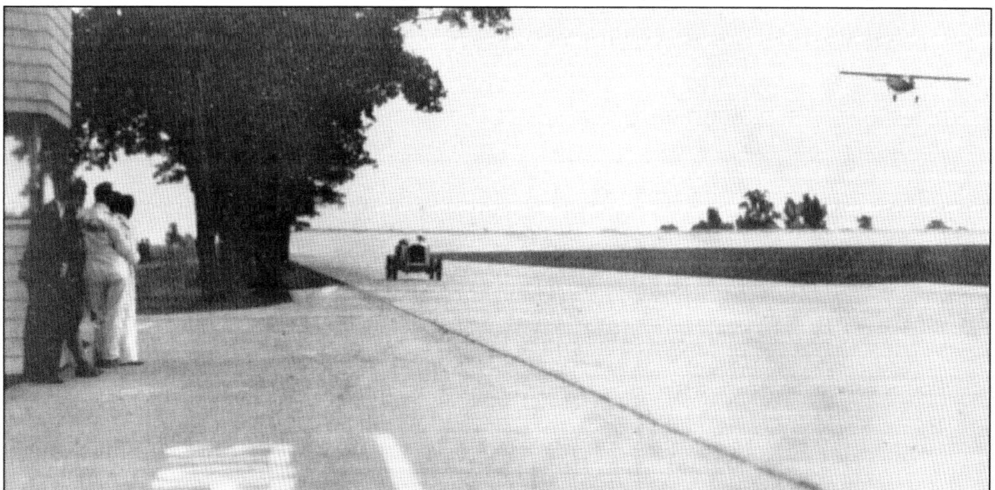

The Vincent Speedster races the Stinson Detroiter down the test track's east straightaway past some on-lookers next to the timing stand in 1929. The late 1920s were the golden years for the Packard Motor Car Company when its cars were outselling all other luxury brands in America and its future appeared as bright and limitless as the sky. (NAHC.)

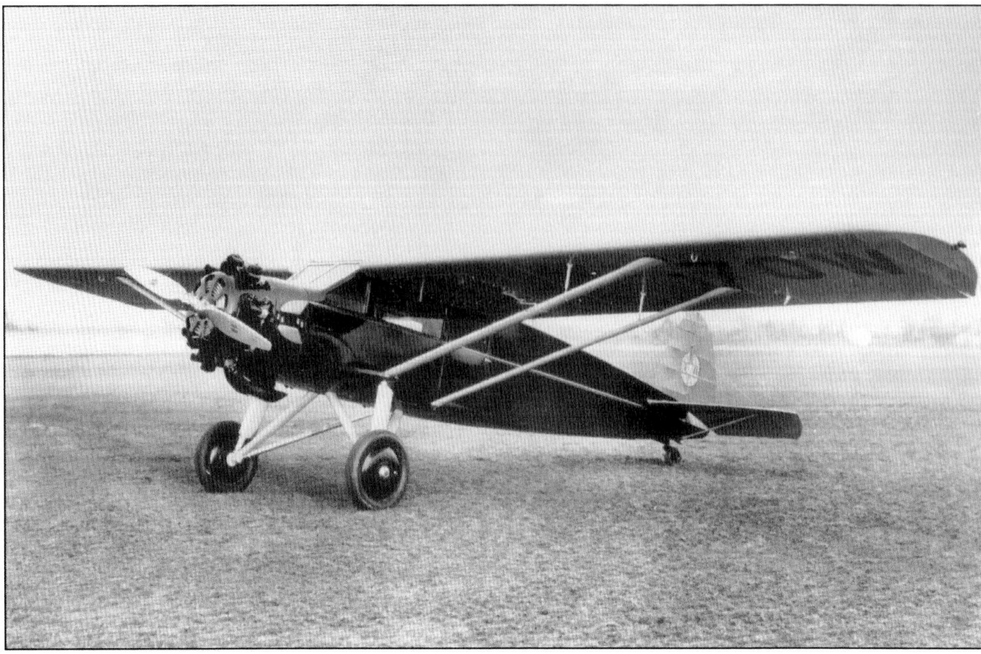

This photograph of a Verville Air Coach NC-70W equipped with the DR-980 engine was taken at the Packard Proving Grounds in early 1930. On April 23, 1930, Capt. Lionel Woolson and two others died in this plane when it crashed in New York during a snowstorm. Seven days later, Col. Jesse Vincent scattered Woolson's ashes over the Packard Proving Grounds. (Robert J. Neal.)

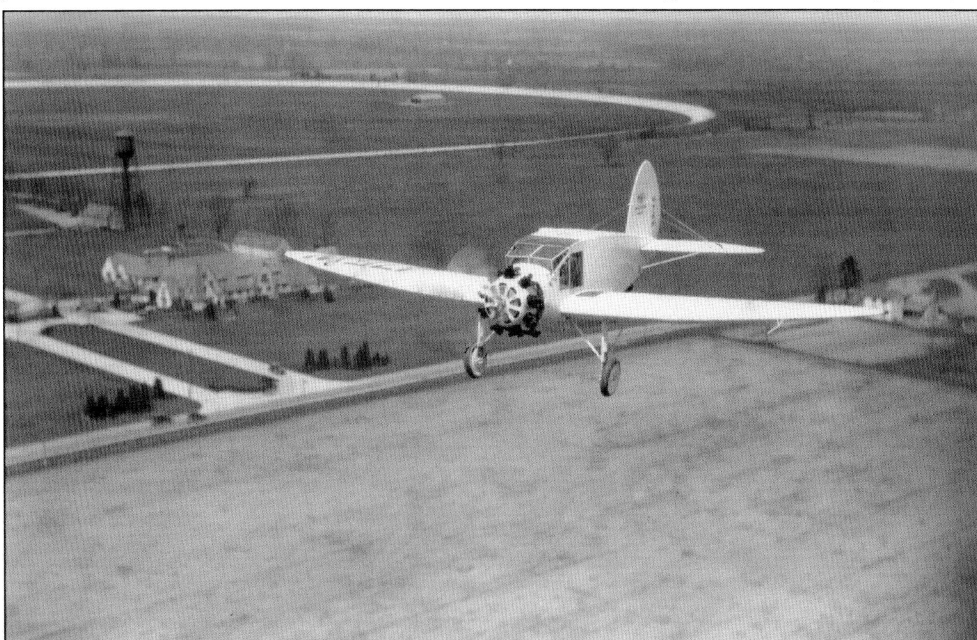

Capt. Lionel Woolson's death, plus the onset of the Great Depression, signaled the end of experimental diesel airplane engine development at the Packard Proving Grounds. The hangar, seen here in the distance behind this Mooney A-1 in 1931, became a storage building for Col. Jesse Vincent's private plane and automobile collection. (Robert J. Neal.)

During the 1930s, the Packard Proving Grounds was entirely dedicated to automotive testing. A 1932 Packard Twin Six sedan climbs "The Hump" on the southwest corner of the site. This steep, 50-foot hill, created to test automobile brakes and transmissions under extreme conditions, was paved on one side and graveled on the other. (NAHC.)

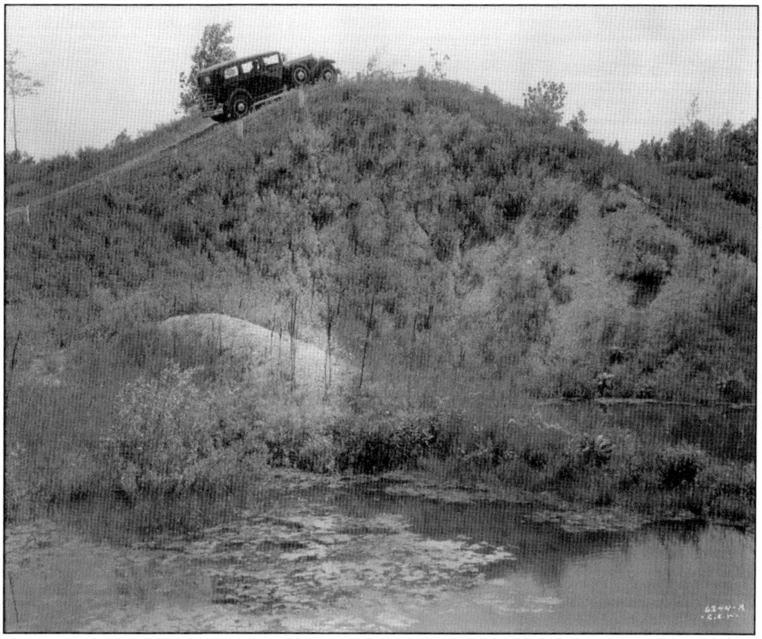

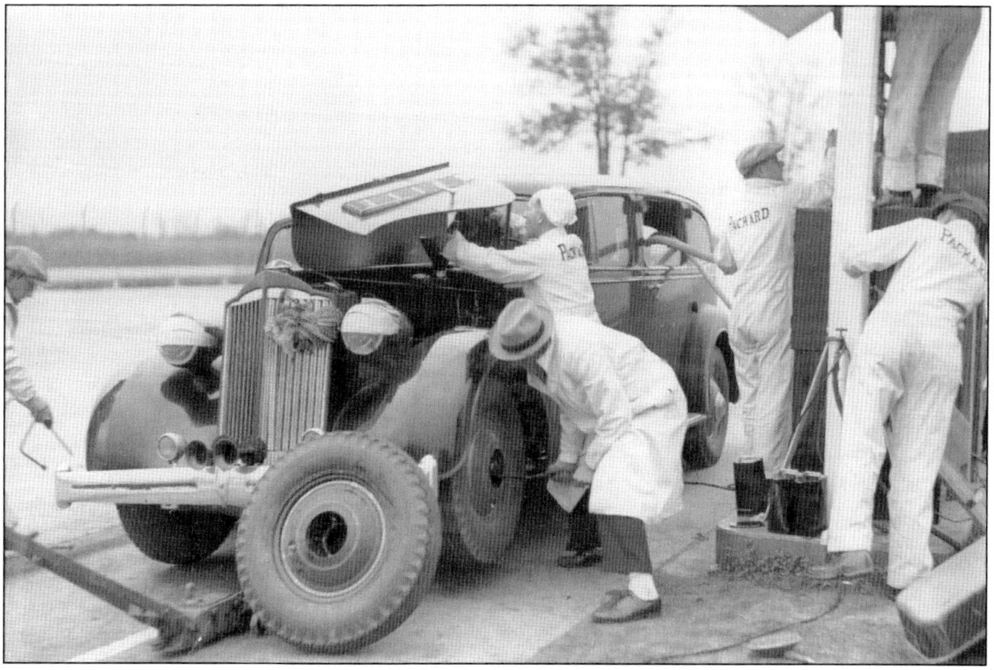

In November 1935, a 1936 Packard sedan was randomly selected off the production line in Detroit and subjected to a grueling 174-hour, 6,121-lap endurance run on the test track. During one of the scheduled pit stops, unidentified Packard Proving Grounds workers perform maintenance tasks while ignoring the pheasant lodged in the front grill. (NAHC.)

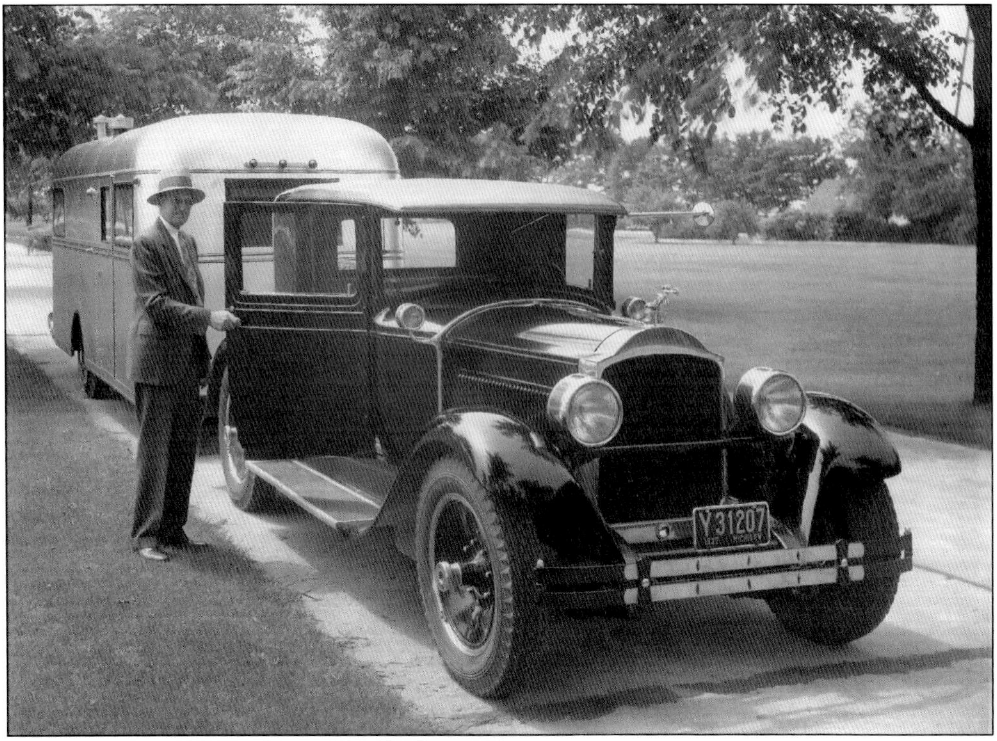


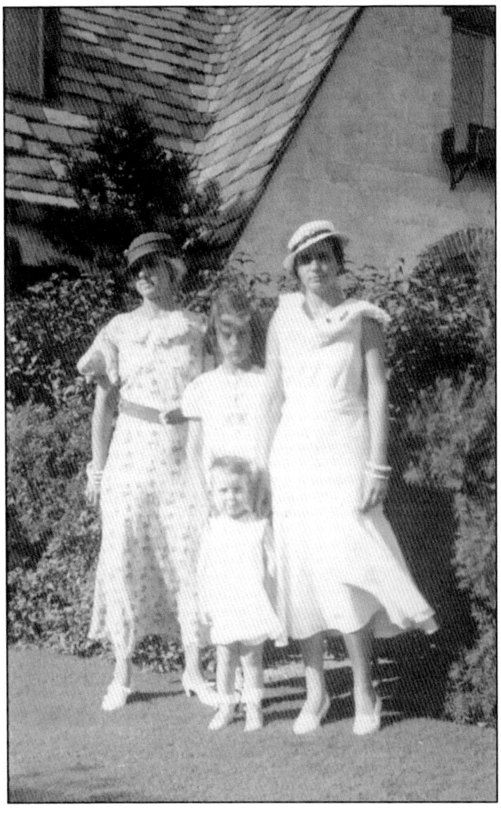

Col. Jesse Vincent's brother Charles Vincent became the Packard Proving Grounds manager. All new automobiles and engineering innovations had to have Charles's stamp of approval before they were offered to the public. Here he is in 1937 at the Packard Proving Grounds with a 1928 Model 526 that was modified to pull the Pierce-Arrow trailer used by the Vincent family for vacations. (Roberta Vincent Mocabee.)

Charles Vincent and his family moved into the gate lodge in 1929. Pictured here in front of the lodge modeling the latest fashions in 1933 are, from left to right, Charles's wife Lucile, 10-year-old daughter Cornelli, and 16-year-old daughter Dorothea; two-year-old daughter Roberta stands in front of Cornelli. The two older daughters both attended Utica High School where Dorothea graduated as class valedictorian in 1934. (Roberta Vincent Mocabee.)

Roberta Vincent was born in Detroit in May 1931 while her family was living at the Packard Proving Grounds. Here is Roberta at five months old with her mother, Lucile, and their dog Fritz in front of the garage and dormitory wing of the gate lodge. The garage was used for testing and storage while the dormitory upstairs housed visiting engineers or unmarried grounds workers. (Roberta Vincent Mocabee.)

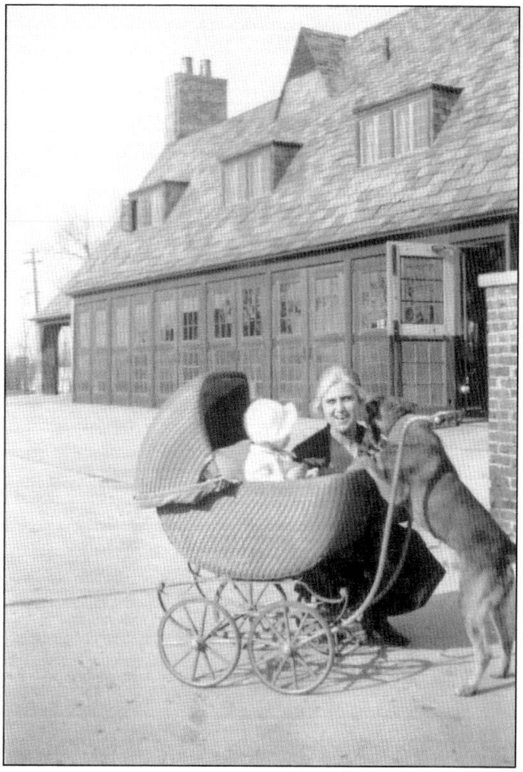

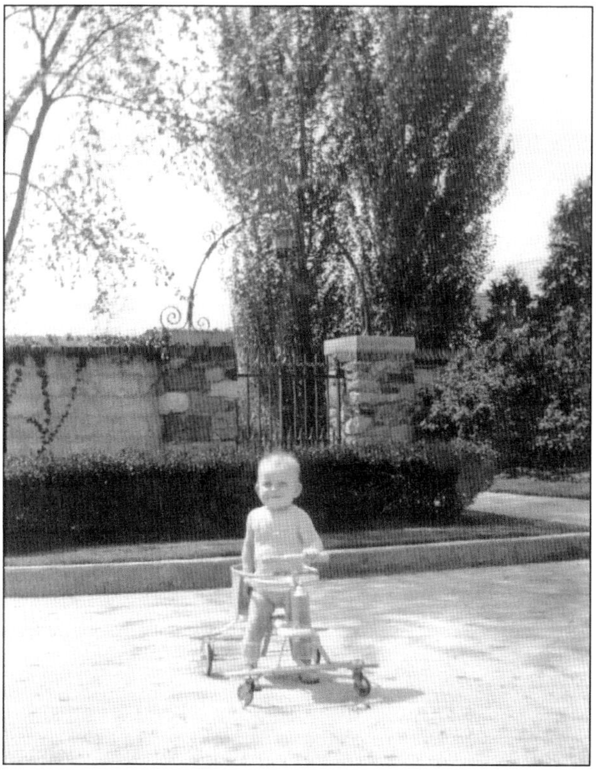

Roberta Vincent rides her scooter by the pedestrian gate near the gate lodge in 1932. She spent the first 10 years of her life at the site under the watchful eyes of her family, tutors, gardeners, and her father's secretary. There were no children her age nearby, but she was happy exploring the many acres of property with her imaginary playmates. (Roberta Vincent Mocabee.)

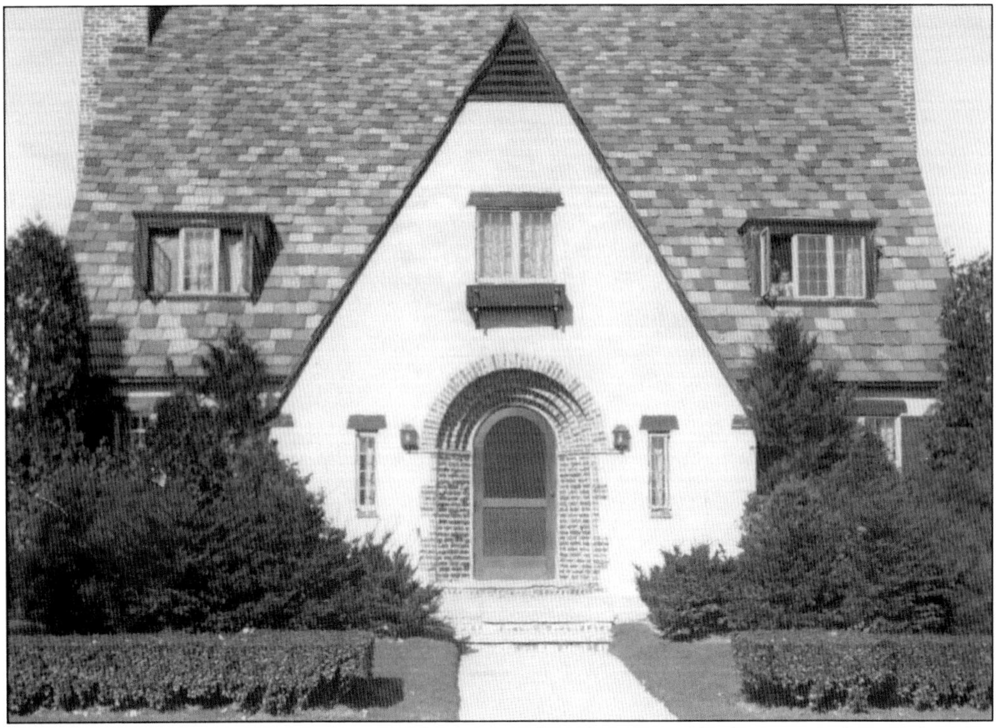

Two-year-old Roberta Vincent waves to the camera from her sisters' bedroom window in the gate lodge. The Vincent family's dining room was to the left and their living room was to the right of the formal front door. Upstairs there were three bedrooms and two bathrooms. Charles and Lucile's bedroom was on the left in this photograph. Roberta's bedroom was in the back above the kitchen. (Roberta Vincent Mocabee.)

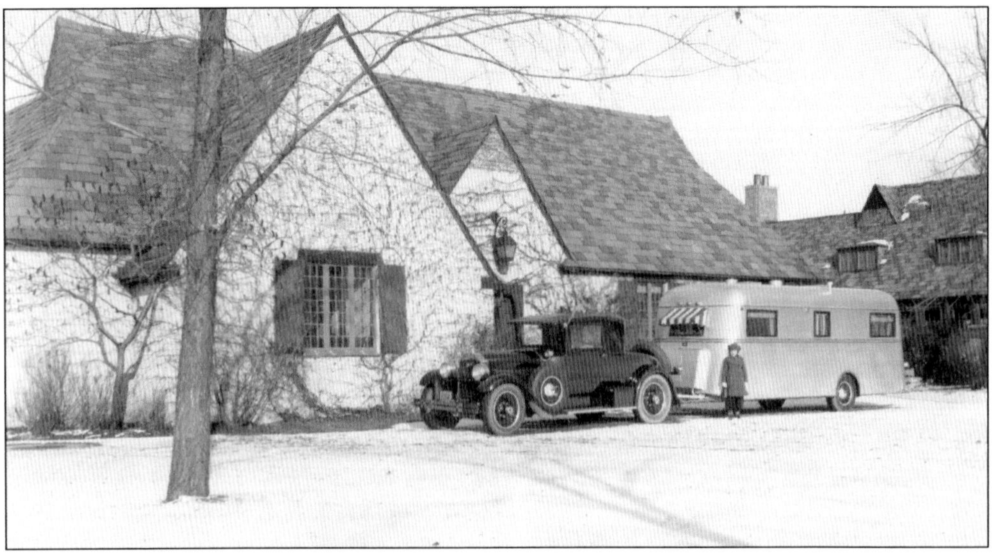

The Vincent family's 1928 Packard Model 526 and Pierce-Arrow trailer are parked in front of the Albert Kahn–designed repair and testing garage that is located behind the gate lodge. This building also housed Charles Vincent's office. Roberta Vincent, standing in front of the trailer, was six years old when this photograph was taken in 1937. (Roberta Vincent Mocabee.)

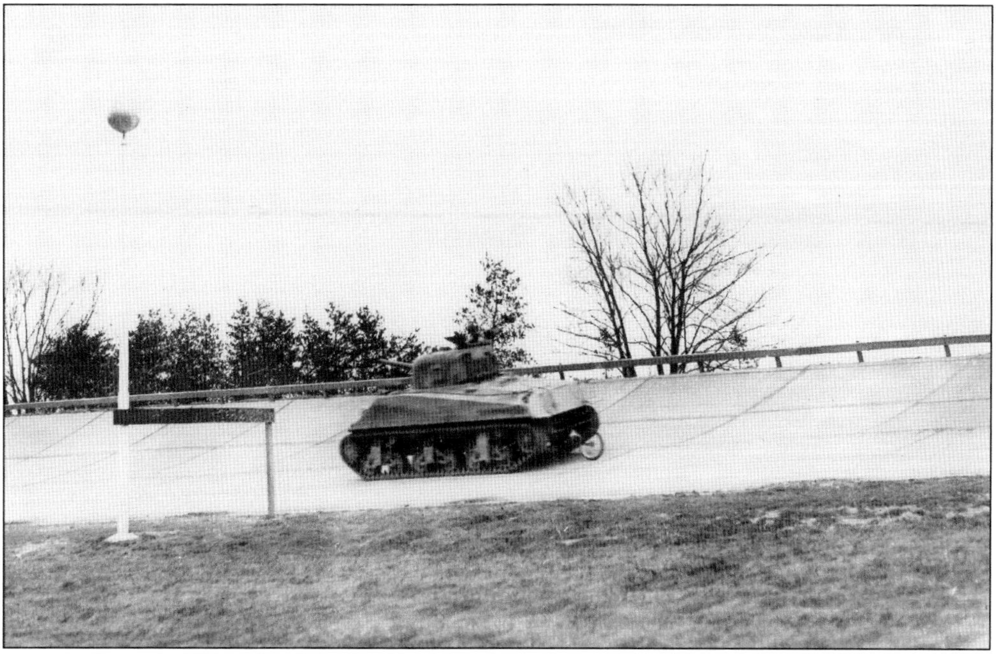

With the onset of World War II, the Vincent family moved out of the gate lodge and the Packard Proving Grounds was leased to Chrysler Defense Engineering to test tanks. Here an M4 Sherman tank makes its way around the test track. To the left of the tank is a pole used for timing laps from the timing stand. (NAHC.)

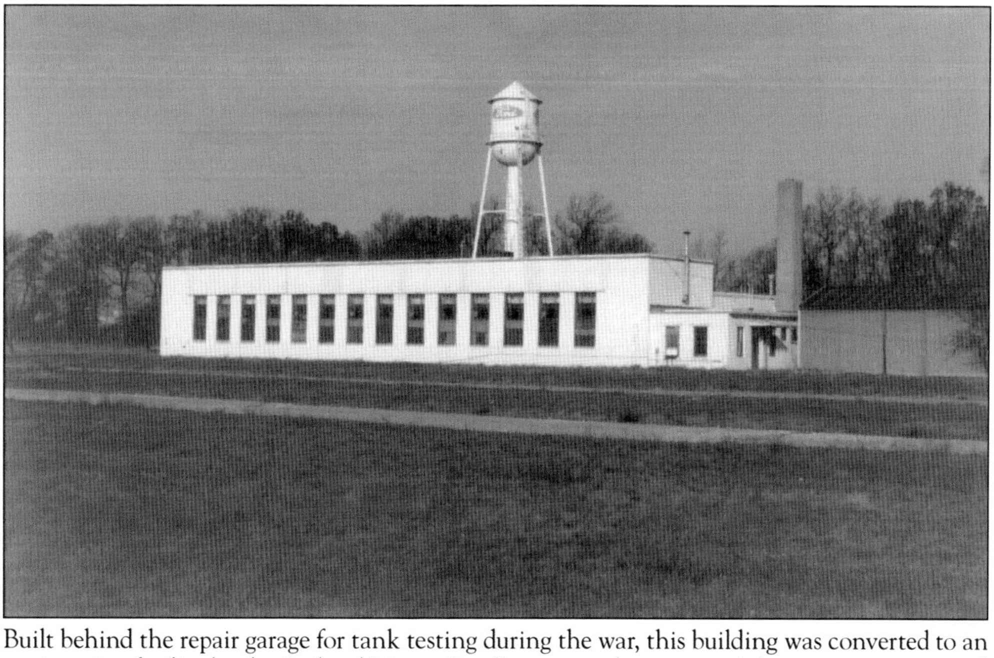

Built behind the repair garage for tank testing during the war, this building was converted to an engineering facility by the Packard Motor Car Company when automobile testing was resumed at the Packard Proving Grounds in 1946. After the war ended, Charles Vincent and his family did not return to the gate lodge, which was subsequently used for offices and conference rooms. (Author's collection.)

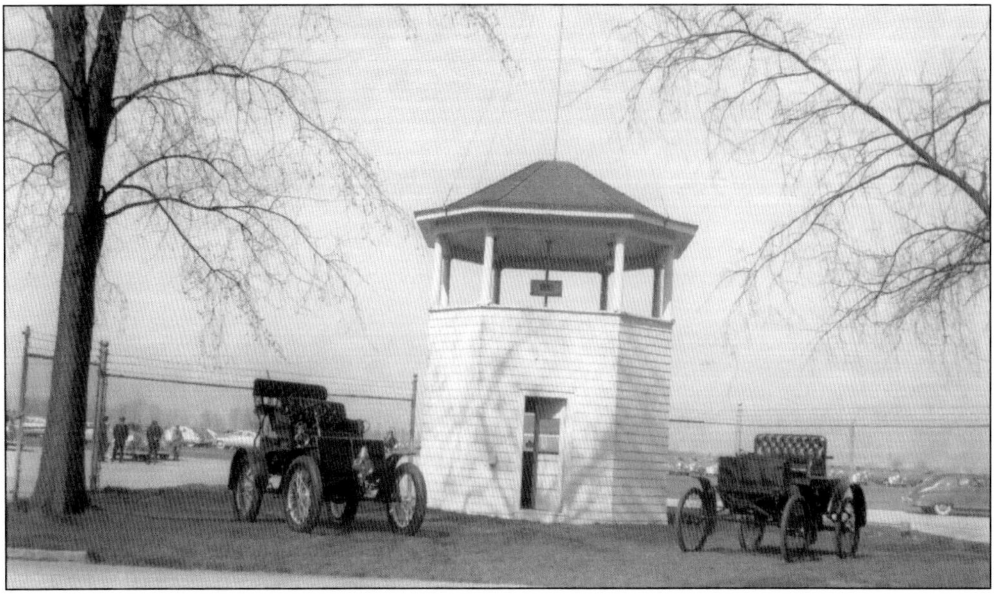

The Packard Motor Car Company celebrated its golden anniversary in 1949 at the Packard Proving Grounds with a display of its earliest models, including an 1899 Packard Number One (right). But the event did little to mask the company's growing problems as it struggled to compete with "The Big Three," who were better positioned to meet the demands of the post-war American consumer. (Craig Nickel.)

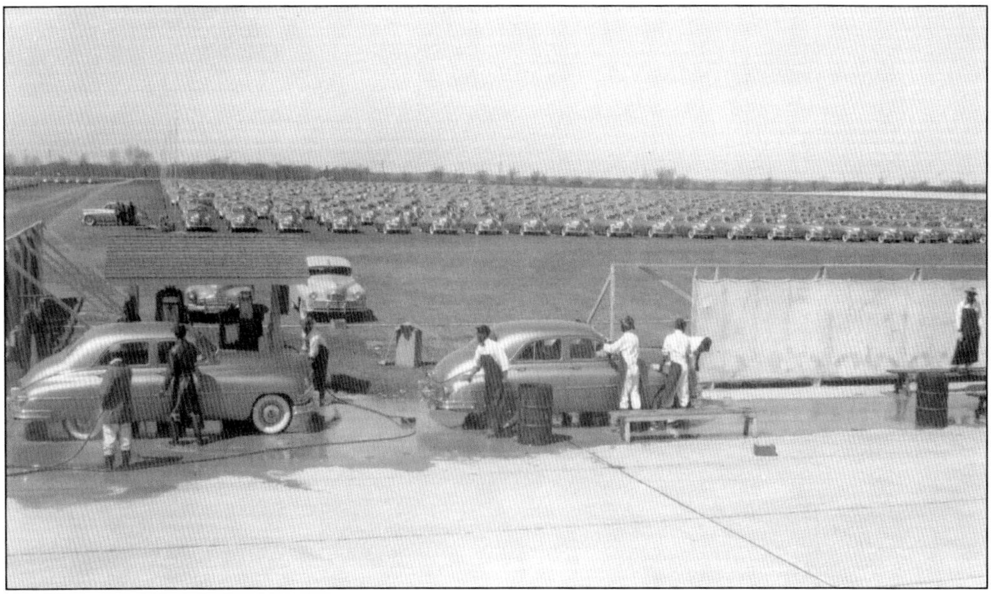

For the anniversary event, 2,000 specially painted gold 1949 Packard sedans were shipped to the Packard Proving Grounds and lined up for a dealer drive-away. Here workers clean the gold automobiles on the test track before they go on display. (Craig Nickel.)

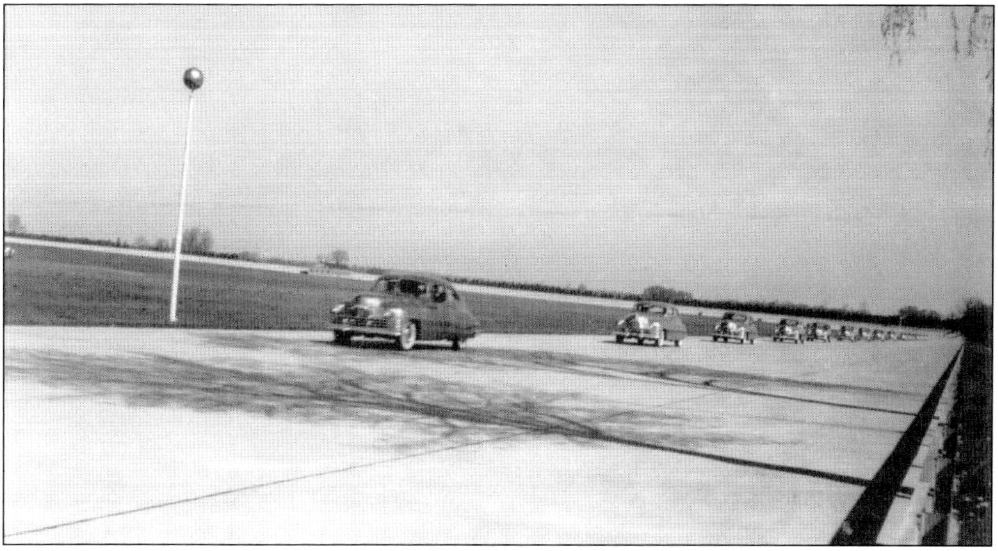

Golden Packard sedans cruise the test track at the Packard Proving Grounds in 1949. By 1950, the golden age of the Packard Motor Company was waning. Throughout the early 1950s, the company would be plagued by management missteps, poor product quality, and a loss of reputation. In an ill-fated move to be more competitive, the Packard Motor Car Company purchased Studebaker in 1954. (Craig Nickel.)

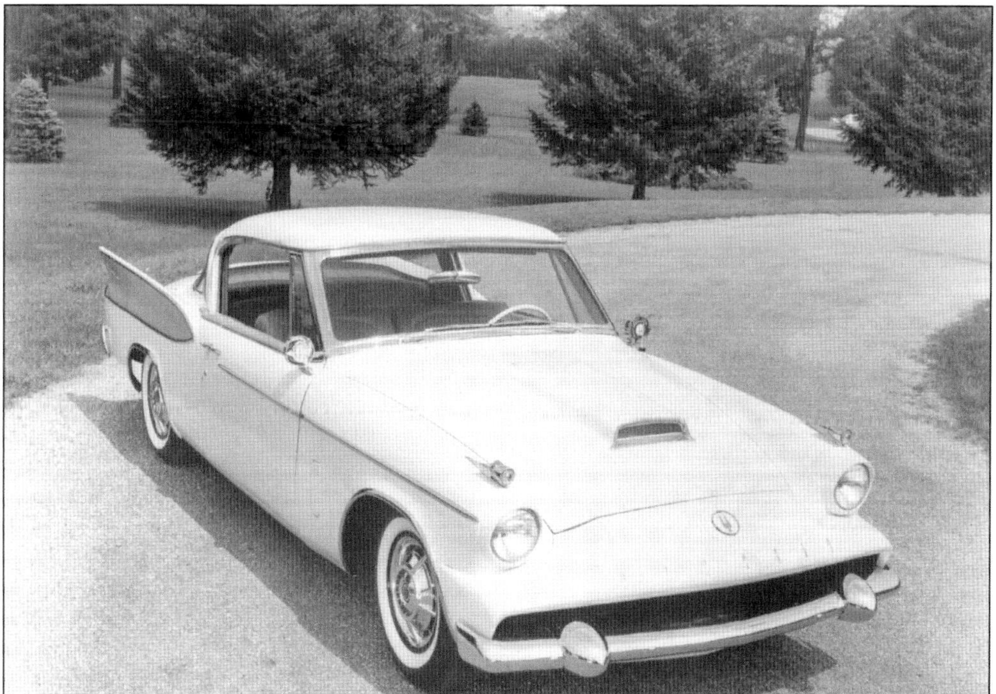

By 1956, the merger with Studebaker was failing and defense contractor Curtiss-Wright Corporation had taken over, transferring automobile manufacturing and testing to South Bend, Indiana. When this 1958 Packard Hawk rolled off the Studebaker-Packard Corporation assembly line in Indiana, the Packard Motor Company had all but ceased to exist. (NAHC.)

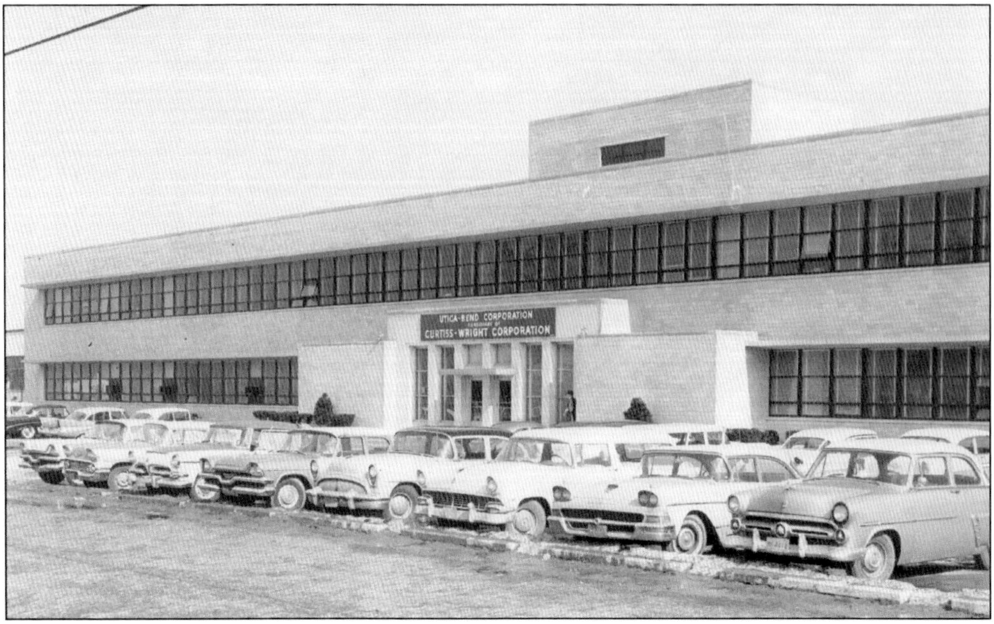


In 1951, the Packard Motor Company built this factory complex at the southeast corner of 23 Mile Road and Mound Road to produce jet, then later automobile, engines. When the Curtiss-Wright Corporation took over the Studebaker-Packard Corporation in 1956, production in the factory complex was shifted back to jet engines and the operations were renamed the Utica-Bend Corporation. (Reprinted with permission of the *Detroit News*.)

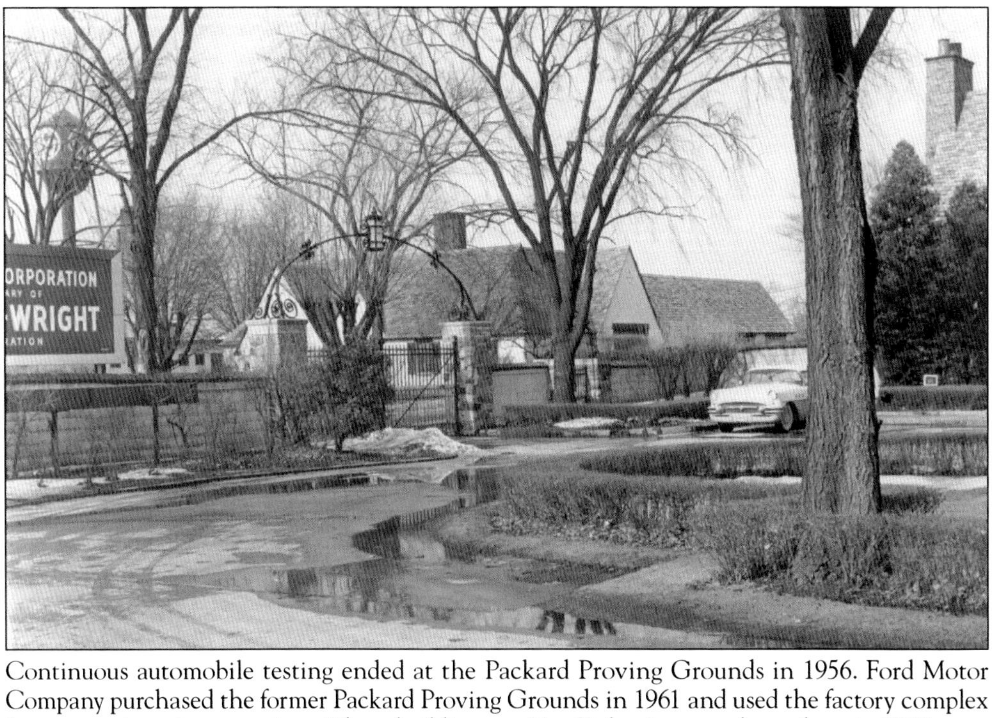


Continuous automobile testing ended at the Packard Proving Grounds in 1956. Ford Motor Company purchased the former Packard Proving Grounds in 1961 and used the factory complex for automotive trim operations. These buildings on Van Dyke Avenue, shown here in 1958, were used for offices, conferences, and storage. (Reprinted with permission of the *Detroit News*.)

# *Seven*

# Spring Hill Farm

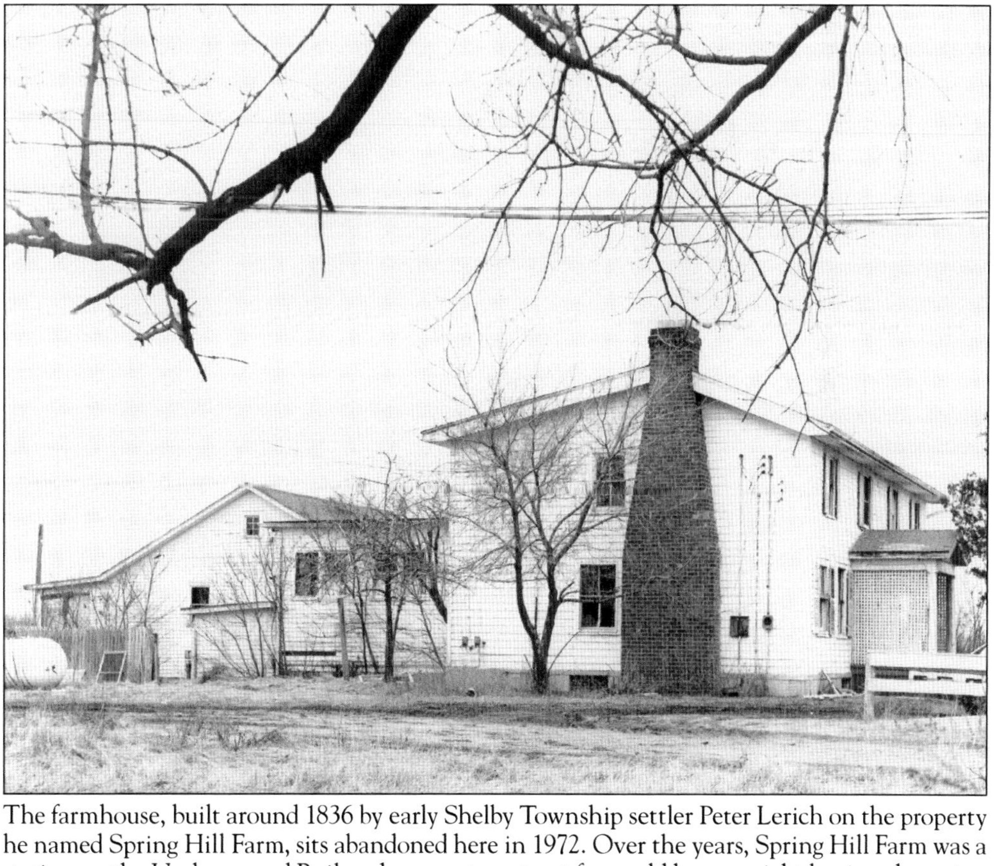

The farmhouse, built around 1836 by early Shelby Township settler Peter Lerich on the property he named Spring Hill Farm, sits abandoned here in 1972. Over the years, Spring Hill Farm was a station on the Underground Railroad, a country retreat for world heavyweight boxing champion Joe Louis, and the site of a Nike missile battery during the Cold War. (Richard Meitz.)

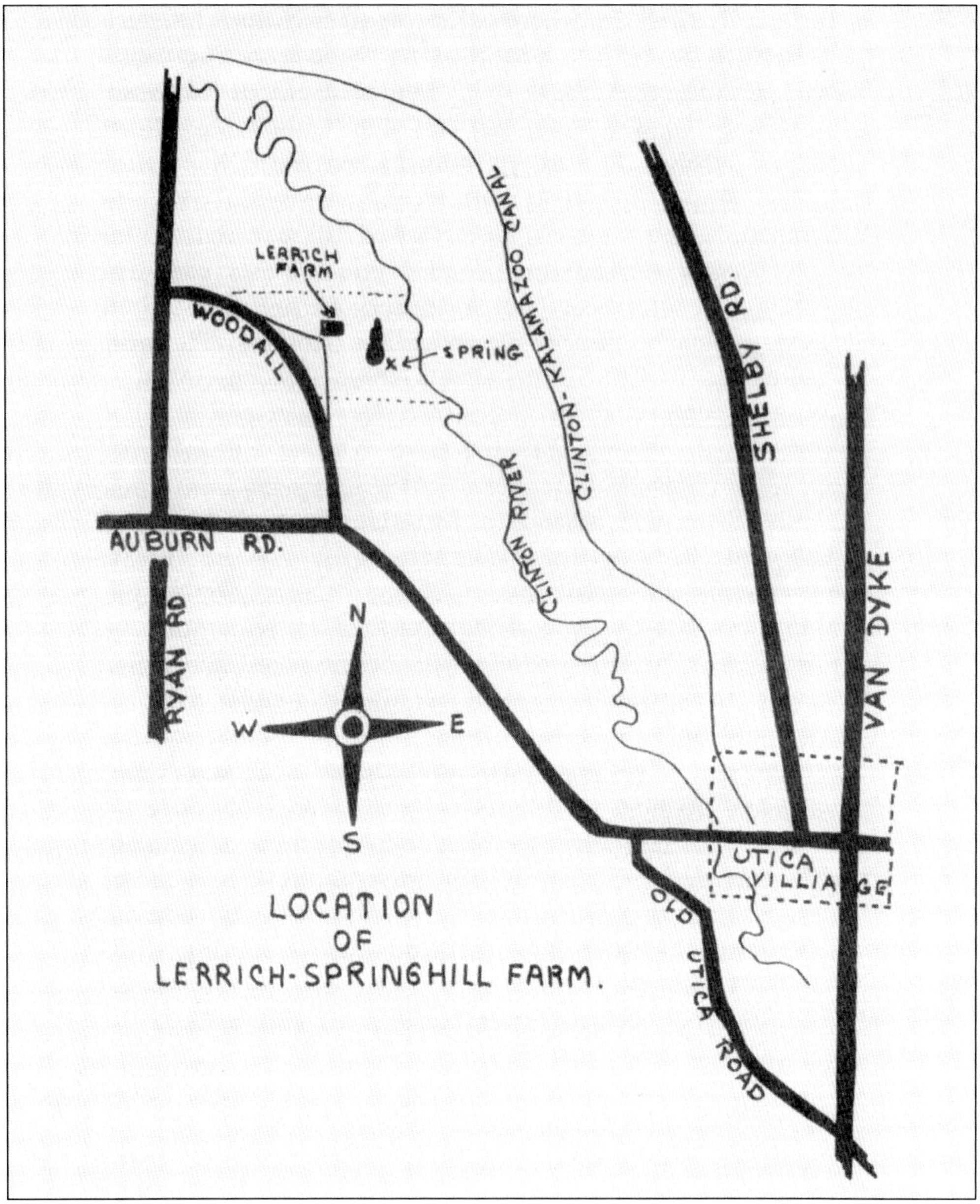


Peter and Sarah Lerich came to Shelby Township from New Jersey in 1835. They purchased 220 acres along the Clinton River in Section 29, adding more land in later years. They built a large farmhouse on a bluff overlooking the river and named their property Spring Hill Farm for the many springs in the hillside. Devout Methodists, the Lerichs strongly believed in temperance (Peter refused to sell his grains to distilleries) and were avid abolitionists. As documented in 1923 by their daughter Liberetta, the Lerich farm was a stop on the Underground Railroad where runaway slaves were hidden and fed on their way to freedom in Canada before and during the Civil War. The runaways stayed overnight in a well-hidden, log-lined cave built into the bluff near a spring that ran below the farmhouse. To help the slaves and railroad agents find the station, sympathetic neighbors and the Lerichs planted a large cedar tree near the spring, which became known as the Beacon Tree. (Macomb County Historical Society and Crocker House Museum.)

Before he bought Spring Hill Farm, Joe Louis owned a share of the Utica Riding Club in Shelby Township. By most accounts, the riding club was located just east of Disco on 24 Mile Road. On June 26, 1938, four days after he beat Max Schmeling in New York City to retain his boxing championship title, Joe Louis helped stage a horse show at the club with other African American horseback-riding enthusiasts. At right, Louis rides one of his thoroughbred horses in the show. Many people from all over the country attended the show, including Louis's wife, Marva Trotter Louis, who was also an accomplished equestrienne. Below she stands (center) smiling for the camera with her husband (to the right of her, in riding boots) and his manager John Roxborough (to the left of Marva), along with several unidentified show attendees. (Both, WPRL.)

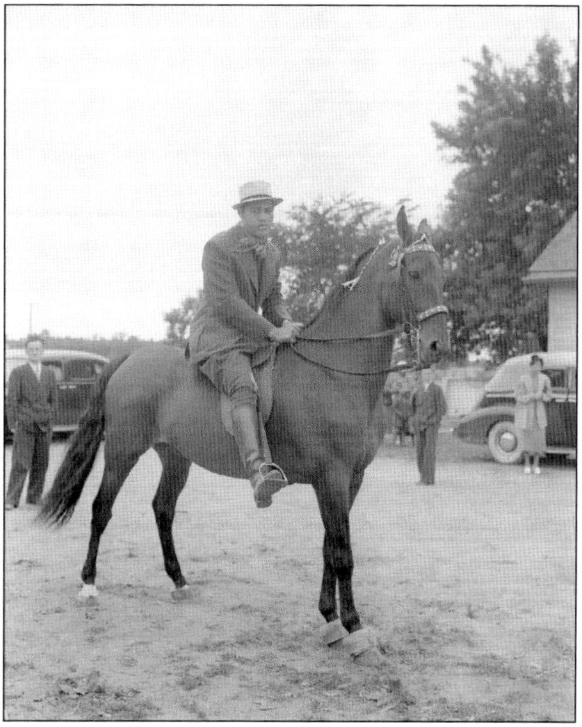

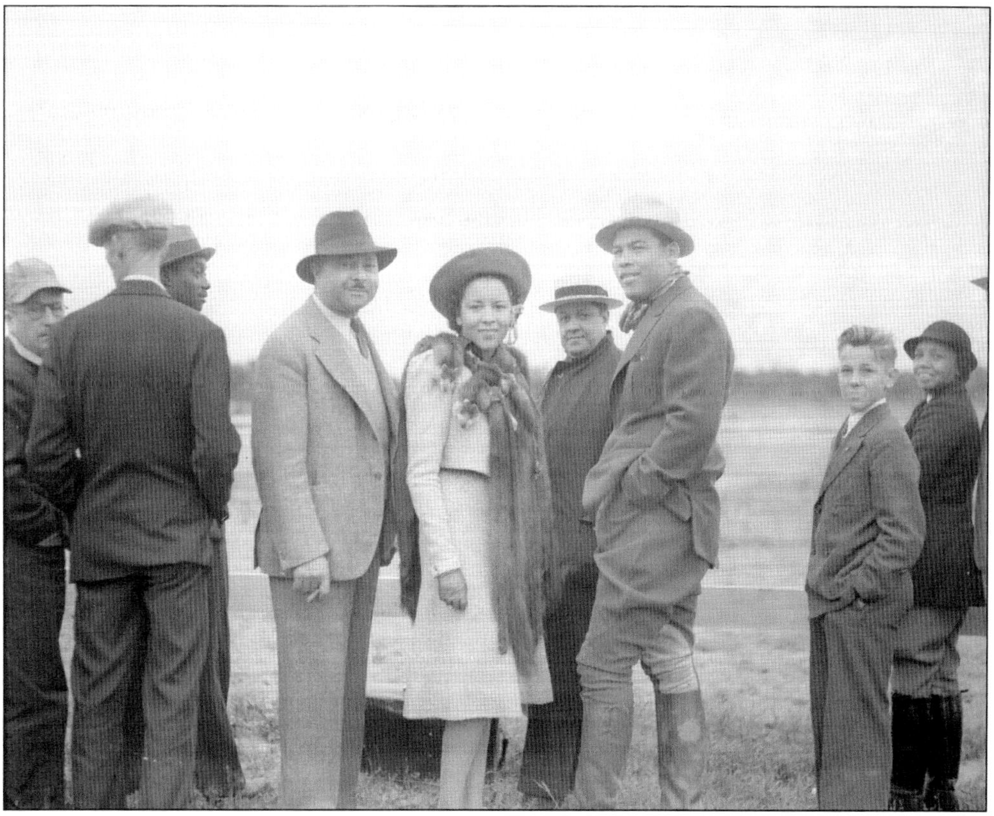

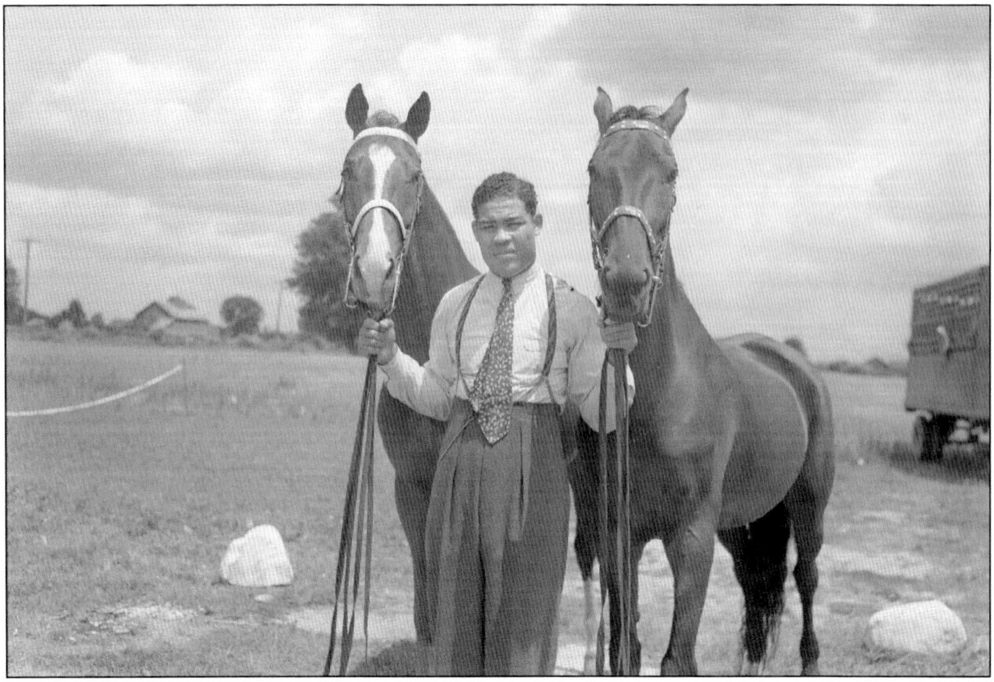

Joe Louis shows off two of his thoroughbreds in Shelby Township in 1938. In 1939, with the help of his manager John Roxborough, Joe Louis bought the 440-acre Spring Hill Farm, where he rode his horses, entertained his friends, and relaxed between matches. At the farm, Louis installed a restaurant, a clubhouse, a dance pavilion, screened barbeque pits with picnic tables, stables, and riding corrals with bleachers. (WPRL.)

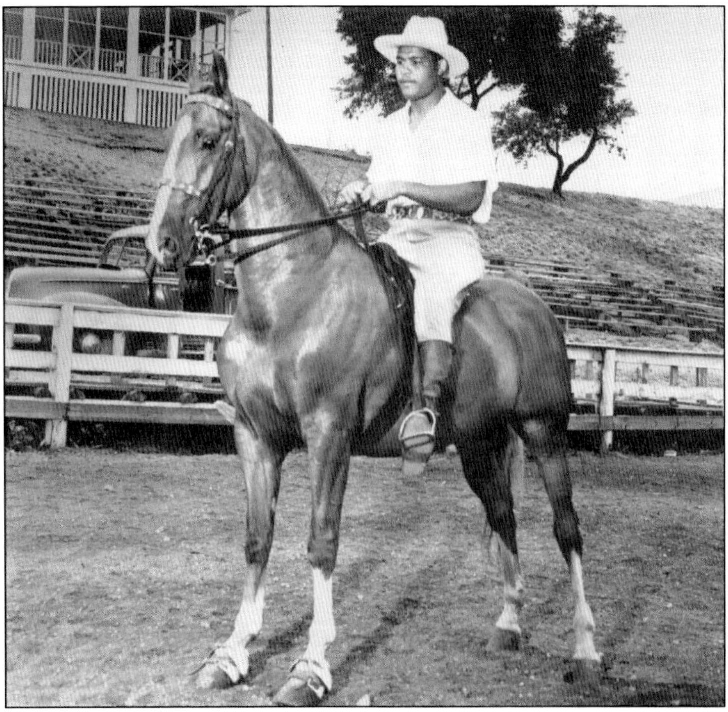

Joe Louis loved horses and horseback riding nearly as much as boxing. Here he poses on a five-gaited American Saddlebred at the corral below the clubhouse at Spring Hill Farm in the early 1940s. Some of his winnings from boxing were used to buy a collection of this popular breed of horse from Kentucky. Louis stabled more than 40 horses of various breeds at the farm. (WPRL.)

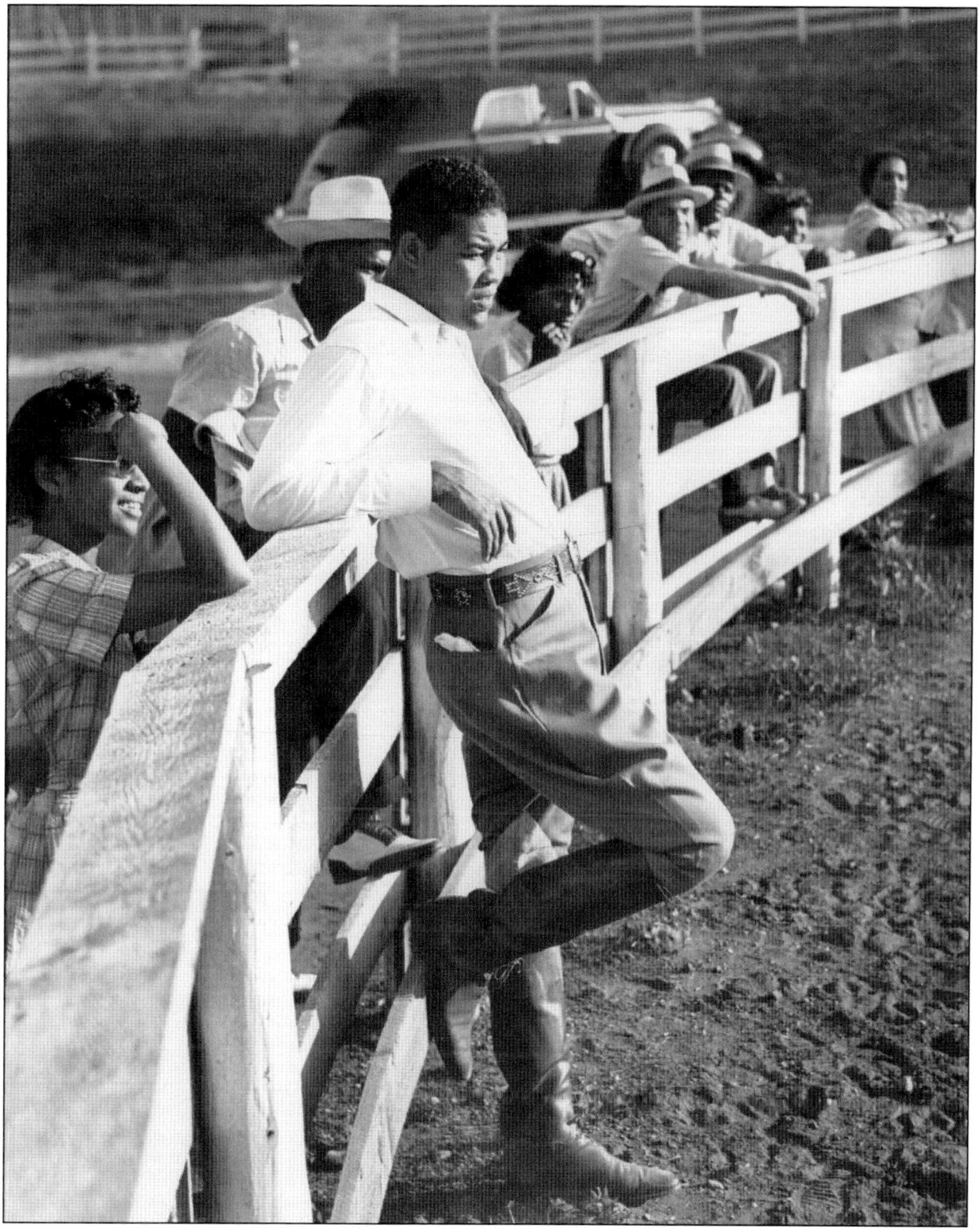

Here is Joe Louis inside one of the corrals at Spring Hill Farm in the early 1940s with several unidentified visitors standing outside. Louis welcomed many visitors to the farm during his ownership years. Families came from Detroit for a day in the country to eat at "Joe's" restaurant, picnic on the grounds, take riding lessons, and attend horse shows. During World War II, Joe Louis took leave of his professional boxing career and his country retreat in Shelby Township to join the army. Toward the end of the war, Louis found himself in deep financial trouble, owing over $100,000 in taxes. In 1944, the Spring Hill Farm property, all but 18 acres and the buildings, was sold to the Michigan State Conservation Department and turned into a park. Some associates of Louis and John Roxborough bought the entertainment venues at the farm and kept them operating until around 1953 when the farm became a private residence. (WPRL.)

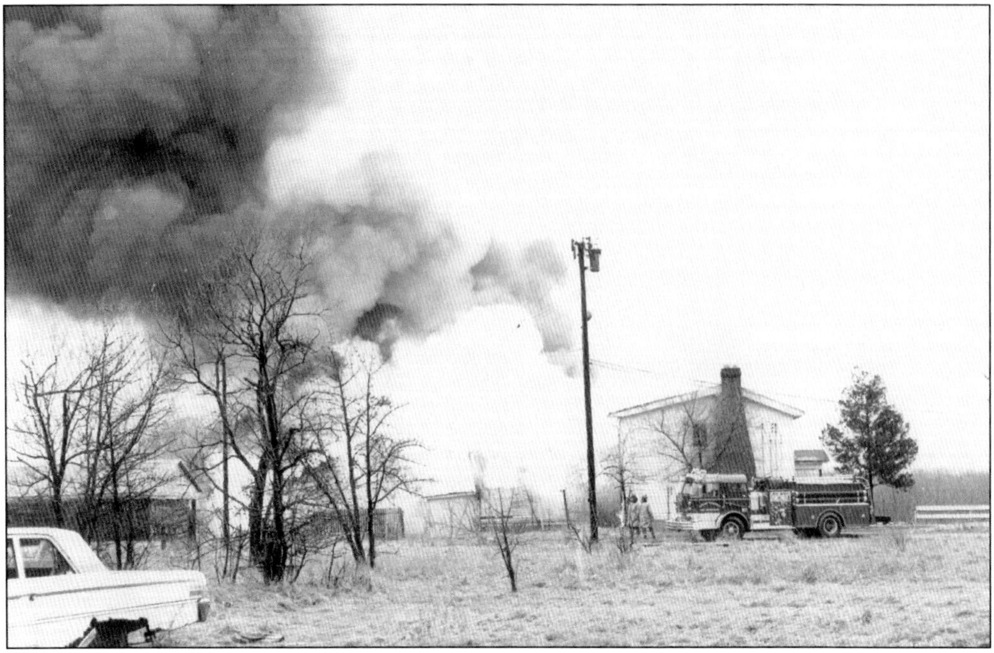

In the afternoon of January 22, 1973, the Spring Hill Farm house caught fire. The building burned quickly and the Shelby Township Fire Department could not get water on it fast enough to put out the flames. The house had been occupied by a succession of renters in its last years and had deteriorated. It had been abandoned for some time when it caught fire. (Richard Meitz.)

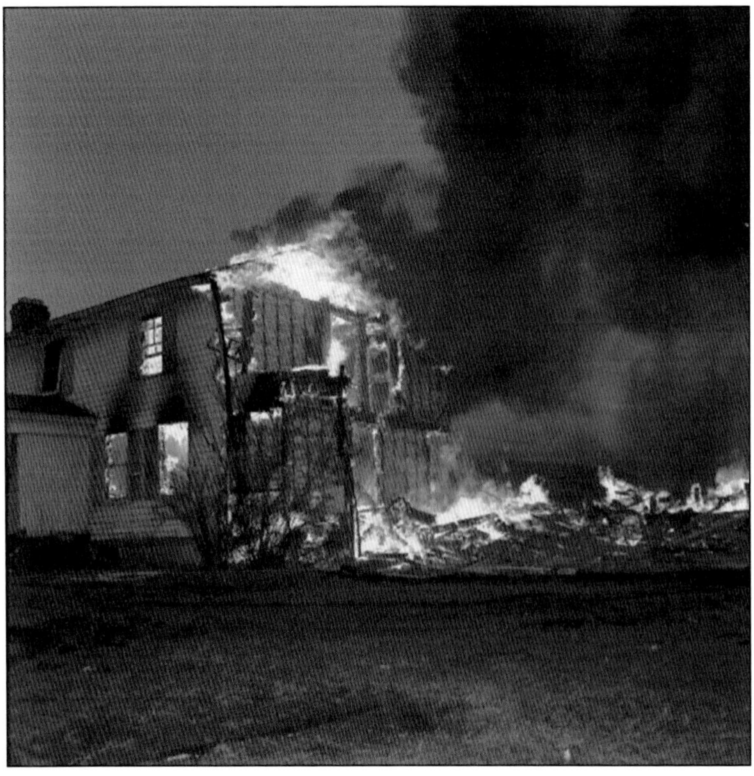

The farmhouse burned into the night. Several of the other farm buildings had burned a few years earlier. The remaining buildings were demolished, and the property was turned over to the Michigan Department of Natural Resources. Today all that is left of the buildings are some cracked foundation slabs. Several springs still flow from the hillside, but the cave that hid runaway slaves is gone. (MD.)

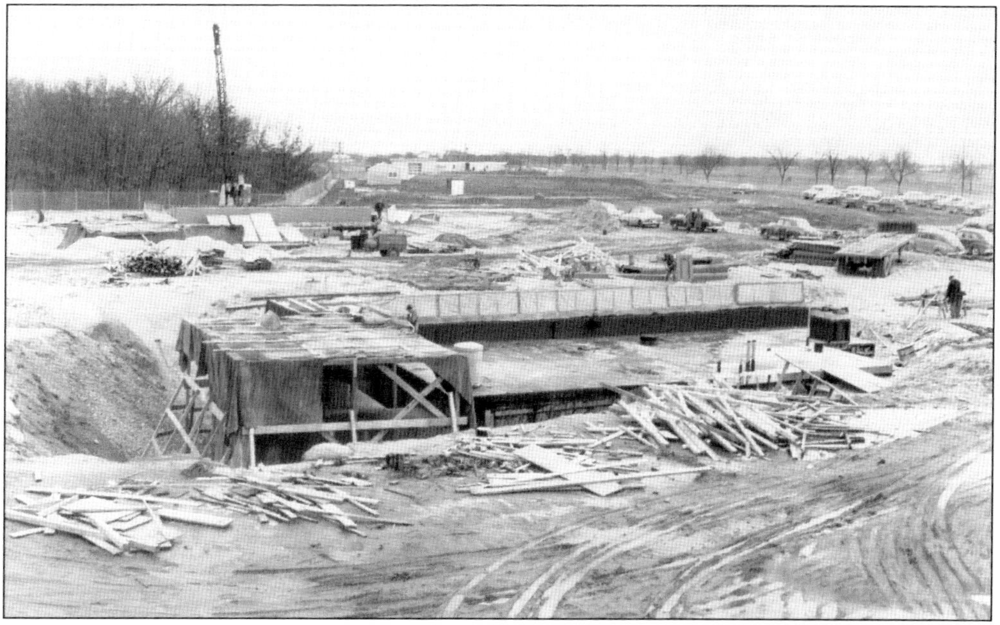

In 1954, Spring Hill Farm was leased to the U.S. Army for use as a Nike missile battery, one of 15 protecting Detroit from attack by Russian bombers. Construction began in October 1954. The site, designated Utica D-06, was occupied in March 1955. Here underground missile storage pits are being built in the launch area, which was located west of the farm buildings on Woodall Road. (MD.)

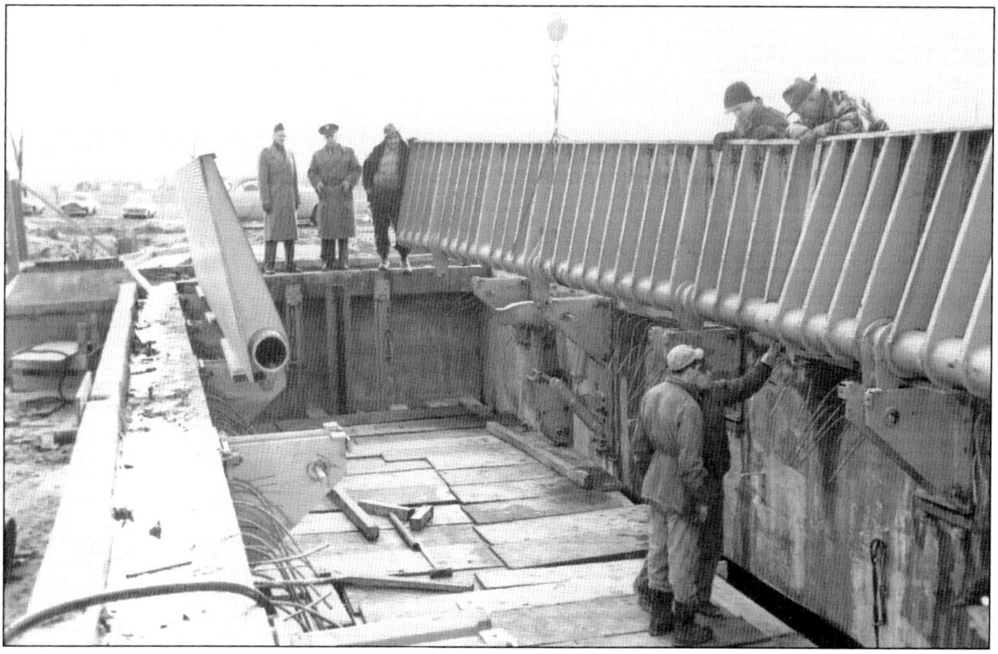

Army officers watch as workers install trapdoors covering a launch pit in 1954. When a missile was ready for launch, the doors would drop down and an elevator would raise the missile to the surface, where it would be manually pushed along a rail to a launcher. Missiles were assembled and fueled in buildings behind protective berms east of the pits. (MD.)

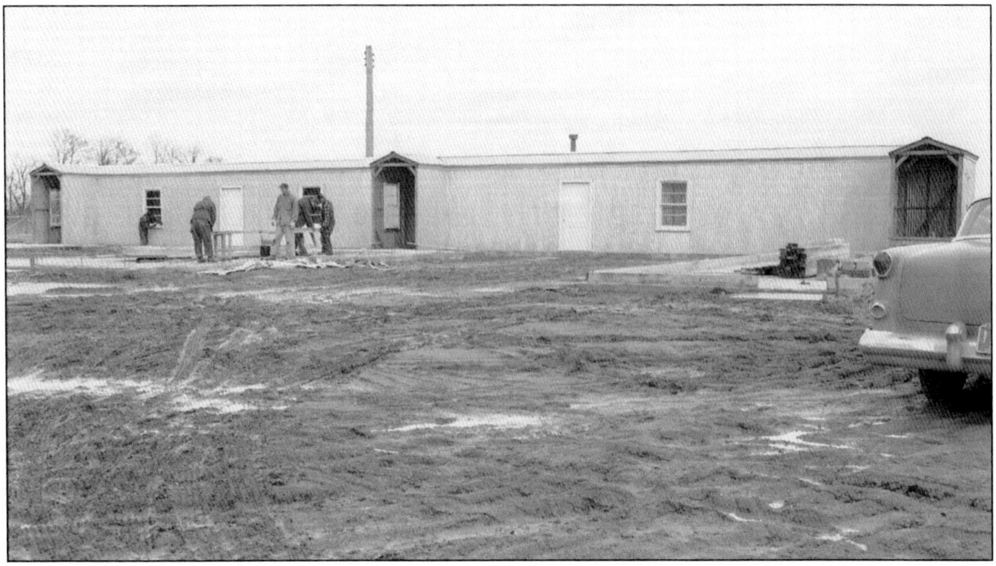

Workers construct a launch support building in the launch area. The Nike site also had an integrated fire control (IFC) area located to the southeast on Woodall Road. The IFC area contained the radars (acquisition, target tracking, and missile tracking) plus equipment and administrative buildings. The two areas were required to be at least 1,000 yards apart for the radar to track outgoing missiles properly. (MD.)

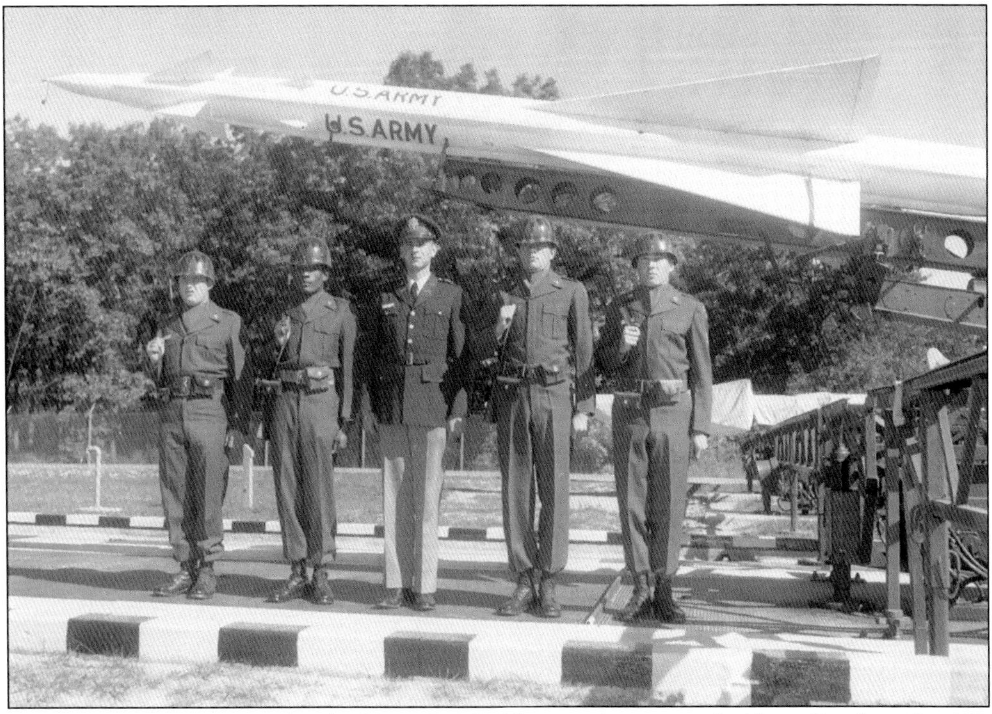


The dedication ceremony for the Utica D-06 Nike missile site was held on October 19, 1957, where Nike Ajax missiles were on display. Around 20 missiles were stored in the underground magazines. Standing at attention on a launch pit cover from left to right are Pfc. Garry LaFaver, Pfc. Roy Byoune, 1st Lt. Robert Gabrielli, Sp3c. Robert Salyer, and Pfc. Allen Vaile. (MD.)

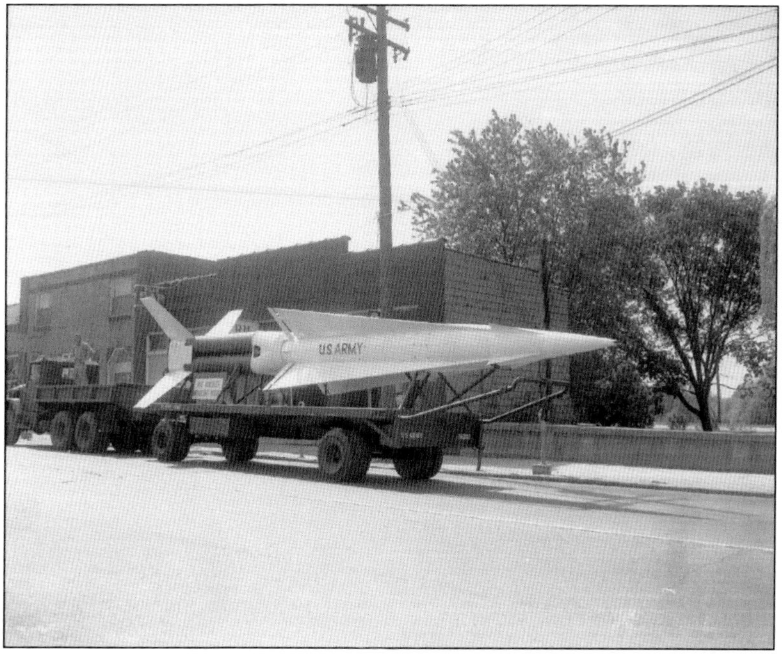


A Nike Hercules missile is towed along Main Street in Utica in 1958. The Hercules was larger and faster than the Ajax and had a greater range; it also had nuclear warhead capability. The conversion from Ajax to Hercules at the Utica D-06 Nike site was completed in April 1961. Due to its larger size, only 12 Hercules missiles could be stored on site. (MD.)

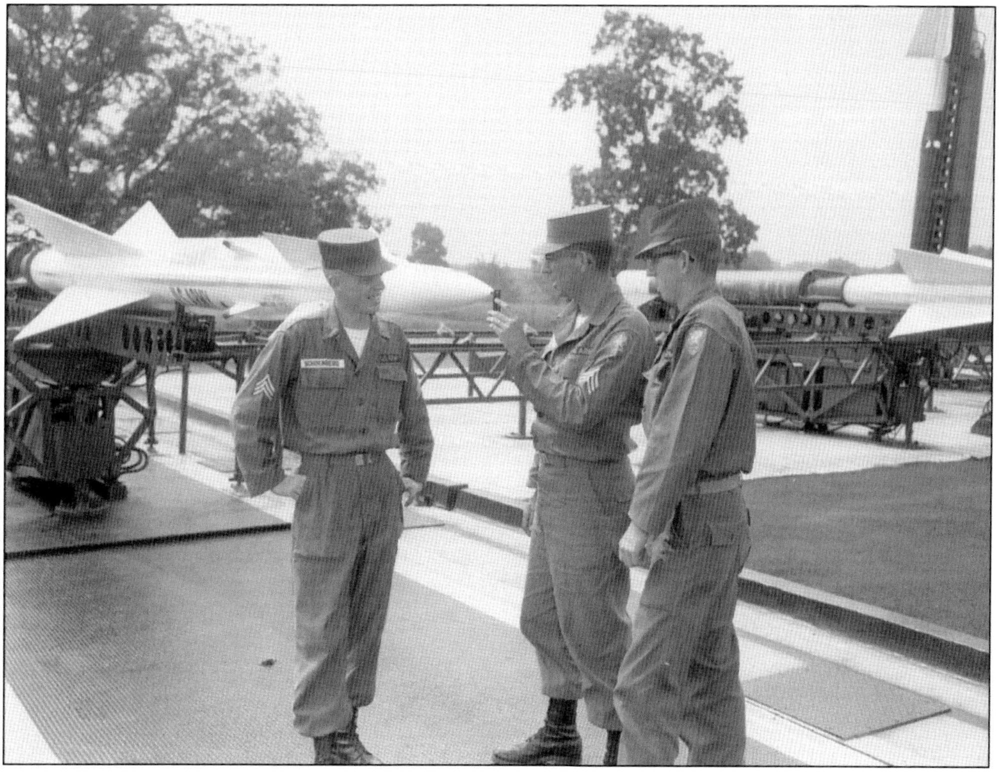

Utica D-06 Nike base personnel take part in training in 1959. Training and drills at the site were ongoing to improve readiness and to learn new technologies, especially when the more advanced Nike Hercules missile system was installed. Also at this time, members of the Michigan Army National Guard were being trained to take over some of the site operations. (MD.)

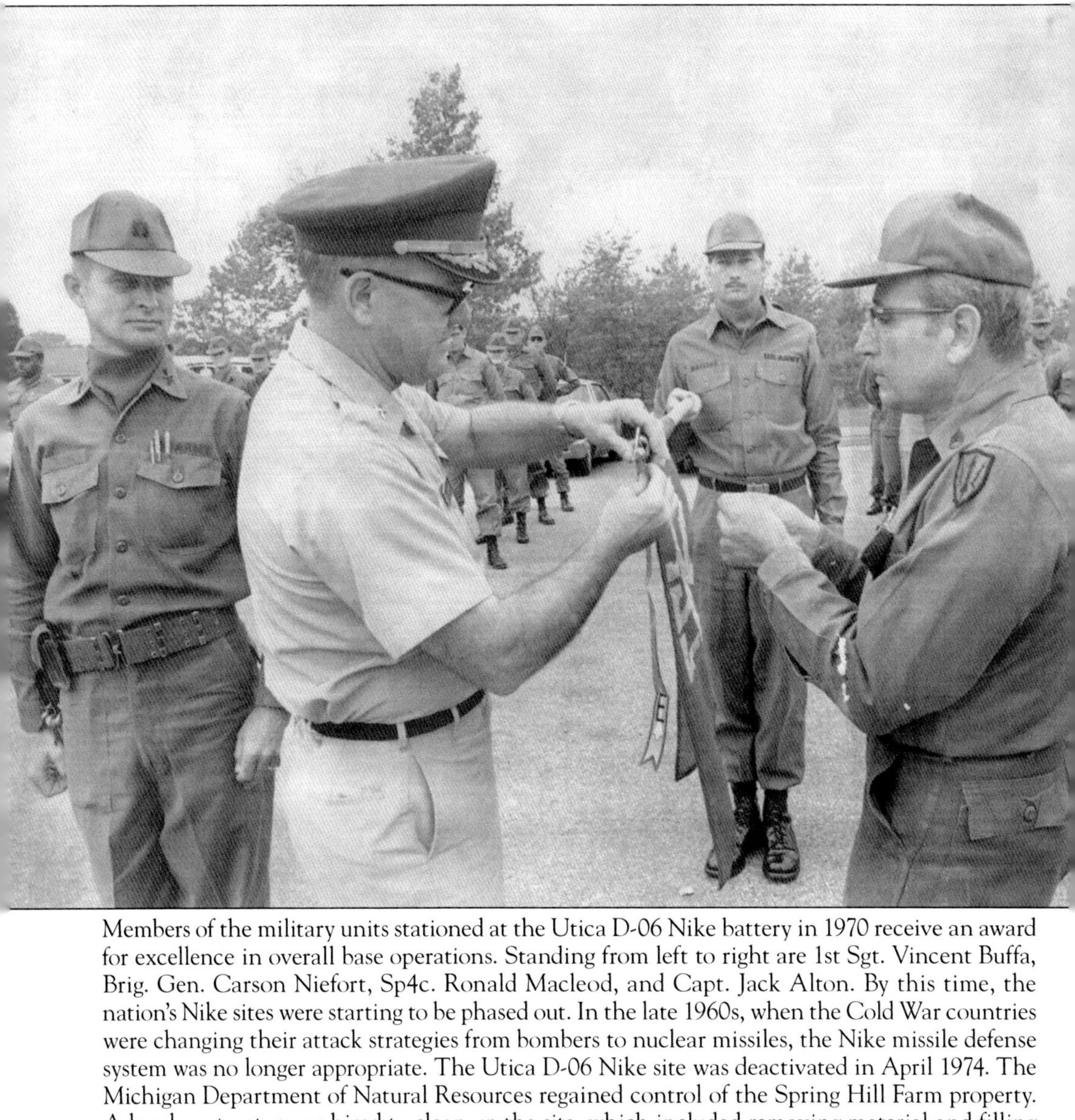

Members of the military units stationed at the Utica D-06 Nike battery in 1970 receive an award for excellence in overall base operations. Standing from left to right are 1st Sgt. Vincent Buffa, Brig. Gen. Carson Niefort, Sp4c. Ronald Macleod, and Capt. Jack Alton. By this time, the nation's Nike sites were starting to be phased out. In the late 1960s, when the Cold War countries were changing their attack strategies from bombers to nuclear missiles, the Nike missile defense system was no longer appropriate. The Utica D-06 Nike site was deactivated in April 1974. The Michigan Department of Natural Resources regained control of the Spring Hill Farm property. A local contractor was hired to clean up the site, which included removing material and filling launch pits. Some traces of the Nike site remain today, such as chain-link fences, radar footings, and the barracks foundations in the IFC area. The radar electronics and equipment building still stands a short distance from the basketball court once used by the servicemen and now used by local children. (*Daily Sentinel.*)

# *Eight*

# SOWING THE SEEDS OF CHANGE

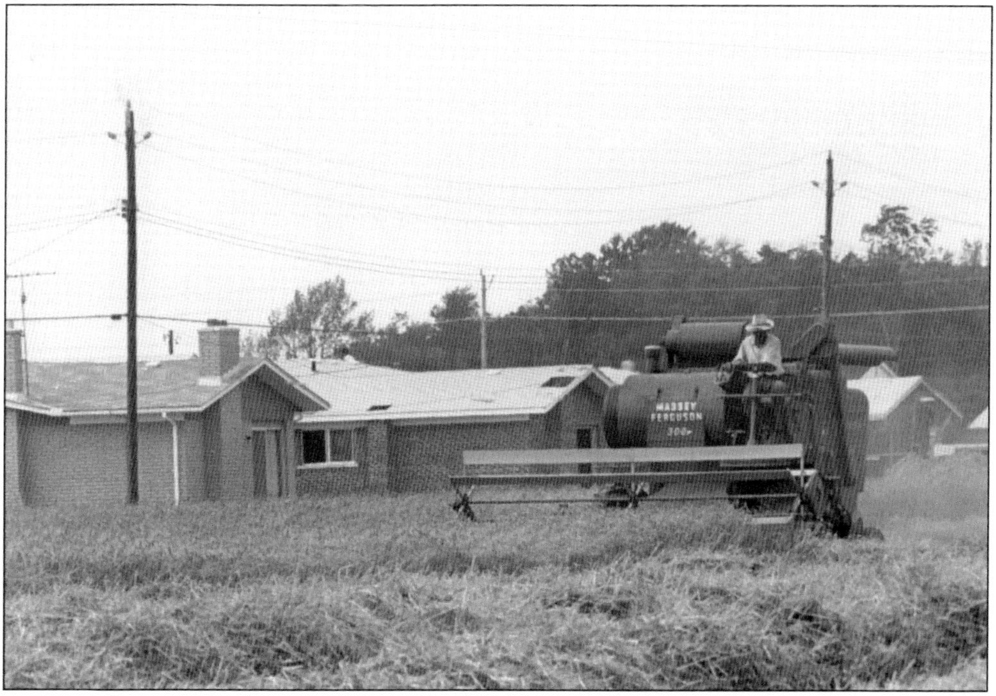

In 1969, a farmer runs a harvester through a field behind a new housing development. This scene was not unusual during the third quarter of the 20th century when Shelby Township transitioned from farmland to housing subdivisions and retail centers as its population increased. Roadways were improved to safely accommodate motor vehicle traffic. New industries and businesses moved in while many agriculture-based businesses folded. (*Daily Sentinel.*)

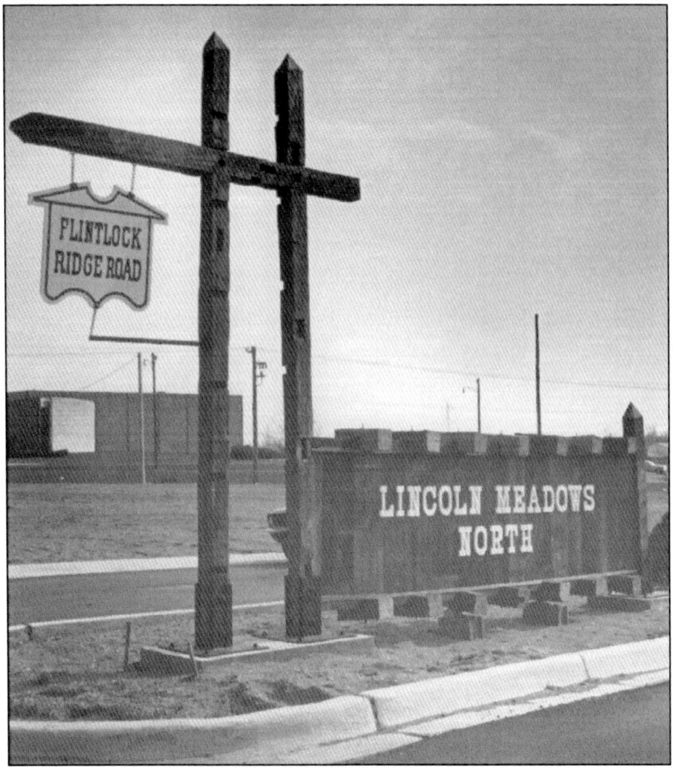


In the 1940s, the township's population doubled, then tripled in the 1950s, and doubled again in the 1960s, fueling the need for more housing. In this 1968 photograph to the left, Lincoln Meadows North is under development on the former Charles Remer farm on Shelby Road. At that time, 48 building lots were offered. A portion of Utica High School is visible behind the new subdivision sign. Below, salesman Ralph Johnson of Four-Way Sales Corporation compares the subdivision plat map with the development already underway. The foundation of one of Charles Remer's barns can still be seen off of Little Turkey Run Road inside the subdivision. (Both, *Daily Sentinel.*)

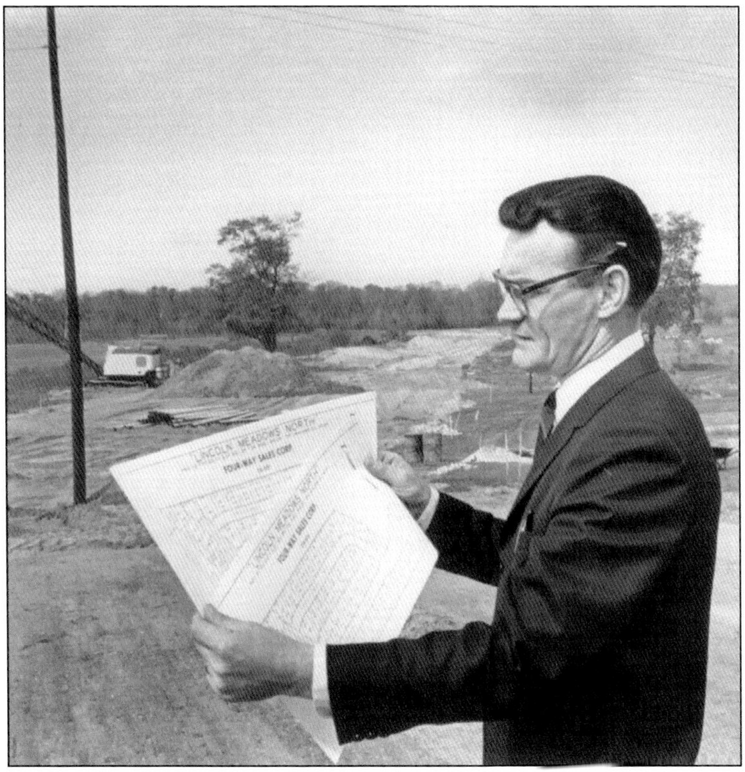

In the early days of Shelby Township, the western end of 23 Mile Road was laid out with right-angle turns to avoid both crossing the Clinton River and bisecting farms. In 1966, these angles, once suitable for slow-moving carriages, were smoothed into curves to allow for faster automobile traffic. Here workmen finish a guardrail around one of the curves. (*Utica Sentinel*; photograph by Wes Stafford.)

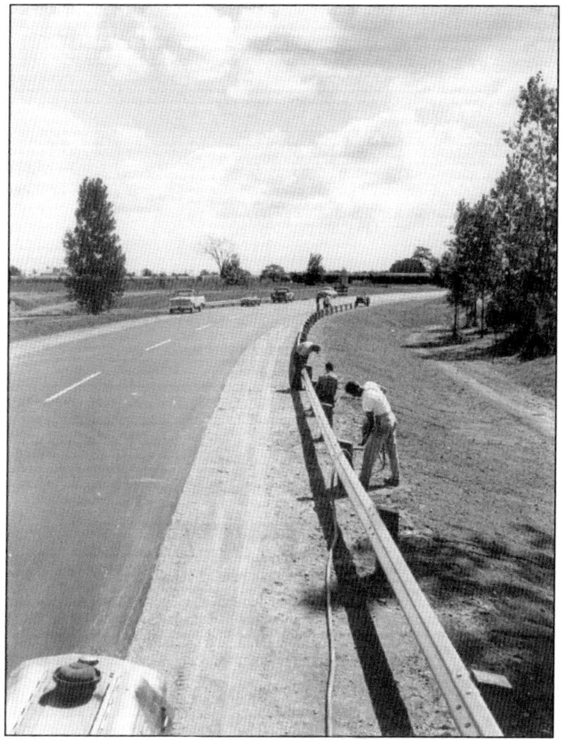

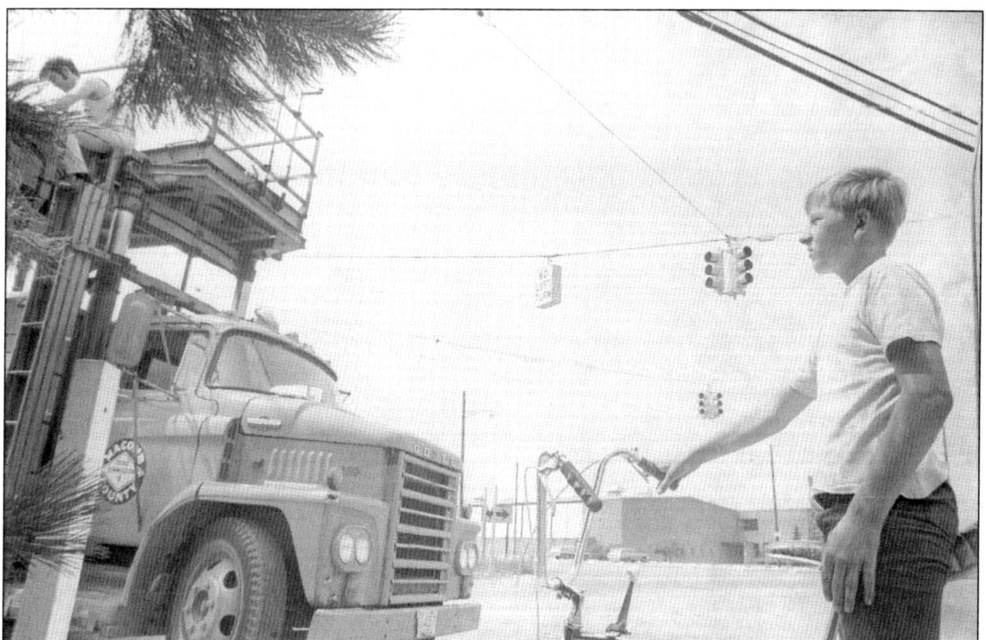

Shelby Township resident Robert Gazda watches as Macomb County Road Commission workers install the first traffic light at the intersection of Shelby and 21 Mile Roads in 1970. Two schools, Utica High and Wiley Elementary, are located at this intersection where automobile traffic had become heavy and dangerous to children crossing to and from school. (*Daily Sentinel*; photograph by Don Polovich.)

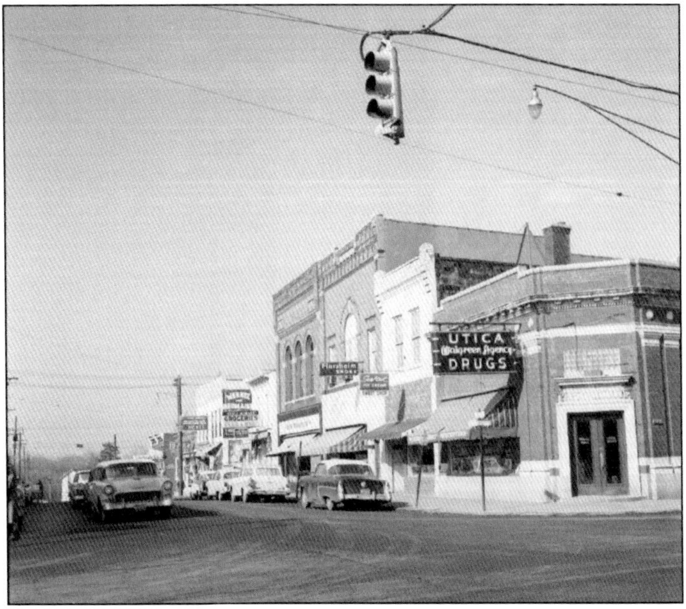


Utica was a bustling city as shown here in 1958 looking west down Main Street from Cass Avenue. Many new businesses popped up alongside several holdovers from earlier times. Shelby Township residents continued to work and shop in downtown Utica, which contributed to the city's growth as well as its growing traffic problems. (WPRL.)

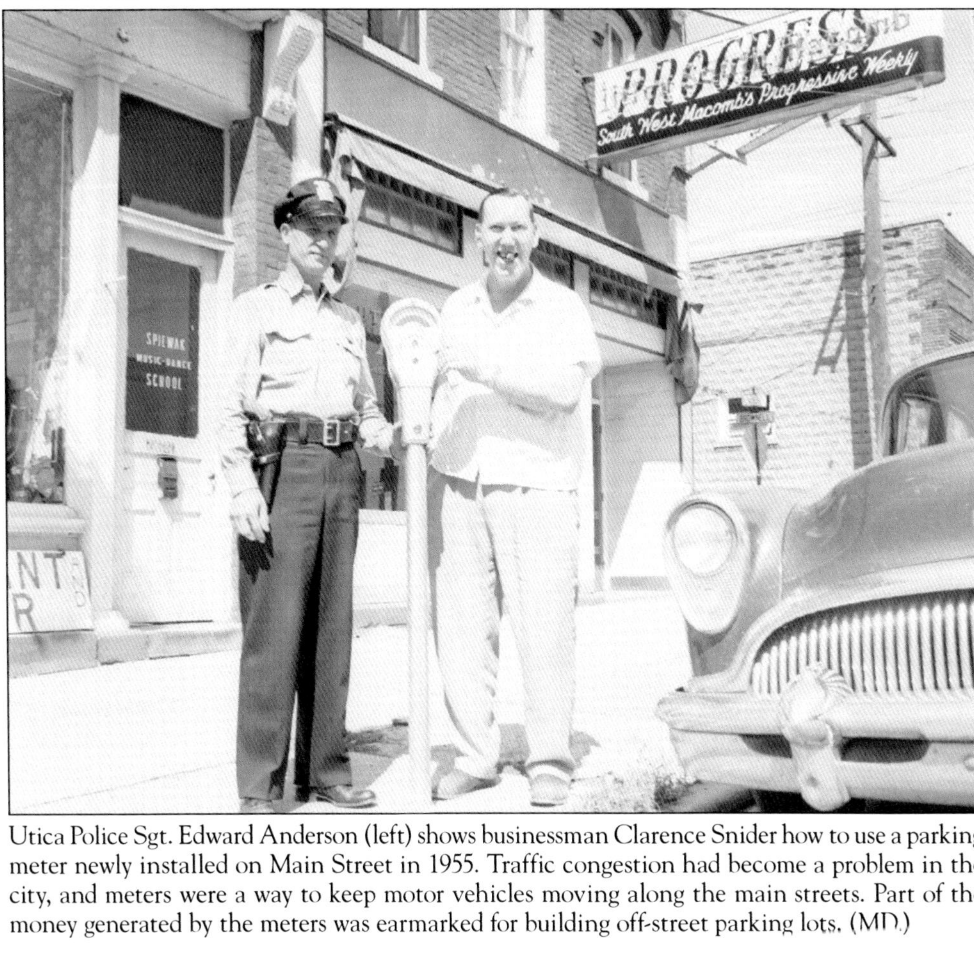


Utica Police Sgt. Edward Anderson (left) shows businessman Clarence Snider how to use a parking meter newly installed on Main Street in 1955. Traffic congestion had become a problem in the city, and meters were a way to keep motor vehicles moving along the main streets. Part of the money generated by the meters was earmarked for building off-street parking lots. (MD.)

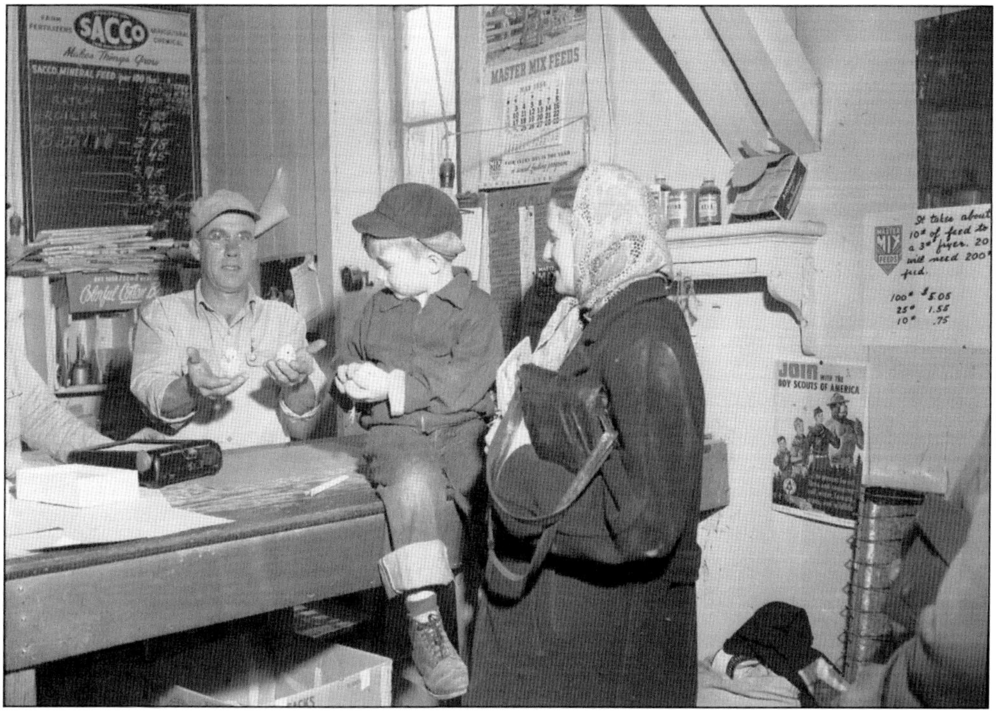


In 1954, the Utica Milling Company ran a promotion for chicken feed by offering 20 free chicks per customer. Above, an unidentified shopkeeper at one of the old mills in Utica holds chicks for two unidentified customers to inspect. As the number of area farms decreased, so did the need for milling and other farm-related services. Milling operations ceased in 1959, and the Utica mills became flour and feed distribution centers. Glenn Crissman, president of the Utica Milling Company, began liquidating the company in early 1961, putting the two mills in Utica, plus the Clinton and Kalamazoo Canal right-of-way, up for sale. Below, the old mill on the south side of Main Street is about to meet the wrecking ball in 1963. (Both, MD.)

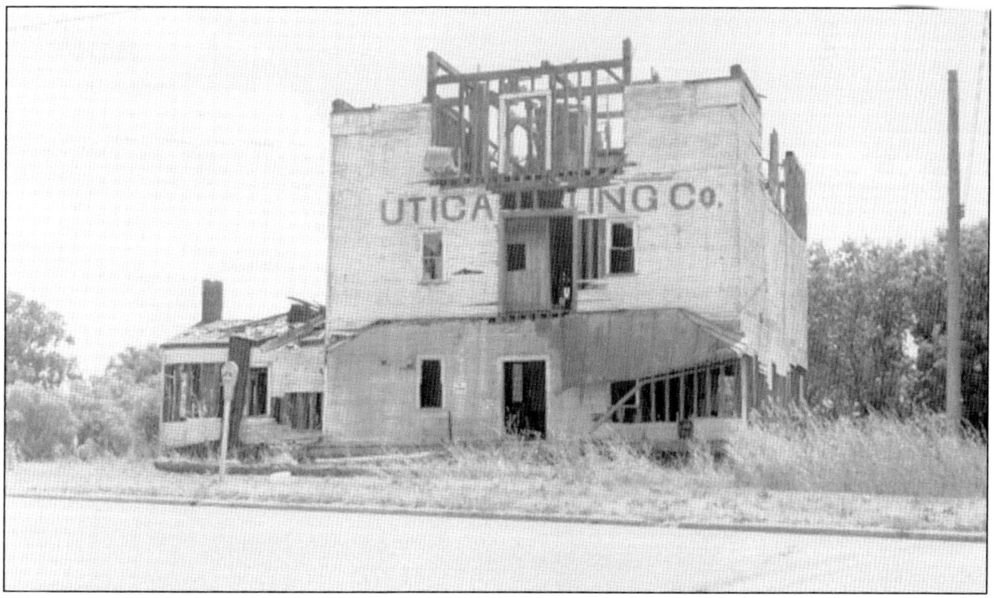

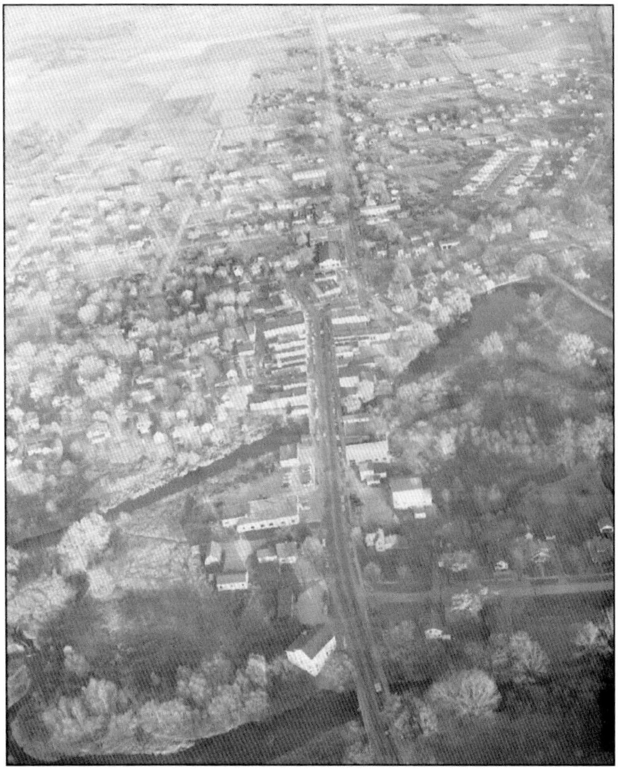

At left is a bird's-eye view of Utica from 1952 looking east along Main Street. The Clinton River flows left to right at the bottom of the photograph. Hall Road, the southern boundary of Shelby Township, connects to Main Street via Van Dyke and Cass Avenues in the center of the photograph. This route was a main thoroughfare connecting points east with Rochester and Pontiac to the west and brought much motor vehicle traffic, for better and for worse, through downtown Utica. In 1957, construction started on the M-59 Freeway designed to connect directly with Hall Road and divert heavy east-west traffic from Utica. Below, in a photograph looking west over Utica, the highway in progress runs south of the city and parallel to Main Street. (Both, MD.)

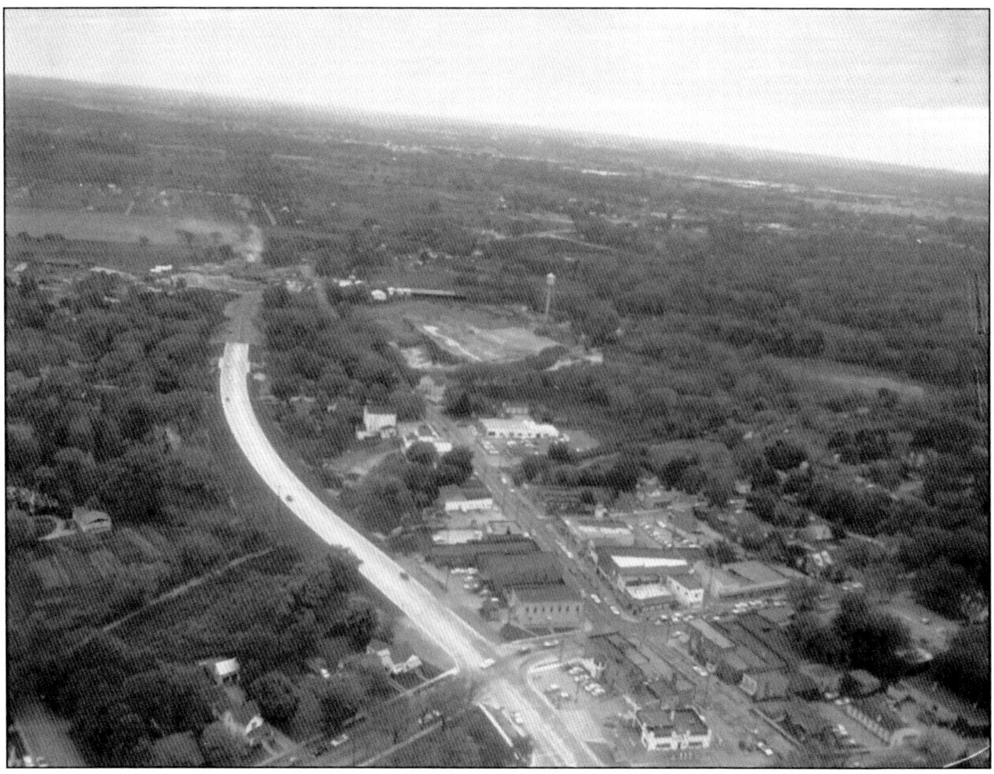

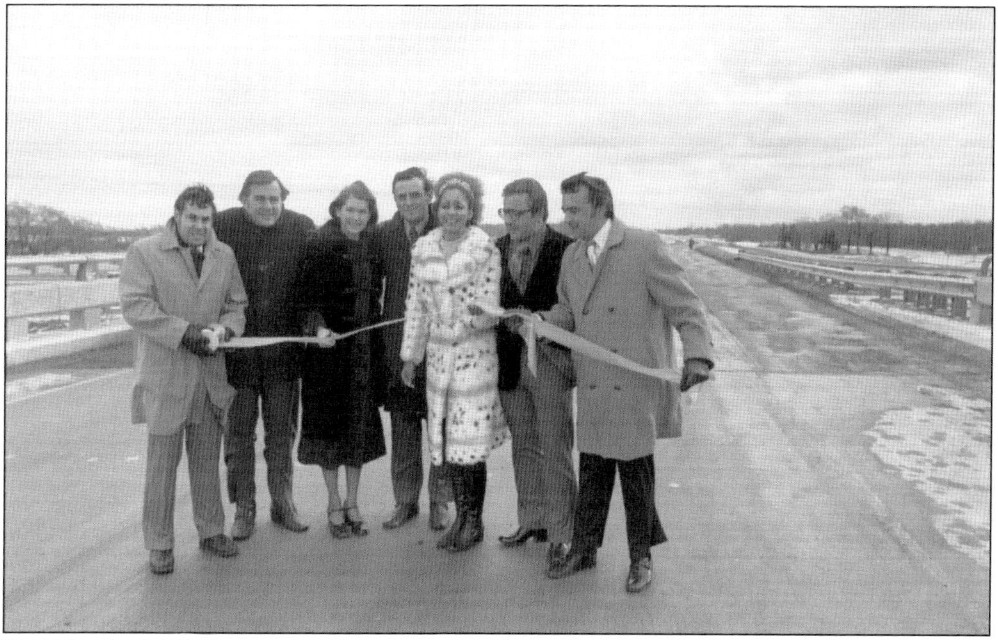

By 1972, the M-59 Freeway had been completed to Pontiac. Standing on the Dequindre Road overpass, local dignitaries join to cut a ribbon dedicating the new freeway. They are, from left to right, Ron Poli, Kirby Holmes, Gail McCauley, George Nickson, Carol Harris, Thomas Guastello, and Donald Bemis. Hall Road was widened in the late 20th century into a multilane boulevard to accommodate increased traffic flow. (MD.)

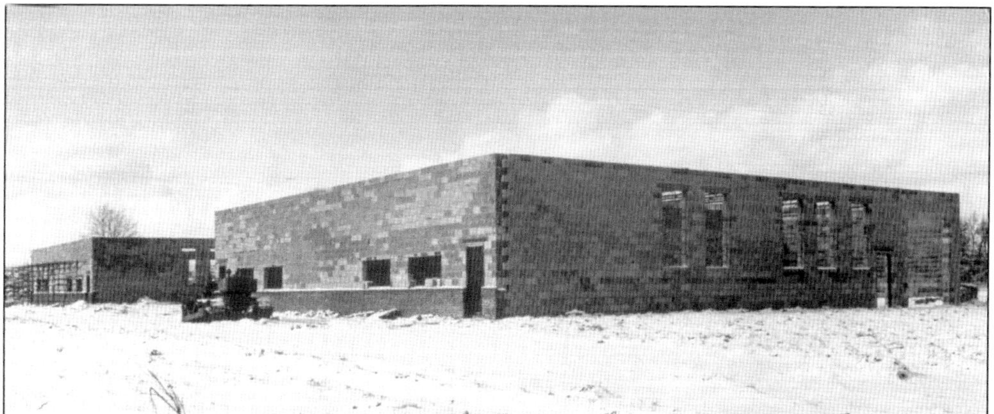

This 1967 photograph shows an industrial complex under construction on Ryan Road just south of 23 Mile Road in Shelby Township on land once farmed by the Cheney and Fangboner families in the 19th century. These buildings were designed to house machine shops and are an example of the new industries coming in to the township that provided well-paying jobs for local residents. (*Daily Sentinel.*)

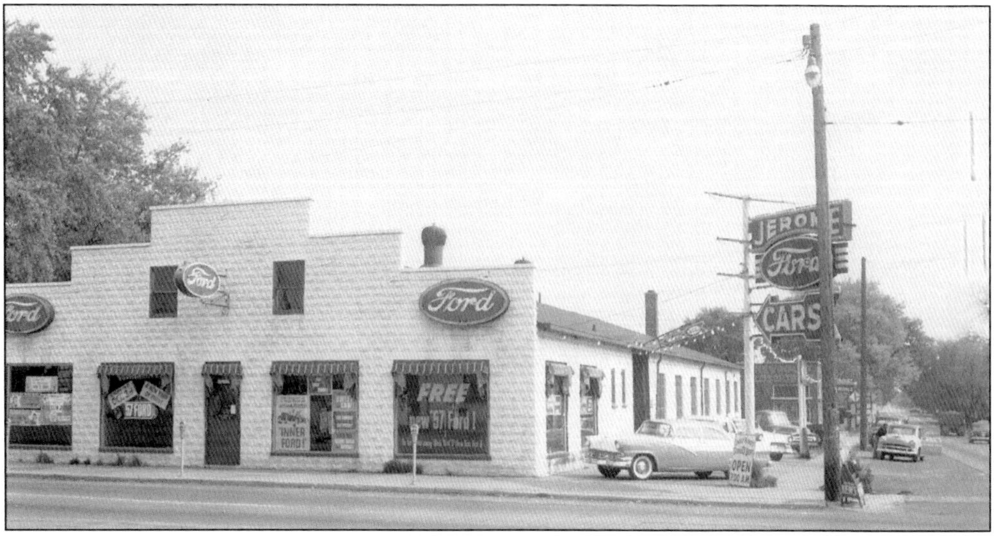


New business also arrived in Shelby Township in the form of automobile dealers and repair shops. Jerome Ford, pictured here in 1956, was on the northeast corner of Van Dyke Avenue and Hall Road. Victor Messmore and Earl Sipperly started the dealership in 1921 and sold farm tractors as well as automobiles. Richard Duncan and Larry Jerome bought the business in 1956. (MD.)

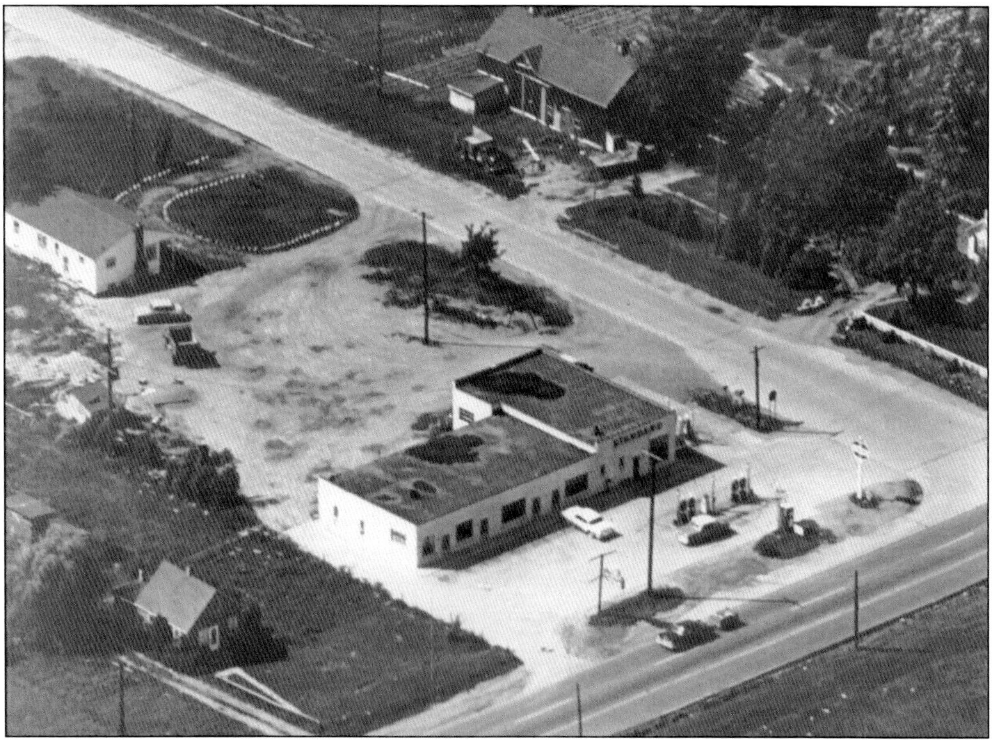

Gasoline and service stations were showing up along well-traveled roads throughout Shelby Township. The Standard Oil station, pictured here around 1956, was located on the southwest corner of 23 Mile Road and Van Dyke Avenue. Started by the Nightingale family in 1946, the station provided fuel and repair service. Attached to it were a barbershop, a beauty shop, and a bar. (Nightingale family.)

When Ford Motor Company purchased the Packard Motor Car facility in Shelby Township in 1961, it became the township's largest employer and taxpayer. In this 1968 photograph, Shelby Township treasurer Jack Millard (left) looks on as Paul Detloff, comptroller of the Ford Motor Company Utica Plant, displays a check for $606,000, which covered the annual township tax bill. (*Daily Sentinel*; photograph by Wes Stafford.)

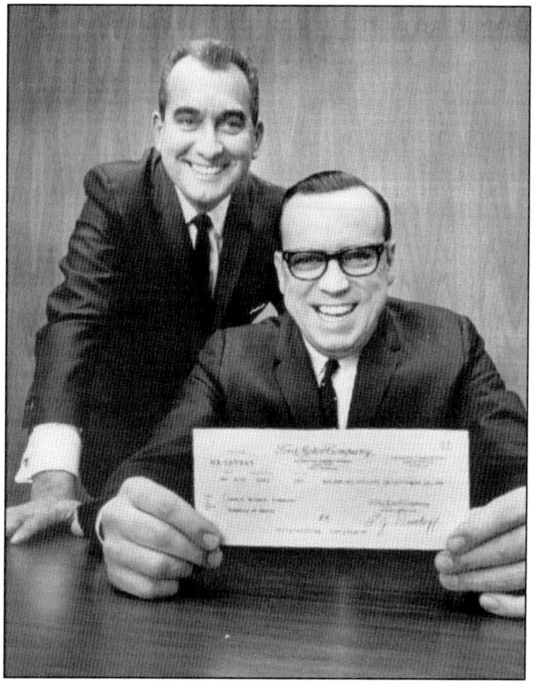

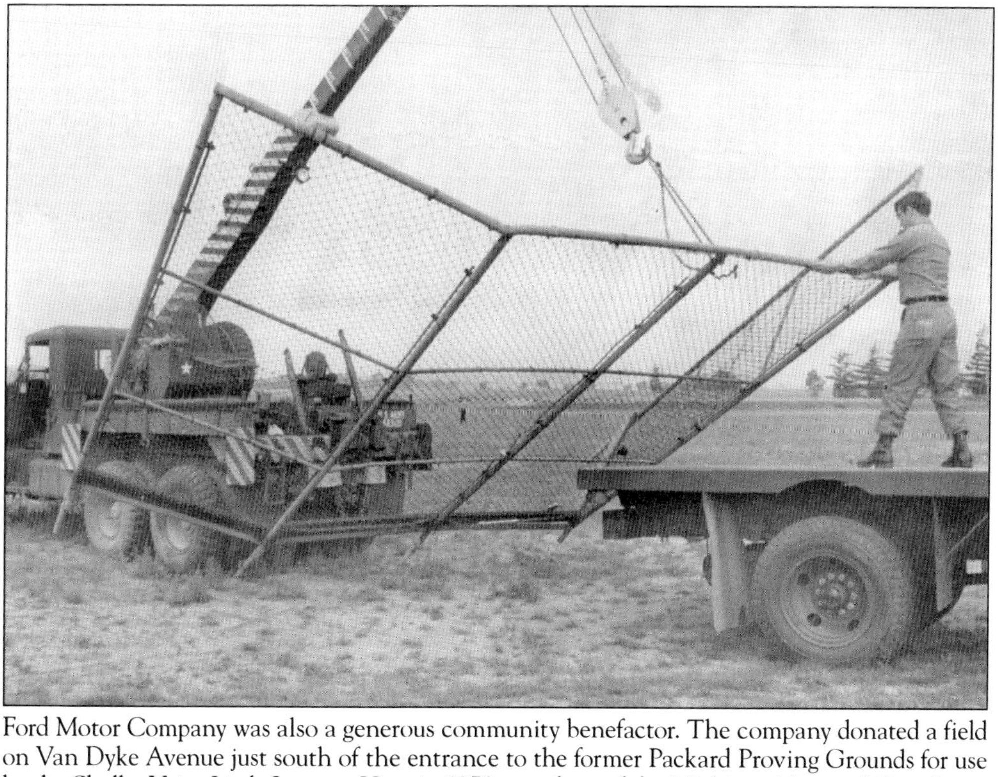

Ford Motor Company was also a generous community benefactor. The company donated a field on Van Dyke Avenue just south of the entrance to the former Packard Proving Grounds for use by the Shelby-Utica Little League. Here in 1970, members of the Michigan National Guard unit stationed at the Nike missile base install a backstop at one of the diamonds at Ford Field. (*Daily Sentinel*; photograph by Don Polovich.)

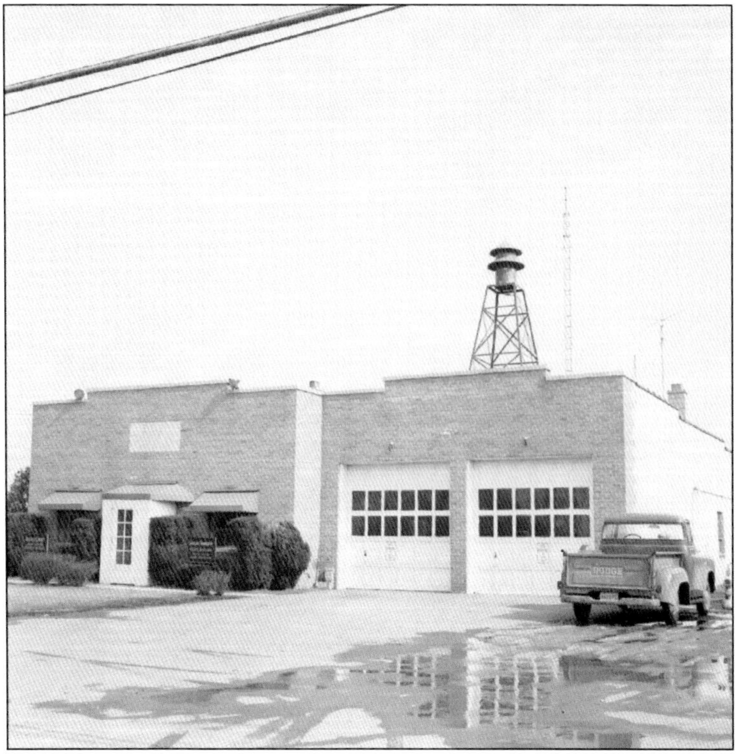

The first Shelby Township town hall was built on Van Dyke Avenue between 22 Mile and 23 Mile Roads in 1948. Before this, board meetings were held at the home of one of the elected officials. The town hall, shown here in 1958, contained offices for the supervisor and other officials plus the township fire and police stations. (WPRL.)

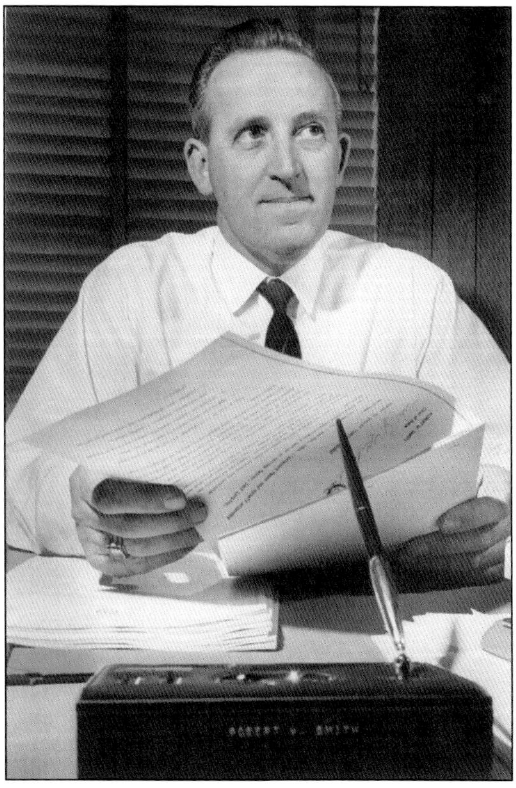

Shelby Township police chief Robert Smith reviews case paperwork at his desk in the town hall in this undated photograph. He was the first and only full-time policeman when the township created its police department in 1954. In 1955, more officers were added to the force, and Smith became the township's first police chief. Chief Smith retired in 1983. (STHC.)

In 1955, members of the Shelby Township police force stand in front of the new patrol car. They are, from left to right, Robert Poynter, Constable Jack Millard, Chief Robert Smith, and Joseph Moore. Before 1954, patrols from the Macomb County Sheriff's Department and the Michigan State Police kept peace in the township. (STHC.)

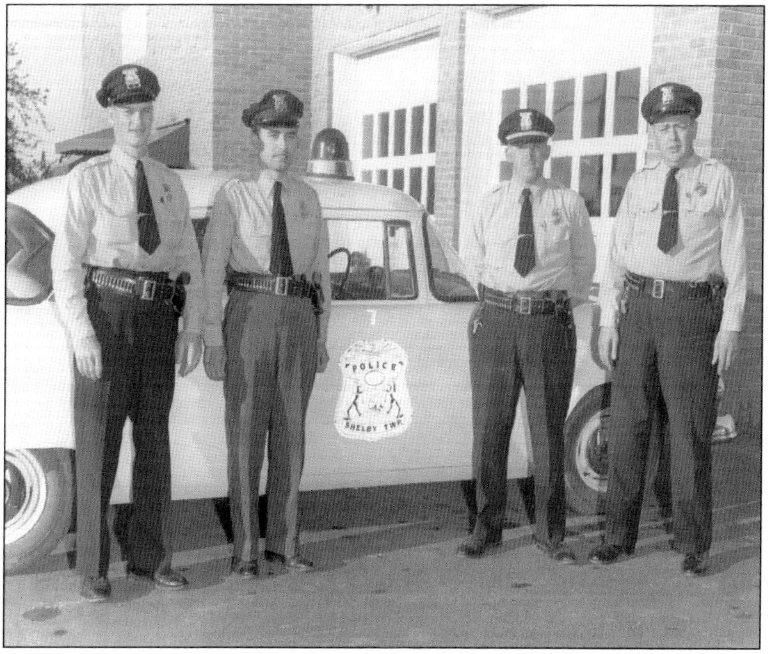


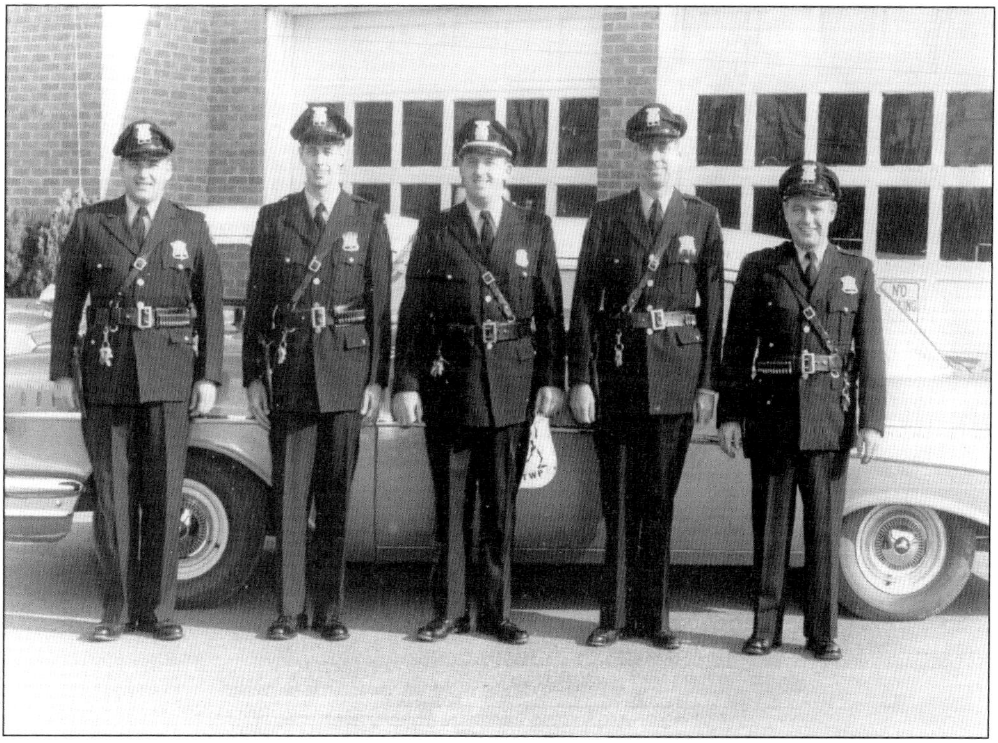

By 1957, the township police force had added a fifth officer. Pictured here in front of the town hall are, from left to right, Edward White, Clendon Mason, Chief Robert Smith, Alfred Hagerman, and Larry Gerou. With the exception of Chief Smith, all the men shown held the rank of patrolman. (STHC.)

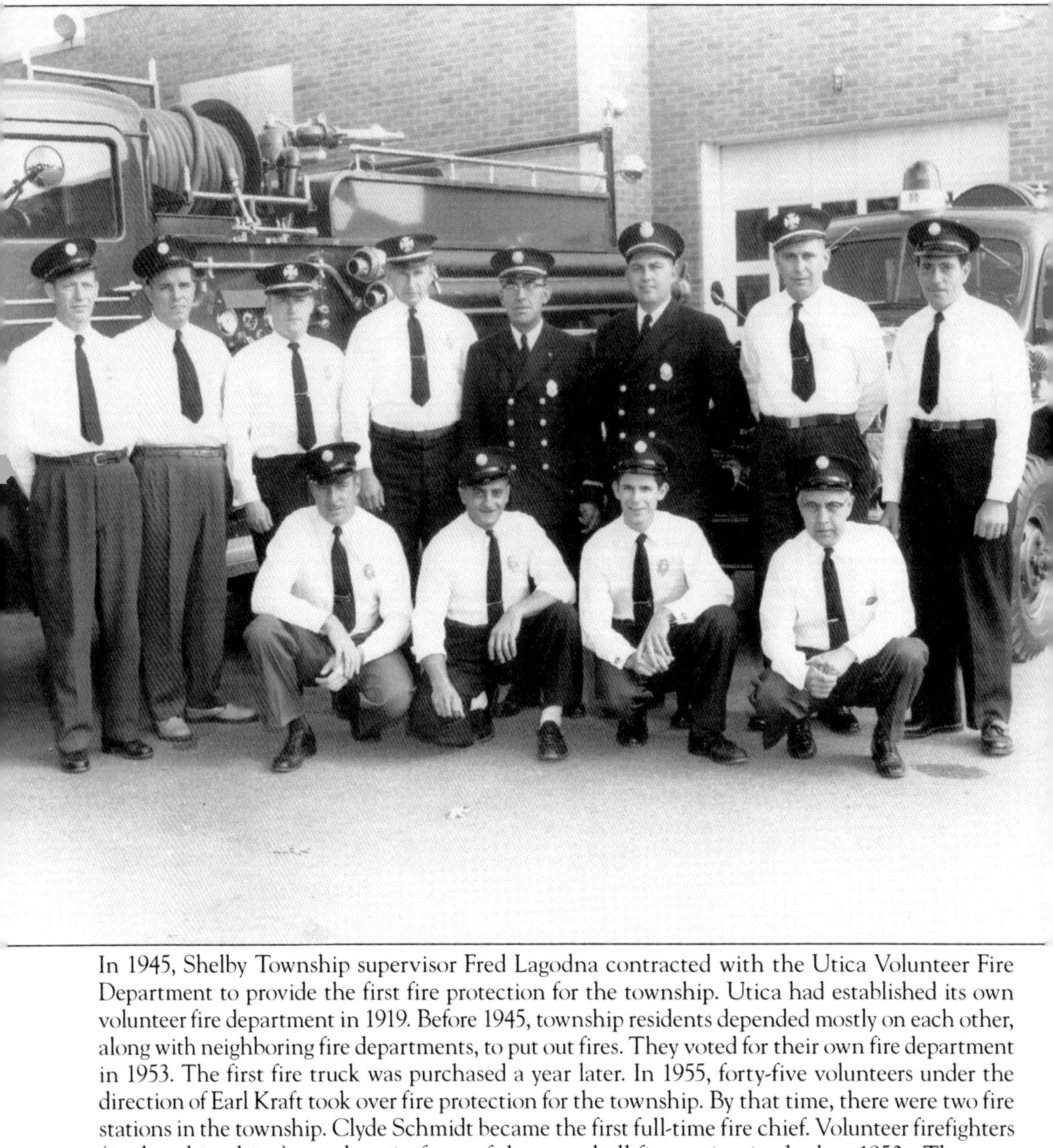

In 1945, Shelby Township supervisor Fred Lagodna contracted with the Utica Volunteer Fire Department to provide the first fire protection for the township. Utica had established its own volunteer fire department in 1919. Before 1945, township residents depended mostly on each other, along with neighboring fire departments, to put out fires. They voted for their own fire department in 1953. The first fire truck was purchased a year later. In 1955, forty-five volunteers under the direction of Earl Kraft took over fire protection for the township. By that time, there were two fire stations in the township. Clyde Schmidt became the first full-time fire chief. Volunteer firefighters (in the white shirts) pose here in front of the town hall fire station in the late 1950s. They are, from left to right, (first row) Joseph DeStrooper, Leo Savarino, Louis Resner, and Adam Leese; (second row) Pete Hoppa, Henry Wojciechowski, Wilbert Teise, William Mrosewski, Fire Marshal Clement Skiba, Chief Clyde Schmidt, Wilfred Meitz, and Paul Licari. (STHC.)

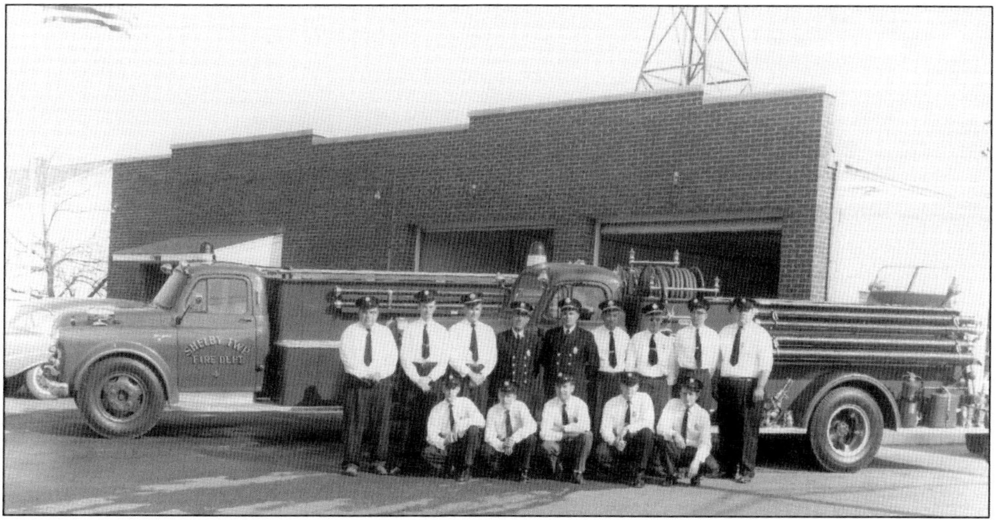

The firefighters from the Ryan Road Fire Station pose for this photograph in the late 1950s. They are, from left to right, (first row) Ronald Skiba, Neil Popkey, Jack Millard, Larry Giacobozzi, and Orville Bushey; (second row) Michael Monicatti Sr., William Rogers, Carlton Stange, Fire Marshal Clement Skiba, Chief Clyde Schmidt, Marvin Meitz, Earl Radtke, Harvey Hansen, and Michael Monicatti Jr. (STHC.)

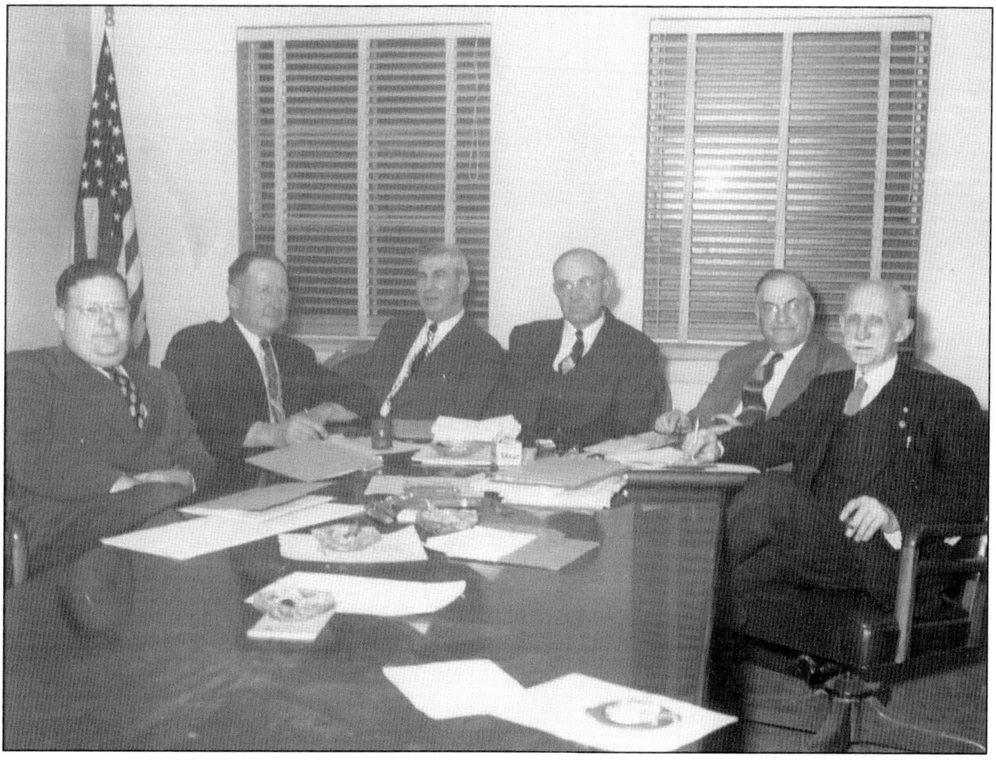

Members of the Shelby Township Board of Trustees discuss township business in a conference room at the town hall around 1950. The members from left to right are attorney George Roberts, justice of the peace Julius C. Kirschbaum, treasurer DeWitt Helferich, supervisor Fred Lagodna, clerk Chester Yenny, and justice of the peace J. Gordon Rankin. (Lynn and Grace Drake.)

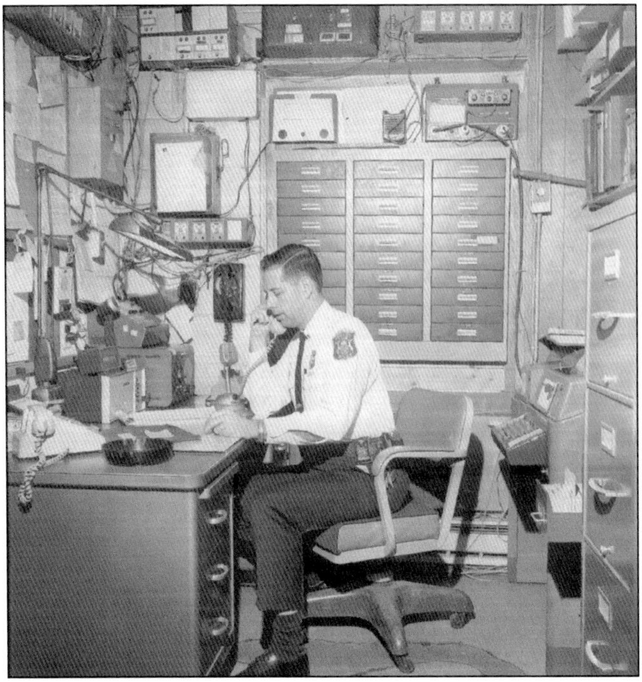

In 1971, Lt. Clendon Mason tries to work in the cramped quarters of the town hall. To keep pace with the growing township population, a larger building was needed to house the growing number of policemen and township government workers. In June 1972, the new Shelby Township municipal complex opened at 24 Mile Road and Van Dyke Avenue in the southeast corner of Disco. (*Daily Sentinel.*)

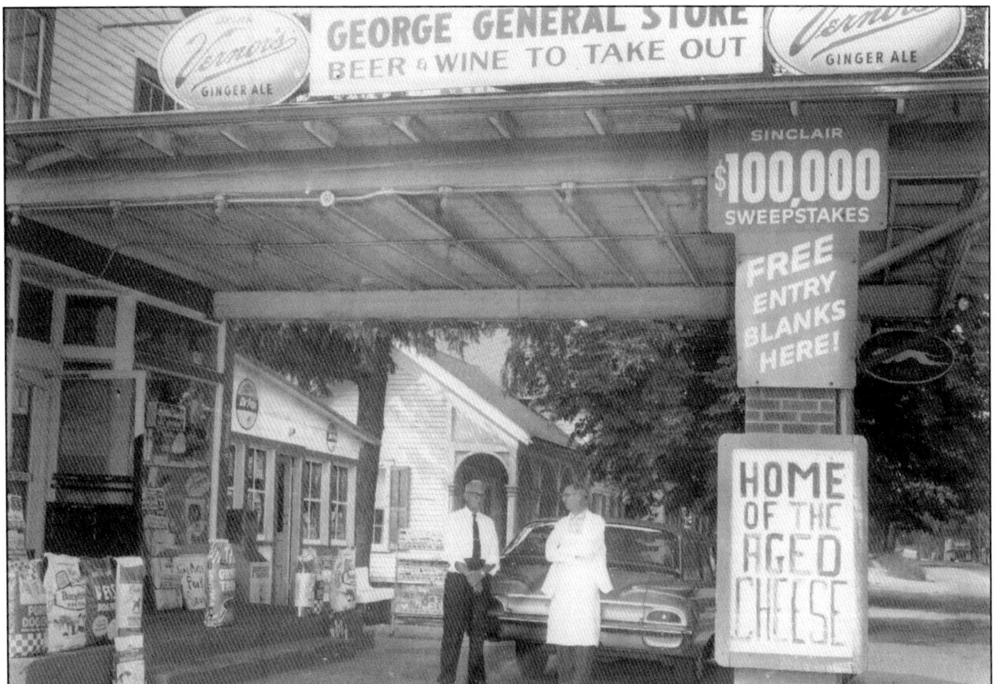


At the old general store in Disco, George Wellhausen (right) talks to an unidentified customer near the gasoline pumps. Wellhausen bought the store from Hugh Switzer around 1953. He sold a variety of foods and general supplies. In 1960, the Wellhausen family began producing and marketing German sausage, which was smoked in the smokehouse behind the store. (George Wellhausen Jr.)

George Wellhausen checks out the old coffee grinder inside his store around 1960. The Wellhausen family sold the business in 1971. The store remained in operation for another 20 years. During this time, most of the old businesses in Disco closed, and many of the old homes and buildings were demolished to make room for future development. (George Wellhausen Jr.)

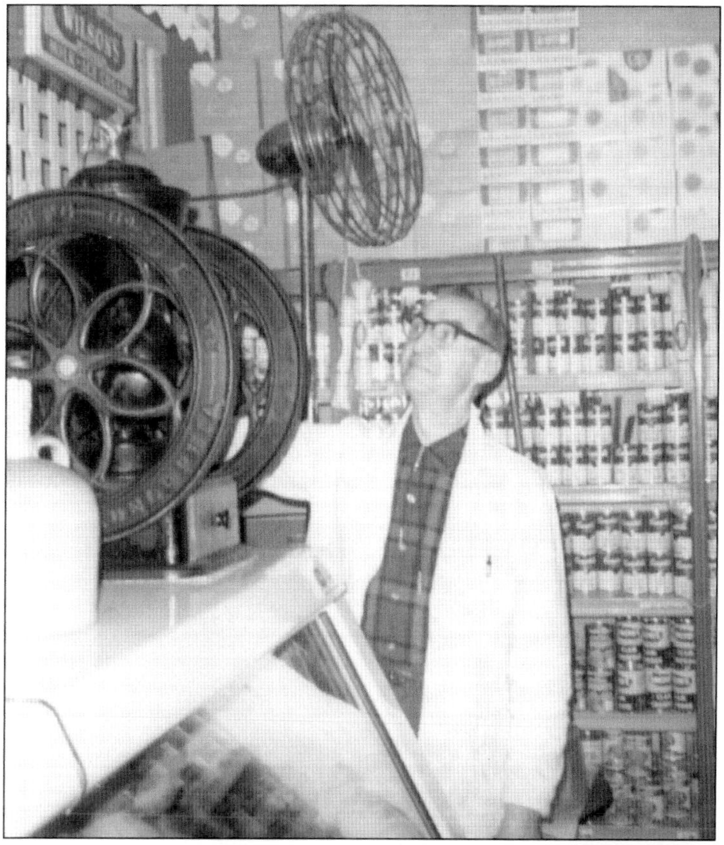

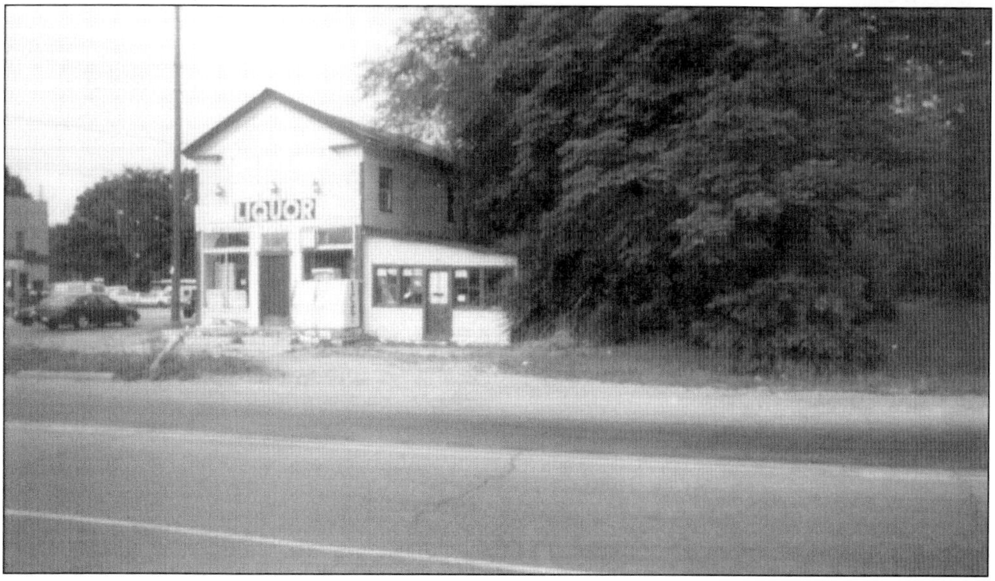


The Disco General Store sits abandoned in 1998. The building was demolished a year later. The road signs that had marked the village of Disco for many years were removed in the mid-1970s so as not to confuse motorists looking for the new township municipal center. The area around 24 Mile Road and Van Dyke Avenue ceased to be known as Disco. (STHC.)

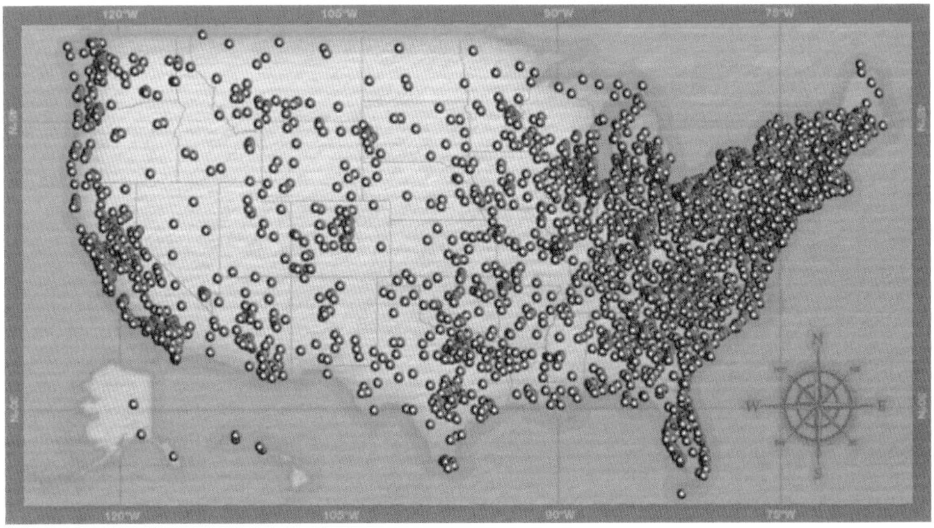